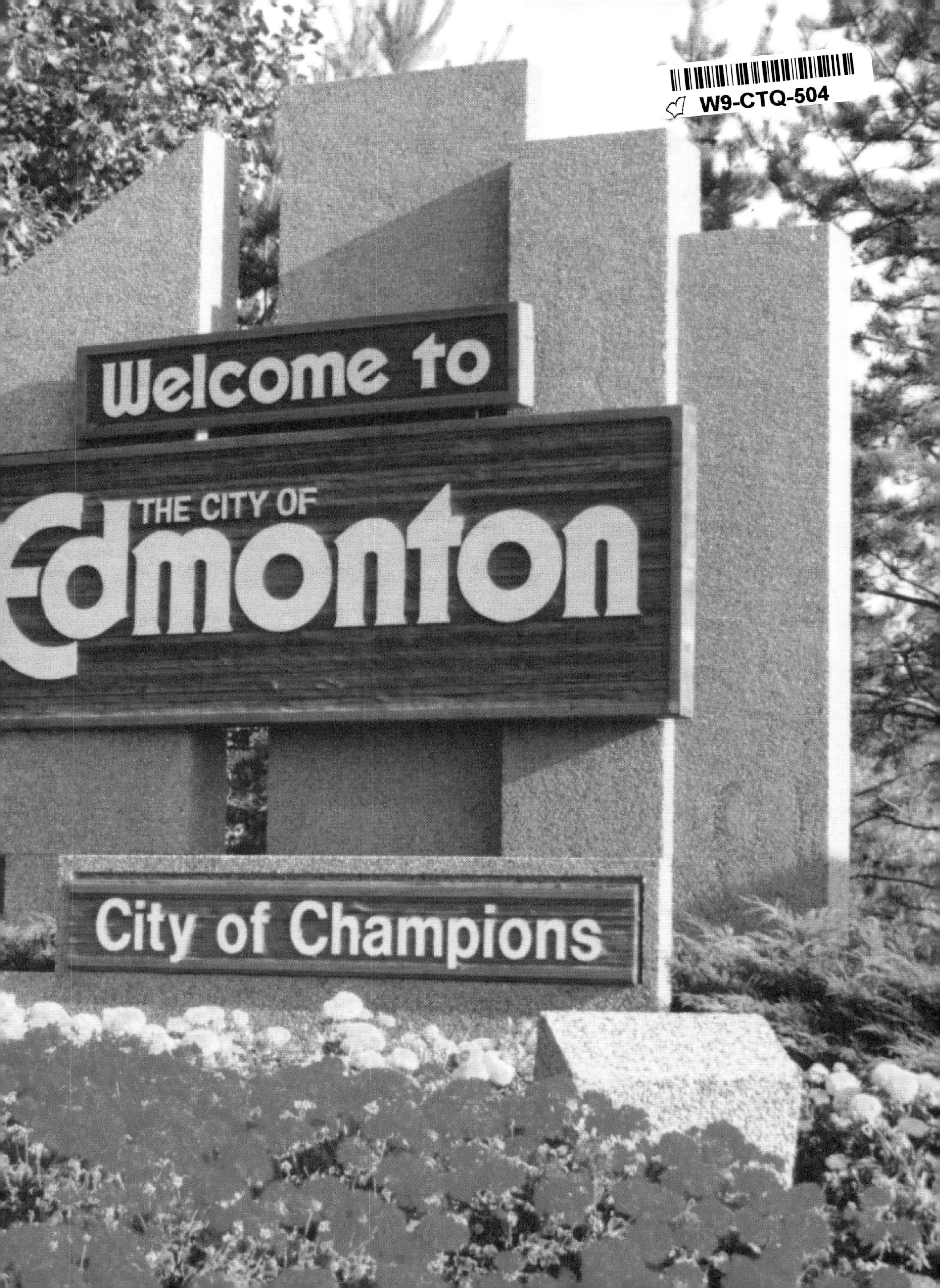
Welcome to
THE CITY OF
Edmonton
City of Champions

City of Champions

Edited by Jamie Wilson
with Allyson Quince

Research Assistant: Sandra Trueman
Illustrations by Heather McLean
'E' logo and inside page design by Studio 3 Graphics Ltd.
Cover design by Jamie Wilson and Marek Konarzewski

Published by City of Champions Inc.

18330 102 Ave.
Edmonton, Alberta
Canada
T5S 2J9
http://www.cityofchampions.ab.ca

Printed in Canada by Quality Colour Press Inc.
18330 102 Ave.
Edmonton, Alberta
Canada

Printed on Luna Gloss 100lb. cover, Luna Gloss 80lb.
text and Resolve Premium Opaque 100lb. from Domtar,
Eddy Specialty Papers.

ISBN 0-9686048-0-3

First Edition, October, 1999

The publishers would like to dedicate this book to John Trueman, a 40-year resident of Edmonton who in 1985 conceived the idea of creating a book called *City of Champions*. He has been persistent in having a unique book of positive information about Edmonton - a book for all Edmontonians. Because of this, we decided to create this book. His concept was that everyone should know that Edmonton is about much more than Oilers and Eskimos - that the city has many champions in a variety of fields, and we should know and appreciate them all.

For 15 years, we have nurtured the idea of producing a book that would showcase all the reasons we're so proud to be Edmontonians. We wanted to create not simply a book about Edmonton, but the definitive list of all the elite championship winners, record holders, and the many people and institutions which are the biggest, best or first of their kind.

We believed that when compiled and combined with the best public and private photographs, the result would be a book that provides interesting and informative material for Edmontonians and visitors alike - material that wouldn't otherwise be known to everyone.

During the extensive research, every attempt was made to contact every known association, sports team, government agency, society and organization for its input. In almost every case, there was excellent co-operation, although some groups had either no records or lacked the resources to provide anything but the barest information. In this process, we have collected an enormous amount of data, and investigated and verified sometimes conflicting information. Due to the magnitude and scope of this project, we apologize should we have inadvertently missed anyone or anything that would have fit into this book. We invite anyone with any such data to contact us so that it can be included in future editions.

We sincerely hope that the City of Champions Inc. has provided a quality book that will be enjoyed by its readers as much as we enjoyed making it available.

City of Champions Inc.

The Premier of Alberta

The Oilers. The Edmonton Grads. The Eskimos. Klondike Days. The Heritage Festival. The Golden Bears. The Cheremosh Ensemble.

These are just a few of the images and memories that spring to mind when Albertans look at their province's capital city of Edmonton. There is one thing these images have in common: they all reflect a city's record of achievement.

From its beautiful river valley to its bustling residential communities, Edmonton is a city that thrives on diversity and seems to succeed at everything it tries. Whether it's a folk festival or an amateur sporting tournament, the people of Edmonton take their projects to heart and turn ideas into achievements. This spirit of hard work, common goals, and productive partnerships has made Edmonton one of Canada's most exciting and accomplished cities.

And it's just going to get better as a new millennium dawns. Edmonton's arts, culture, sports and volunteer sectors have served notice to the world that they intend to build on their past achievements, not rest on them. This book captures the achievements of the past and details the promise of the future for the citizens of Edmonton. Edmontonians can be proud of the record of success recorded here - it illustrates the pioneering spirit and sense of adventure that characterize Alberta's capital.

On behalf of the Government of Alberta, I am pleased to use this opportunity to wish all the citizens of Edmonton the very best as your city embarks on the journey of the 21st century. Like all Albertans, I look forward to seeing the achievements the city has planned for the future.

Sincerely yours,

Ralph Klein

The Mayor of Edmonton

I would like to thank *City of Champions* for highlighting our city's many achievements. This book serves to remind us all of just how far we have come and how much we have accomplished. Edmonton's reputation as the City of Champions refers to more than our great sports teams, individual athletes and the major international sporting events we continue to host. It also refers to the culture, educational institutions, festivals, parks, business leaders and the incredible goodwill and community involvement of our citizens.

I am proud to be Edmonton's mayor as we close the second millenium and enter the third. It is a time when people are reflecting on the past and dreaming of what the future will hold. *City of Champions* will act as an historical marker for future generations of Edmontonians, capturing the pride and promise we see in our city.

This book showcases what makes Edmonton the greatest city in the greatest province in the greatest country in the world.

Everyone who calls themselves an Edmontonian should own a copy!

Yours truly,

Bill Smith

Just to be sure the record's straight, I have to proclaim having been born in Calgary. My parents, Ben and Laura, decided that I (and my four siblings) should have a sort of dual hometown-ship, so my dad accepted a transfer and promotion to Edmonton.

How lucky can you get? Having the two most liveable places in the world as your birthplace and your living-place; that's how lucky.

It's the people of Edmonton, not just the teams and winners of honours in every conceivable field of endeavour, who are the real champions. They're the ones who allow and then support, encourage, and protect the new ideas; the pursuit of the impossible; the actual doing of the unachievable. And they're the ones who, in mind-boggling numbers, voluntarily work harder than anybody knows to sustain the formidable (small-c) culture of this best of all possible cities.

It is a daily joy to work and live in River City among these remarkable people, to whom I personally owe everything. In this book, you can read about and see the tip of the iceberg.

Tommy Banks

Thousands of extraordinary citizens work in the shadow of every celebrity, quietly doing their best to build the relationships that make Edmonton thrive. When I see one of our well-known local philanthropists on the evening news, I'm as proud as anyone to discover that another important contribution to the city's welfare has been made. And I'm equally impressed when I see dedicated volunteers and Samaritans making vital contributions to the well being of their fellow Edmontonians. They look after our beautiful River Valley, drive revelers home during Operation Rednose, participate in the MS Walk or the Run for the Cure, take tickets or work security at the Folk or Fringe festivals, organize bake sales, give to the food bank, donate blood, and so much more. Edmontonians take enormous pride in making this lovely city a truly wonderful place to live.

This really is a City of Champions—too many champions to count, each one priceless. I'm proud to be a member of such a giving, caring community.

Lois E. Hole

Lois E. Hole, C.M.
Chancellor, University of Alberta

Contents

Amateur Sports (continued)

Festivals

Arts & Leisure

Contents

By the Numbers

The name City of Champions doesn't just come from Edmonton's history of sporting achievements. There are many people, places and events which have combined to make the city unique. Edmonton is a northern, resource-based centre that has led the way in areas ranging from population growth to computer systems.

The city's downtown arts district (centered on the grassy Sir Winston Churchill Square) has won its share of accolades, and has become a mecca for crowds during major events, or just a place for those checking out the trailblazing cultural scene.

Even in these terms of raw data and civic achievements, the numbers are impressive.

(Photo courtesy Edmonton International Street Performers Festival)

By the Numbers

Population

Edmonton is the fifth largest city in Canada, with a population of about 635,000. The Metro Edmonton area (which includes the city itself and neighbouring communities such as The Hamlet of Sherwood Park and The City of St. Albert) has a population of about 907,000. Edmonton is the largest metropolitan centre between Toronto and Vancouver.

As one of Canada's fastest-growing urban centres, Metropolitan Edmonton is expected to have a population of 1,000,000 by 2007.

Edmonton was incorporated as a town in 1892 with a population of 700 people. The Klondike Gold Rush of 1897 brought thousands of businessmen to Edmonton on their way north and in 1904 Edmonton was incorporated as a city with a population of 8,350.

Its population had increased to 11,400 when Edmonton was selected as the provincial capital in 1906. The city quickly developed a role as a service centre for the growing agricultural economy, resulting in further population growth. When Strathcona and North Edmonton were annexed in 1912, the city grew by another 5,580 people reaching a population of 53,611 that year.

Edmonton's biggest boom came with the 1947 discovery of oil in Leduc, a community just outside of Edmonton, and the city became the production centre of Canada's petrochemical industry. Within a decade Edmonton became one of the largest cities in Canada with a population increase

Edmonton's spectacular North Saskatchewan River Valley is the jewel in the crown of downtown Edmonton. The valley's parks system is the biggest of its kind in North America.
(Photo by Allyson Quince)

during the 1950s of 123,264 people. In 1956 Edmonton was reportedly one of the two fastest growing metropolitan areas in Canada and by 1959 the population reached 260,733.

This trend, along with the baby boom between 1947 and 1967, resulted in a continual increase in population through the 1960s. These factors combined with the annexation of the small neighbouring communities of Beverly in 1961 (population 8,970) and Jasper Place in 1964 (population 37,580) led to a population increase of 161,685 people during the 1960s, giving Greater Edmonton a population of more than 422,000 by 1969.

Population growth slowed during the 1970s but Edmonton still saw an increase of 68,941 people to 491,359 by 1979. Growth picked up during the 1980s, with the city's population increasing by 92,513 to hit 583,872 by 1989. The City of Edmonton's population is forecast to increase at an average rate of 1.3 per cent per year, reaching 679,700 by 2003.

Metro Edmonton covers 9,537 square kilometres (3,682 square miles) and encompasses 20 municipalities. The area's population is expected to grow by 1.4 per cent each year, reaching 955,900 by 2003.

Land Use

Edmonton is the most spacious city in Canada. The population density of Edmonton is 920 people per square kilometre (355 per square mile), the lowest in Canada and far below Toronto's population density of 6,729 per square kilometre (2,597 per square mile).

The city proper covers 670 square kilometres (259 square miles) of land, with the most outstanding feature of the city's land use being its North Saskatchewan River Valley parks system. With 7,425 hectares (18,348 acres) of parkland, it is the longest expanse of continuous urban parkland in North America. In total, Edmonton has 896 parks comprising 11,086 hectares (27,393 acres) and has the second-most parkland per capita of Canada's major cities.

The largest category of permitted land use in Edmonton, other than roadways, is agricultural.

Land use distribution in the city is 47 per cent for agricultural, 18.9 per cent for residential, 8.6 per cent for vacant or undeveloped land, 7.2 per cent for recreational and open spaces, six per cent for industrial, 4.6 per cent for transportation, 3.4 per cent for institutional, 3.3 per cent for commercial and 1.1 per cent for utilities. One land-use record for the city is an entry in *Ripley's Believe it or Not*. With 16 churches, 96 St. is acknowledged as "Church Street" by *Ripley's*.

Affordability

Edmonton is one of the most affordable major cities in the world. Predicted CMHC local housing market indicators for 1999 put Edmonton's average single new house price at $175,500 and the average single MLS (pre-owned homes) price at $132,900.

Edmonton also has one of the lowest residential tax rates of major Canadian cities and with approximately 41 per cent of resale homes priced at less than $100,000, Edmonton has a national reputation of having a real estate market with exceptional value. In the rental sector, Edmonton has the lowest apartment rental rates of major Canadian cities, and the lowest housing rental rates of major world cities surveyed by Runzheimer International.

Although not a record-setter on it's own, the Valley Zoo is one of the best-loved attractions in Edmonton's North Saskatchewan River Valley. Lucy the elephant is one of the main reasons people come back again and again to the zoo.
(Photo courtesy City of Edmonton)

Weather

Edmonton is one of Canada's sunniest cities, getting an average of 2,315 hours of sunlight per year. Due largely to the fact that it is Canada's northernmost major city, the average June day sees up to 17 hours of sunlight. Average temperatures in summer range from a high of 23C (73.4F) to a low of 12C (53.6F). The hottest day was on June 29, 1937, with a record of 37.2C (99F).

But being so far north (Lat. N:53° 32' and Long. W:113° 29') also means having colder than normal temperatures. A persistent snow cover typically lasts from mid-November to mid-March. A white Christmas is almost guaranteed in Edmonton, with a 98 per cent chance of having snow on the ground on that date. On average, there is a snow cover of 16 cm (6.3") on Christmas Day. But Christmas Day of 1970 set the record with a snow cover of 43cm (16.9").

In winter, temperatures average from a high of only -11C (12.2F) to a low of -19C (-2.2F). The coldest day on record was -49.4C (-57F) on January 19, 1886. The worst wind chill on record occurred on December 15, 1964 with a reading of -67C (-88.6F) or a heat loss of 2,732 watts per square metre.

Edmonton experienced a cold-winter record in 1969 with 26 consecutive days reading below -18C (-0.4F). But in 1984 the city recorded its mildest January-to-March period with temperatures more than 7C above normal. On Environment Canada's climate severity index, Edmonton rates a 37 (with 1 being very mild and 100 being very severe), just below Toronto at 35 and above Ottawa

Cycling is just one of the many leisure activities available in the river valley parks system.
(Photo courtesy City of Edmonton Archives)

at 43. Reportedly more than 60 per cent of harsh winter days in Edmonton are due to the wind chill factor.

On average, July is the hottest month of the year in Edmonton and January is the coldest.

The month with the most rainfall on average is July and the highest average snowfall occurs in January. Edmonton has annual averages of 349.3mm (14.1") of rainfall, and 129.6cm (50") of snowfall (measured on the ground).

The heaviest rainfall in Edmonton (since 1937) took place on July 31, 1953 with 114mm (4.5") of rain. The city's worst snowfall on record was in 1942 when a total of 495.3mm (19.5") fell between 2 a.m. on November 15, and 10 a.m. on November 16. On average, Edmonton has 21 hours of freezing precipitation a year, 35 hours of thunderstorm activity and chinooks on 12 days per winter.

Statistics also show that Edmonton enjoys a spell of warm fall weather three years out of every four, typically between September 19 and 26. Usually the good weather lasts for more than six days.

A Giving City

Edmontonians set the standard for good works. The Edmonton Food Bank, which as the Edmonton Gleaners Association has supplied food to needy families since 1981, was the first food bank in Canada.

The Alberta Capital Region United Way raised $12.4 million in 1998 through its 5,400 volunteers. That was a 20-per-cent boost in donations over the previous year, a record increase for any charity running in Alberta.

Started in February 1952, the Volunteer Centre of Edmonton is one of the oldest organizations of its kind in Canada. The centre refers approximately 4,000 volunteers to its 280 agencies each year. In 1998, the largest-ever global conference on volunteering was held in Edmonton with 2,700 delegates from more than 100 countries in attendance.

About 40 per cent of Edmontonians are formal volunteers, although that doesn't include the countless other unrecorded hours of volunteer work done in the city. Based on Edmonton's population that means that approximately 249,000 volunteers serve in formal positions each year. Each local volunteer contributes an estimated 147 hours of time annually, which translates into about 37 million hours of volunteer time served. If each hour is given a value of $10, the cost of volunteer hours in the city would be $370 million, an amount close to what the city takes in annually for residential and business taxes.

A Winning City

One of the city's outstanding achievements was Edmonton being the first major municipality in North America to embark on a long-range financial planning process, which resulted in the city receiving a straight-A report card from the Canadian Bond Rating Service. Other awards won by the city include:

1999

City Manager Bruce Thom won the Award of Excellence from the International City/County Management

Association. This prize, recognizing the world's top civic administrator, has never before been won by a Canadian.

Plan Edmonton (the city's 10-year general development plan) won the Award of Excellence from the Alberta Association of the Canadian Institute of Planners (AACIP).

Edmonton Transit driver Al Waselenchuk won the Canadian Urban Transit Association's National Bus Roadeo title, as the most skilled bus driver in the country. He won the regional title in 1999 and 1998.

1998

Edmonton was named as the most beautiful city in Canada in the national Communities in Bloom contest for the second year in a row. Edmonton won in the over-300,000 population category.

Special recognition was awarded to the city by the Canadian non-profit organization for its strong community partnerships and its success in controlling Dutch Elm disease. The Town of Stony Plain, just west of Edmonton, also won the national Communities in Bloom title, in the category of towns with 5,000 to 10,000 people.

The Capital City Downtown Plan won the AACIP Award as well as the 1997 Award of Merit from the International Downtown Association. Edmonton was one of only four cities in the world to receive the award. The five-year plan to revitalize the downtown is designed to promote continued economic development, provide for more parks and increase the downtown's residential population.

It also hopes to encourage arts, culture and entertainment, improve

The boom-and-bust cycle of Edmonton's past has lessened with the growth of non-resource industries. A side effect is how new construction activity such as this luxury high-rise project has once again become a common sight.
(Photo by Allyson Quince)

The Old Strathcona district is full of fun shops and historic buildings, such as the Dominion Hotel Building. The area centered on Whyte Ave. has become a culture and recreation magnet for the entire city.
(Photo by Allyson Quince)

parking, and preserve architectural heritage.

The City of Edmonton's Planning and Development Department's one-stop public information service system (known by the acronym of POSSE) won the 1998 Award of Excellence from the public-sector Canadian Information Productivity Awards - Canada's most prestigious information technology awards.

POSSE was also inducted into the Smithsonian Institution. POSSE also won the 1997 Award for Excellence and Innovation from the Urban and Regional Information Systems Association in Washington D.C. The system also received the Study Award from the Bertelsmann Foundation in Germany as one of the top 10 computer innovation systems in the local government category in North America.

1997

The city won a provincial Emerald Award for the renovation project on the High Level Bridge. The project used cutting-edge technology and techniques to safely strip away and dispose of toxic paint that had been used in the bridge's construction.

The Edmonton Police Service (EPS) Forensic Identification Section's photograph of tissue fragments on the inside of a gun barrel won the Tiller Award for Excellence in Law Enforcement Photography.

The city won the Alan Ridge Award for Merit for excellence in records and information management from the Association of Records Managers and Administrators.

1996

The city won the International Institute of Municipal Clerks Technology Award of Excellence for recognizing areas for improvement, developing solutions and following through.

On August 15, Edmonton opened Canada's first ECO Station to collect household hazardous wastes, furniture, broken appliances, yard waste, household refuse and recyclable material at a one-stop recycling and disposal facility year round.

The ECO Station is recognized as the most comprehensive facility of its kind in Canada.

The city's Historic Resource Management Team's preservation program was given the Heritage Canada Achievement Award for helping to preserve the city's past.

1995

The Canadian Institute of Planners awarded the city the Eric W. Thrift Award for Planning Excellence, for the Boyle St./MacCauley Redevelopment Plan. The award cited the effect the plan had in strengthening the inner-city neighbourhood's community ties.

Outstanding dedication to special-needs children won Staff Sgt. David Stewart of the Edmonton Police Service the 1995 Kiwanis Club award for outstanding community and volunteer service by police officers.

The 35-year EPS veteran, with his wife Deborah, has provided a safe haven over the years for numerous children with handicaps or from abusive backgrounds.

1992

The AACIP gave the city's Planning and Development department an award for its policy of street improvements.

1990

The city's policy to encourage the designation and preservation of historic resources has received two awards as the best of its kind.

One of the awards came from The Canadian Institute of Planners. The second of the awards was presented by the AACIP.

Although not an award per se, Edmonton set an environmental precedent when it became the first city in North America to recycle cardboard milk cartons.

Quick Facts

Edmontonians are believed to be the most ecologically minded people in Canada, using less water per person than any other city in the country.

Professional Sports

Edmonton has a tradition of sporting achievement. From the city's beginnings, this legacy has been the foundation of a professional sports community that has always attained excellence.

The Eskimos, Oilers, Drillers and Trappers are the four big professional sports franchises in Edmonton today. They are just the latest of the pro teams that have each given the city some of its most exciting memories.

Whether through team wins, or by the standout play of individuals such as Eskimo legend Jackie Parker (left) and Wayne Gretzky (right), professional sports has been one of the most visible ways in which Edmonton has earned the title 'City of Champions.'

(Photo courtesy W.B. Ranson)

Professional Sports

While many non-Edmontonians think only of hockey when it comes to notable Edmonton sports teams, the city has a long history in several different sports.

Edmonton Eskimo Football Club

No current professional sports organization in Edmonton has the history and winning tradition of the Canadian Football League's Edmonton Eskimo Football Club.

Both on and off the field, the team fondly known as the Eskimos (or Esks) is known as Canada's most successful professional football franchise.

The team has won more championships than any other current professional sports organization in Edmonton, and is a perennial fan favourite.

The Eskimos' history began in 1892, when the club was organized as a rugby team, and defeated an established Calgary club. Beating Calgary was a trend that has continued for more than 100 years. In 1895, Edmonton won its first Alberta Rugby Football championship.

With the new century came changes and more victories, and the organization won its second Alberta Rugby Football championship in 1908.

The team's name was officially changed to Eskimo in 1910, and the organization became part of the Western Canada Rugby Football Union (WCRFU) that was established in 1911. The team won the 1913 Alberta Rugby Football championship, its third such title.

There were no games during World War One, but the WCRFU was re-started in 1919. The Esks became the first western-based team to take part in the Grey Cup, in 1921, but lost to the home team Toronto Argonauts 23-0. The Esks appeared in the Grey Cup game again the following year, losing to Queen's University 13-1.

The team officially disbanded after 1923, but played rugby in the local league until 1928. After losing the

An early but undated photograph of the Edmonton Eskimo Team.
(Photo courtesy City of Edmonton Archives)

Alberta Rugby Football championship in 1924, the Eskimos won the Alberta title for a sixth time in 1928.

Edmonton's Joe Cook tossed the first forward pass for a touchdown, in a 1929 game. The Eskimos were part of the Western Interprovincial Football Union from 1938 to 1940, but in blue-and-white uniforms.

After dropping out of the WIFU (which ceased operations during the Second World War), the Edmonton Eskimo Rugby Football Club became a publicly owned company in 1948. Shares were a dollar each, and 20,000 were available. Local legends such as Joe Shoctor and Henry Singer became involved with the organization, which has remained a community owned club ever since.

The team rejoined the WIFU in 1949. The Esks adopted the current colours of green and gold that year when they had to borrow uniforms from the University of Alberta, and decided to stick with the now-famous green and gold colour scheme.

The Eskimos didn't win any championships during the next few years, but one notable achievement was halfback Billy Vessels receiving the first Schenley Award, in 1953, as the league's outstanding player.

The modern winning tradition began in 1954, with the famous Grey Cup win over the heavily favoured Montreal Alouettes. The game is best known for Jackie Parker's last-minute fumble recovery for a touchdown. Bob Dean kicked the convert and the Eskimos won the team's first Grey Cup championship.

The Esks won the second cup title the next year, and Normie Kwong won

Henry "Gizmo" Williams is a multiple record-holder, and one of the most-loved Eskimos of all time.
(Photo courtesy Edmonton Eskimo Football Club)

the Schenley Award as the outstanding Canadian player.

The Canadian Football Council was officially formed in 1956, and the Eskimos (led by quarterback and future Premier of Alberta Don Getty) celebrated by winning the team's third Grey Cup in a row, beating Montreal. Kwong again won the Schenley as

Kicker Dave Cutler; one of the most prolific scorers in Eskimo history.
(Photo courtesy Edmonton Eskimo Football Club)

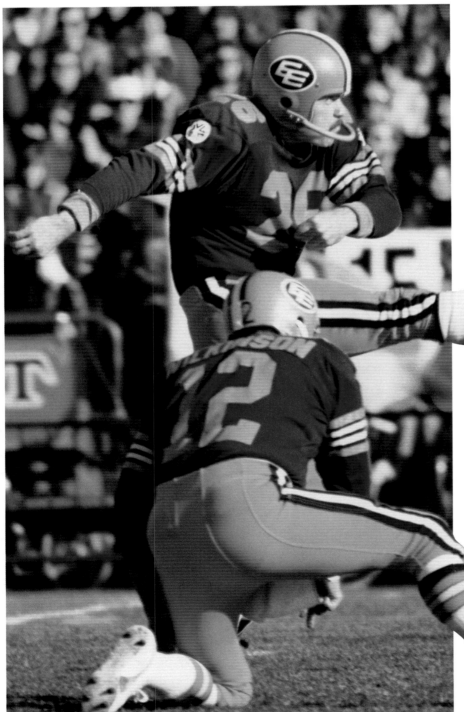

outstanding Canadian. Another outstanding player of this era was Rollie Miles, who was named to the league's all-star team eight times.

Although the team didn't make it to the Grey Cup in 1957, Jackie Parker was named the league's outstanding player, and Johnny Bright won the league's rushing title. Parker and Bright repeated their Schenley Award wins the next year. Parker would again win the title of league's best player, in 1960.

The 1960s saw little success for the Eskimos as a team, but there were some personal highlights for the players.

Among those highlights was Bill Mitchell setting a CFL record for the longest field goal, at 58 yards, in 1964. The record stood for six years, until Esk Dave Cutler kicked a 59-yard field goal in 1970. Cutler would set another league record in 1973, kicking 32 field goals in a season. George McGowan would tie the CFL record of 15 receptions in a game, and win the Schenley Award as the league's outstanding player.

Although Grey Cup wins still eluded the team, individual awards continued. Tom Wilkinson won the Schenley as the league's outstanding player in 1974.

The late 1970s and early 1980s were a golden era for the Eskimos, both for individual players and as a team. The Grey Cup title once again went to Edmonton in 1975 (its fourth championship) when the team beat Montreal 9-8.

The team's remarkable, and

unchallenged, string of five consecutive Grey Cup victories began in 1978, when the Eskimos beat Montreal 21-13. The second in a row came in 1979, as the Esks once again defeated Montreal, this time 17-9. The third in a row was in 1980, with a 48-10 win over Hamilton. 1981 saw the team with its fourth title in the sequence, with a 26-23 win over Ottawa (the team's 14-1-1 season was also a league record). The fifth title in a row came after an unremarkable 3-5 start in the 1982 season. The Eskimos won all remaining eight games, and beat Toronto 32-16 in the Grey Cup game.

Future NFL great, quarterback Warren Moon was voted the outstanding player and James Parker won the Schenley Award as the league's outstanding defensive player.

The team created the Wall of Honour at Commonwealth Stadium in 1983. Tom Wilkinson was the first player honoured.

Edmonton hosted its first Grey Cup game in 1984, but the team had been eliminated in the division semi-finals.

A banner year for the Eskimos came in 1987.

As well as winning its tenth Grey Cup title, the team set many records. Brian Kelly set the CFL career record for most yards receiving (11,169), most touchdown receptions (97), most 100-yard receiving games (41) and most 1,000-yard seasons (six). Henry "Gizmo" Williams set league records for most punt returns for touchdowns in a season (five), and

Warren Moon was not only a championship Eskimo quarterback, he went on to greatness in the National Football League.

(Photo courtesy Edmonton Eskimo Football Club)

most punt returns for touchdowns in a quarter and a game (both two).

The Eskimo's official fortieth anniversary came in 1989, and the team broke its own league record for season wins, notching 16 victories in that season. Other team records set that year included most points (644), most touchdowns (70) and most yards gained (7,951).

Also that year, Tracy Ham set a league record for the most rushing yards by a quarterback, with 1,051.

Eskimo players would set more individual records, and the team's last big victory came in 1993, winning the Grey Cup with a 33-23 victory over Winnipeg.

Canadian Eskimo players have set records, winning the most Outstanding Canadian awards by taking 11 of the trophies since they were first handed out in 1974. Willie Pless has won the award more times (five) than any other player.

One of the newest record-holders is

The 1978 Grey Cup Champions. Back row, left to right: Brian Fryer, Pat McNeil, Gregg Butler, Hector Pothier, Joe Hollimon, Warren Moon, Danny Kepley, George McGowan and Jim Duncan. Third Row, left to right: Don Warrington, Pete Lavorato, John Farlinger, Dave Fennell, David Boone, Bruce Lemmerman, John Konihowski, Tom Scott, York Hentschel, Ted Milian and Barry Kowalski. Second Row, left to right: Stewart Kirtio, Mike Paush, Dwayne Mandrusiak, Jim Adams, Derrick Glanton, Bill Stevenson, Stuart Lang, Willie Martin, Waddell Smith, Larry Washington, Jim Germany, Ed Jones, Tom Towns, Hank Ilesic, Ian Bryans, Brian Kelly, Dave Cutler, Hamish Wright, Tom Pon and Jimmy Buckanesky. Front row, left to right: Charlie Turner, Ron Estay, Tom Wilkinson, Angelo Santucci, Don Matthews, Hugh Campbell, Matt Baldwin, Dan Daniel, Quincy Moffat, Larry Highbaugh, Dale Potter, Eric Upton and Bob Howes. Absent: Assistant coaches Joe Faragalli and Cal Murphy.

(Photo courtesy Edmonton Eskimo Football Club)

coach Don Matthews. Beginning his first season as the Eskimo head coach in 1999, Matthews came in already holding the CFL record for the most wins as a coach, with 148. Every game he wins with Edmonton will extend that record. Eagle Keys has third place for wins as a head coach, with 131 wins. He coached the Esks from 1959 to 1963.

Legendary Eskimo coach Joe Faragalli holds the record for the most wins in a season, when the Eskimos set the league standard of 16 (against two losses) in 1990.

Hugh Campbell (president and CEO) holds the record for consecutive first-place finishes as a head coach, when the Esks took the title six times in a row, from 1977 to 1982. That same remarkable stretch left Campbell with the record for having most consecutive Grey Cup wins (five) and appearances (six) among head coaches.

Even the Eskimos field, Commonwealth Stadium, has set a record. The 1997 Grey Cup had the

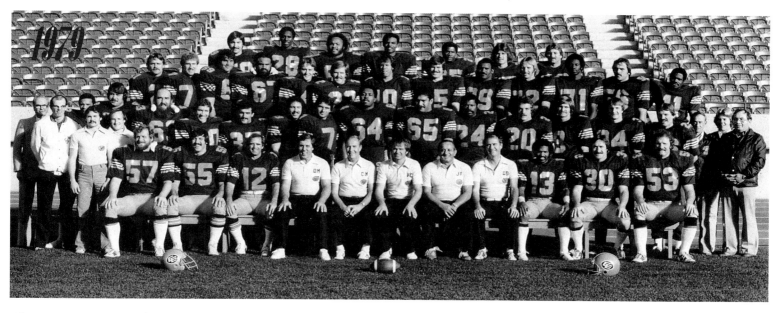

The 1979 Grey Cup Champions. Back row left to right: Leo Blanchard, Gregg Butler, Jimmy Walker, Warren Moon, Jim Germany, Marco Cyncar and Danny Kepley. Third row left to right: Don Warrington, Brian Fryer, York Hentschel, Mike Wilson, Dave Zacharko, Tom Scott, Bruce Lemmerman, Stuart Lang, Joe Hollimon, John Konihowski, Waddell Smith, Ted Milian and Jimmy Rogers. Second row left to right: Quincy Moffat, Jim Adams, Jerome Stanton, Dwayne Mandrusiak, Bill Stevenson, Dennis Dickau, Hector Pothier, Brian Kelly, Emilio Fraietta, Angelo Santucci, Pete Lavorato, David Boone, Dave Fennell, Ed Jones, Tom Towns, Hank Ilesic, Ian Bryans, Dave Cutler, Buck Buckanesky, Mike Paush and Tom Pon. Front row left to right: Eric Upton, Ron Estay, Tom Wilkinson, Don Matthews, Cal Murphy, Hugh Campbell, Joe Faragalli, Dan Daniel, Larry Highbaugh, Dale Potter and Bob Howes. Missing: Carl Crennel.

(Photo courtesy Edmonton Eskimo Football Club)

1982

The 1982 Grey Cup Champions (above). Back row, left to right: Leo Blanchard, Ken Walter, Harry Doering, Mark deBrueys, Dan Kearns, Dan Butcher, Tom Tuinei, Warren Moon, Marco Cyncar, James Parker, Bill Manchuk and Danny Kepley. Third row, left to right: Brian Fryer, Brian Kelly, Mike Levenseller, Craig Mallender, Tom Scott, Greg Marshall, Dave Fennell, David Boone, Mike Williams, Ralph Dixon, Ted Milian and Neil Lumsden. Second row, left to right: Bill Stevenson, Clif Olander, Rod Connop, Hector Pothier, Nereo Bolzon, Angelo Santucci, Emilio Fraietta, Mike McLeod, Ed Jones, Tom Towns, Wendell Williams, Gary Hayes, Jim Germany, Dave Cutler and Joe Hollimon. Front row, left to right: Hank Ilesic, Sean Kehoe, Waddell Smith, Don Matthews, Bruce Lemmerman, Hugh Campbell, Cal Murphy, Gene Gaines, Larry Highbaugh, Dale Potter and Eric Upton.

(Photo courtesy Edmonton Eskimo Football Club)

The 1981 Grey Cup Champions (right). Back row, left to right: Leo Blanchard, Ken Walter, Dan Kearns, John Pointer, Hank Ilesic, Warren Moon, Joe Hollimon, James Parker, Bill Manchuk and Danny Kepley. Third row, left to right: Brian Kelly, Stuart Lang, Waddell Smith, Tom Scott, Mark Wald, David Boone, David Fennell, Marco Cyncar, Sean Kehoe, Ted Milian and Neil Lumsden. Second row, left to right: Bill Stevenson, Brian Fryer, Brian Broomell, Hector Pothier, Pete Lavorato, Angelo Santucci, Emilio Fraietta, Mike McLeod, Ed Jones, Tom Towns, Jim Germany, Dave Cutler and Gary Hayes. Front row, left to right: Eric Upton, Ron Estay, Tom Wilkinson, Don Matthews, Bruce Lemmerman, Hugh Campbell, Cal Murphy, Dan Daniel, Larry Highbaugh, Dale Potter and Bob Howes.

(Photo courtesy Edmonton Eskimo Football Club)

The 1980 Grey Cup Champions (above). Back row, left to right: Leo Blanchard, Danny Buggs, Robert Barber, David Boone, York Hentschel, David Fennell, Harry Walters and Danny Kepley. Third row, left to right: Brian Fryer, Brian Broomell, Don Warrington, Randy Simmrin, Stuart Lang, Dan Kearns, Tom Scott, Hank Ilesic, Mark Wald, Warren Moon, James Parker, Mike Wilson, Joe Hollimon, Ted Milian, Jim Germany, John Konihowski and Neil Lumsden. Second row, left to right: Brian Kelly, Bill Stevenson, Gregg Butler, Hector Pothier, Pete Lavorato, Angelo Santucci, Emilio Fraietta, Mike McLeod, Maurice Burton, Ed Jones, Tom Towns, Ernest Pough and Dave Cutler. Front row, left to right: Eric Upton, Ron Estay, Tom Wilkinson, Don Matthews, Cal Murphy, Hugh Campbell, Joe Faragalli, Dan Daniel, Larry Highbaugh, Dale Potter, Bob Howes. Absent are Waddell Smith and Dan Yochum.

(Photo courtesy Edmonton Eskimo Football Club)

highest attendance of any league championship game, with 60,431 fans.

Edmonton Oilers

The Edmonton Oilers have brought the city its greatest international attention, and were integral in its most intense period of pro-sports success. It all began when the legendary Bill Hunter brought them here as a World Hockey Association franchise in 1972.

Joining the National Hockey League when the WHA was amalgamated in 1979, the team almost immediately began to dominate the professional hockey world.

The Oilers was the first of the old WHA teams to win the

One of the greatest players in NHL history, Mark Messier is one of many Oilers who were an invaluable part of the team's glory years.
(Photo courtesy Edmonton Oilers Hockey Club)

Stanley Cup, doing it faster than any expansion team.

The Oilers have so far won five Stanley Cup championships (1983/84, 1984/85, 1986/87, 1987/88 and 1989/90). A wave of the

team's championship banners hangs from the rafters at Skyreach Centre - their home rink. As well as the Stanley Cup wins, the team took the title for first place in the regular season standings three times, won six Campbell Conference championships and took eight Smythe Division championships.

Oilers players have been the source of countless hours of charity work and community service over the years. One of the groundbreaking efforts came when Glenn Anderson aligned himself with the Cross Cancer Institute. He sponsored the unique idea of having individuals and businesses donate increasing amounts of cash for cancer research every time he added to his points total. He also provided personal memorabilia for a special room at the institute to help lift the spirits of patients and their families.

The Oilers of the mid-1980s have been called the best hockey team the world has ever seen. While the unofficial title may be argued, Oilers players hold or have tied 26 regular-season, and 28 playoff league records. Here are the more notable achievements.

Team Records:
Most goals in a season - 446 (1983/84).
Highest goals-per-game average in a season - 5.58 (446 goals in 80 games) (1983/84).
Most shorthanded goals in one season - 36 (1983/84).
Most scoring points in one season - 1,182 (1983/84).

Jari Kurri, Wayne Gretzky and Glenn Anderson pose (photo left) after they set the record for the most 50-or-more goal scorers on a team in one season (in both 1983/84 and 1985/86). The impromptu team portrait (photo below) came after the 1987/88 Stanley Cup win. It was initiated by Gretzky, and was the last time he was photographed playing as an Edmonton Oilers member.
(Photos courtesy Edmonton Oilers Hockey Club)

Most assists in one season - 736 (1983/84).

Most 50-or-more scorers in one season - 3. 1983/84: Wayne Gretzky (87) Glenn Anderson (54) and Jari Kurri (52). 1985/86: Jari Kurri (68) Glenn Anderson (54) and Wayne Gretzky (52).

Longest undefeated streak at the start of a season - 15 games (12 wins, 3 ties) (1984/85).

Fewest games in a season without scoring a goal - 0 (1980/81, 1981/82, 1986/87).

Individual Records:

Most goals in a season - 92, Wayne Gretzky (1981/82).

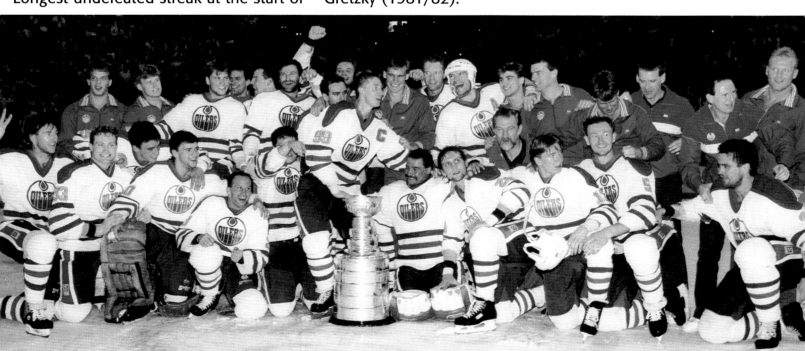

Star player Kevin Lowe (above) in 1999 became head coach.

(Photo courtesy Edmonton Oilers Hockey Club)

Most goals in a season by a defenceman - 48, Paul Coffey (1985/86).

Most assists in a season - 163, Wayne Gretzky (1985/86).

Most points in a season - 215, Wayne Gretzky (1985/86).

Most games scoring three goals or better in a season - 10, Wayne Gretzky (1981/82, and 1983/84).

Fastest two shorthanded goals - 12 seconds apart, Esa Tikkanen (vs. Toronto, 1988).

Longest consecutive-game point-scoring streak - 51 games, Wayne Gretzky (1983/84).

Most assists in a game - 7, Wayne Gretzky (three times, in 1980, 1985, 1986).

Most assists by a goalkeeper in one season - 14, Grant Fuhr (1983/84).

Most playoff points in one year - 47, Wayne Gretzky (1984/85).

Most playoff goals in one year - 19, Jari Kurri (1984/85).

Most playoff assists in one year - 31, Wayne Gretzky (1987/88).

Most shorthanded goals in one playoff year - 3, both Wayne Gretzky (1982-83) and Todd Marchant (1996-97).

Most powerplay goals in one playoff game - 3, Jari Kurri (1987).

Most assists in one playoff game - 6, Wayne Gretzky (1987).

Most points in one playoff game period - 4, both Wayne Gretzky (1987)

Todd Marchant (photo above) is one of the current Oilers with an entry in the NHL record books.
(Photo courtesy Edmonton Oilers Hockey Club)

Some of the current owners of the Edmonton Oilers. Back, left to right: Manuel Balsa, Gary Gregg, Art Mihalcheon, Dick Paine, Tom Mayson, Ron Hodgson, Tim Melton. Front, left to right: Ernie Elko, Ed Bean, Simon Sochatsky, Cal Nichols, Jim Hole, Bruce Saville, Jim Woods, Bill Butler, and Linda Hughes. Not shown are: Dave Addie, Neal Allen, Jakob Ambrosius, Gordon Buchanan, Dick Colf, Mike Dalton, Don Hamilton, Gerald Knoll, Walter Kuchar, Larry Makelki, Al Owen, Marcel Roberge, Harold Roozen, Rusty Stalwick, Barry Weaver, Keith Weaver, Jim Zanello, Todd McFarlane, Roger Roberge, Ted Barrett, and anonymous.

(Photo courtesy The Edmonton Journal)

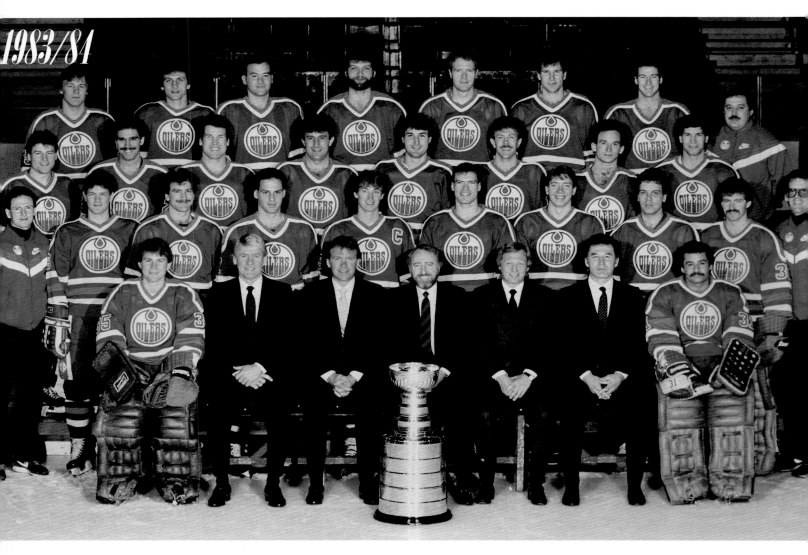

1983/84

The *1983/84 Stanley Cup Champions. Front row, left to right: Andy Moog, John Muckler, Glen Sather, Peter Pocklington, Bruce MacGregor, Ted Green and Grant Fuhr. Second row, left to right: Barrie Stafford, Pat Hughes, Glenn Anderson, Lee Fogolin, Wayne Gretzky, Mark Messier, Jari Kurri, Dave Lumley, Mike Zanier and Peter Millar. Third row, left to right: Pat Conacher, Charlie Huddy, Dave Hunter, Jaroslav Pouzar, Paul Coffey, Willy Lindstrom, Ken Linseman and Larry Melnyk. Fourth row, left to right: Raimo Summanen, Kevin McClelland, Rick Chartraw, Dave Semenko, Randy Gregg, Don Jackson, Kevin Lowe and Lyle Kulchisky.*

(Photo courtesy Edmonton Oilers Hockey Club)

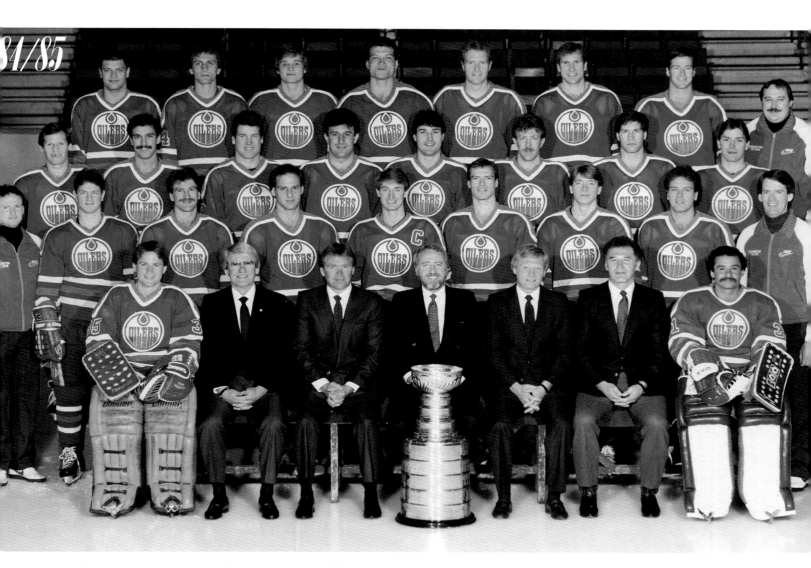

The 1984/85 Stanley Cup Champions. Front row, left to right: Andy Moog, John Muckler, Glen Sather, Peter Pocklington, Bruce MacGregor, Ted Green and Grant Fuhr. Second row, left to right: Barrie Stafford, Pat Hughes, Glenn Anderson, Lee Fogolin, Wayne Gretzky, Mark Messier, Jari Kurri, Dave Lumley and Peter Millar. Third row, left to right: Mark Napier, Charlie Huddy, Dave Hunter, Jaroslav Pouzar, Paul Coffey, Willy Lindstrom, Larry Melnyk and Billy Carroll. Back row, left to right: Esa Tikkanen, Kevin McClelland, Mike Krushelnyski, Dave Semenko, Randy Gregg, Don Jackson, Kevin Lowe and Lyle Kulchisky.

(Photo courtesy Edmonton Oilers Hockey Club)

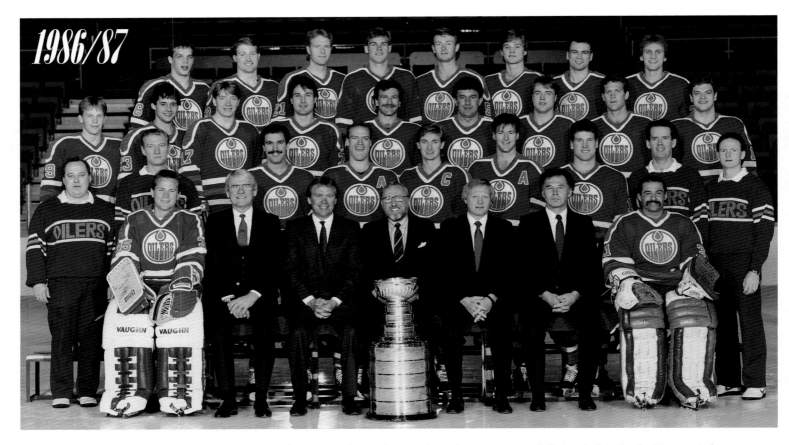

The 1986/87 Stanley Cup Champions (above). Front row, left to right: Andy Moog, John Muckler, Glen Sather, Peter Pocklington, Bruce MacGregor, Ted Green and Grant Fuhr. Second row, left to right: Lyle Kulchisky, Juergen Merz, Charlie Huddy, Mark Messier, Wayne Gretzky, Kevin Lowe, Dave Hunter, Peter Millar and Barrie Stafford. Third Row, left to right: Reijo Routsalainen, Moe Lemay, Jari Kurri, Paul Coffey, Glenn Anderson, Jaroslav Pouzar, Kent Nilsson, Craig MacTavish and Esa Tikkanen. Back row, left to right: Kelly Buchberger, Marty McSorley, Randy Gregg, Jeff Beukeboom, Steve Smith, Mike Krushelnyski, Craig Muni and Kevin McClelland.

(Photo courtesy Edmonton Oilers Hockey Club)

1987/88

The *1987/88 Stanley Cup Champions* (above). Front row, left to right: Bill Ranford, John Muckler, Glen Sather, Peter Pocklington, Bruce MacGregor, Ted Green and Grant Fuhr. Second row, left to right: Lyle Kulchisky, Juergen Merz, Charlie Huddy, Glenn Anderson, Mark Messier, Wayne Gretzky, Kevin Lowe, Jari Kurri, Keith Acton, Peter Millar and Barrie Stafford. Third row, left to right: Dave Hannan, Geoff Courtnall, Craig MacTavish, Marty McSorley, Kevin McClelland, Normand Lacombe and Esa Tikkanen. Back row, left to right: Craig Muni, Craig Simpson, Steve Smith, Jeff Beukeboom, Randy Gregg, Mike Krushelnyski and Daryl Reaugh.

(Photo courtesy Edmonton Oilers Hockey Club)

The *1989/90 Stanley Cup Champions* (left). Front row, left to right: Grant Fuhr, Jari Kurri, Mark Messier, Ron Low, John Muckler, Glen Sather, Bill Ranford, Peter Pocklington, Bruce MacGregor, Ted Green, Kevin Lowe, Glenn Anderson and Eldon Reddick. Second row, left to right: Lyle Kulchisky, Ken Lowe, Reijo Routsalainen, Charlie Huddy, Petr Klima, Craig Simpson, Craig MacTavish, Joe Murphy, Esa Tikkanen, Adam Graves, Martin Gelinas, Mark Lamb, Stewart Poirier and Barrie Stafford. Back row, left to right: Kelly Buchberger, Geoff Smith, Steve Smith, Randy Gregg, Dave Brown, Jeff Beukeboom, Vladimir Ruzicka and Craig Muni.

(Photo courtesy Edmonton Oilers Hockey Club)

and Glenn Anderson (1988).
Most playoff wins by a goaltender in
one playoff year - 16, both Grant Fuhr
(1988) and Bill Ranford (1990).

The Oilers have some non-playing
achievements as well, such as becoming
the NHL's first and only community-
owned team in 1998, when it was
purchased by a group of 37 local
businesspeople and ordinary citizens
from Edmonton and across Northern
Alberta.

The unprecedented move came
when then-owner Peter Pocklington was
facing financial collapse, and his bank
(Alberta Treasury Branches) took over
the team and other assets, putting them
up for sale to the highest bidder.

Luckily for Edmonton, an earlier deal
Pocklington made to gain concessions
from the city had him sign a deal that if
the team was to be sold, a local buyer

would be given first option to purchase
the team for US $70 million.

When a Houston businessman
arrived to buy the team, there were
fears that no one person or group in
Edmonton could come up with the cash.

In a move that showed loyalty to the
city over sheer profit-making, a group of
local entrepreneurs - led by Cal Nichols,
Jim Hole, Ed Bean and Bruce Saville -
stepped up to form a conglomerate of
buyers.

Wheeling and dealing until literally
the last minute of the deadline imposed
by Pocklington's earlier deal, they came
up with the cash and loans to secure
the team. It was an arrangement the
NHL was unfamiliar with, but the
businessmen persuaded the league that
it would work.

The success of the takeover -
although stunning - wasn't a surprise to

Edmonton's first major hockey championship in 1948 created a legacy of excellence. There were other celebrations in the years to come as more titles were won. This mid-1950s photo shows players (left to right) Larry Wilson, Glenn Hall, Jim Anderson and Al Arbour.
(Photo courtesy City of Edmonton Archives)

people who knew the group.

Nichols had led a different group a few years earlier that had saved the Oilers from financial troubles, by boosting the number of season tickets sold, and doing it in record time.

Other notable achievements included the 1989 NHL All-Star game, generally considered one of the finest ever put together. It was the last time the NHL allowed a member club to completely organize and run the event.

Another achievement was the last-minute staging of the NHL entry draft in 1995. The event was held in Edmonton because of the move of the original hosts, the Winnipeg Jets, to Arizona.

Even before the Edmonton Oilers brought worldwide attention and championships to the city, there were many professional and semi-professional junior teams that brought championships to Edmonton. Here's a rundown of the teams and some of their accomplishments.

Edmonton Hockey Club

The earliest recorded official hockey team in the city, it was the first Alberta team to play for the Stanley Cup. After winning the championship of Western Canada, the club played challenge matches for the cup in 1908 and 1910, but lost both times.

Edmonton Hustlers

This was the city's main hockey team in the 1910s and 1920s, but there were no championships.

Edmonton Flyers

Playing first as amateurs and later as a professional farm team for the Detroit

Edmonton Flyers Captain Gordon Watt accepts the Allan Cup.
(Photo courtesy City of Edmonton Archives)

Red Wings, the Flyers was the best game in town from its start in 1939 through to the 1962/63 season.

The high point came when the Flyers brought Edmonton its first taste of hockey championship, winning the 1948 Allan Cup (the national amateur championship). The series was a walkover, with the Flyers, led by captain Gordon Watt, winning four games to one over the Ottawa Senators.

The event was a watershed in Edmonton's sports history. It was estimated at the time that more than 60,000 people (about half of the city's population) showed up to cheer the team in a victory parade along Jasper Avenue.

The Flyers fans saw many future NHL stars make their career starts here. These players included Al Rollins (goalkeeper on the 1948 Allan Cup-winning team) who went on to win the 1954 Vezina and Hart Trophies in the National Hockey League with the Chicago Black Hawks.

Another player was Al Arbour, who would later gain fame as the coach and general manager of the New York Islanders during its glory years.

The Flyers also won the 1952/53 Western Hockey League title, and the next season became the first team to win both the regular-season title and the league championship (beating the Calgary Stampeders). Notable players from this era included future NHL greats Glenn Hall, Johnny Bucyk and Norm Ullman. The last title won by the Flyers was the 1961/62 league championship.

One of the people associated with the team as a non-player was trainer Tiger Goldstick. One of Edmonton's many colourful sporting characters, Goldstick was involved in many sports

The Edmonton Ice was the city's last link to its junior-hockey glory years. (Photo courtesy Northlands)

(notably baseball), and was a tireless sports booster who would later found a children's sports charity and have a city sports field named in his honour.

Edmonton Oil Kings

With the demise of the Flyers, the focus of professional hockey fell on the Oil Kings junior team. The team was formed in 1950, but played only special matches and did not join the Western Canada Junior Hockey League until the next season.

Only two years after entering the league, the Oil Kings won the league title, but lost the Memorial Cup series to St. Catherines. Norm Ullman and Johnny Bucyk were early Oil Kings (and Flyers) players who would make it to the NHL. At the time, players didn't have agents, but Oil Kings manager Leo LeClerc helped both players negotiate their NHL contracts, making him arguably the first player agent. Other names to become famous in Edmonton hockey circles were manager Bill Hunter (who would bring the Oilers to town), Pat Quinn (NHL coach) and Glen Sather, the current Oilers general manager.

The team's first Memorial Cup came in the 1962/63 season, in its fourth straight attempt. The second Memorial Cup championship came in 1966, when Bill Hunter had become the team's manager. The next major title was the 1970/71 Western Canada Hockey League championship. During this time, the Oil Kings would play for the Memorial Cup more times than any other Alberta team.

After years of being the dominant hockey team in Alberta, the team played in its last Memorial Cup in 1971/72.

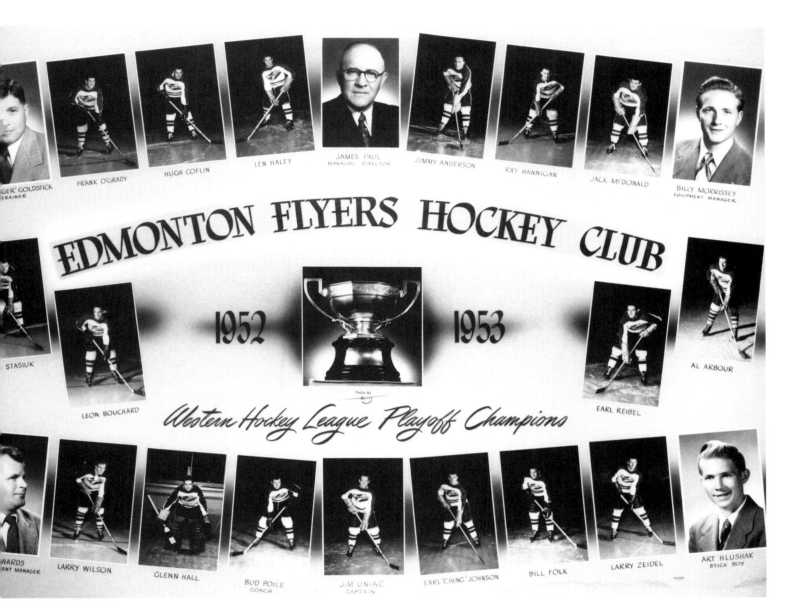

52/53 Edmonton Flyers team picture shows a veritable who's who of the city's sports legends. Several of the players *d here went on to successful non-hockey careers either in Edmonton, or as National Hockey League stars.*

(Photo courtesy City of Edmonton Archives)

Edmonton Nuggets/Monarchs

One of the city's leading teams of the late 1960s (the name was changed partway through its existence), the team played in the Western Canada Senior Hockey League. There were no championships.

Edmonton Ice

Playing from 1996 - 1998, the Ice was the first major junior team in Edmonton since the advent of the Oilers.

The team did not win any championships before moving to British Columbia.

Edmonton Drillers

Edmonton has been called the soccer capital of Canada.

Commonwealth Stadium, the country's best natural-turf facility, is the home of Canada's national soccer team. Canada's top-level international matches are played in Edmonton, routinely seeing the largest crowds for such events.

Professional soccer has a history of success in Edmonton, which has been involved in the sport from its beginnings as a national professional movement. Currently, professional soccer is represented in Edmonton by the Drillers indoor team - a member of the National Professional Soccer League.

The team - which plays in Skyreach Centre - was established in 1996 when the Chicago Power was purchased and brought to the city. The name was a revival of a name used by the defunct 1980-81 NASL championship indoor soccer team.

The Drillers' first game was on November 1, 1996, and its first season ended with a 21-19 record (the team lost in the conference semi-final to St. Louis).

But there were some records set by the team. The first year saw Domenic Mobilio lead the league in power play goals, with nine. Goalkeeper Scott Hileman led the league with a low 10.09 average.

Awards earned by the team in the first year include: Ross Ongaro, Coach of the Year; Carmen D'Onofrio, runner-up for Rookie of the Year and named to the league's All-NPSL Rookie team; Shayne Campbell and Martin Dugas were named Second Team Rookie All-Stars; and Goalkeeper Hileman (team MVP) was named to the third.

The team went into the 1998 playoffs as the division champions. That season saw the Drillers have the best record in the National Conference, and Ongaro was again named coach of the year.

The current Drillers team has a connection to the very start of professional soccer in Edmonton.

That began in 1979, when entrepreneur Peter Pocklington bought the Oakland Stompers of the North American Soccer League for US$3.8 million, renamed them the Drillers, and had them play both indoor and outdoor games.

The team steadily improved, and brought the city its first professional soccer title, in 1981, by winning the North American indoor soccer championship.

The team also went to the finals the following year, but was defeated.

With almost no fan base in North America, the league seemed doomed from the start, and the team folded in 1984.

The next professional soccer team in Edmonton was the Eagles, an outdoor team that played in the Canadian Professional Soccer League.

Playing in Clarke Stadium, the team brought more soccer success to Edmonton, winning the league championship at the end of a string of 14 straight wins in the 1983/84 season. But the entire league folded due to financial problems.

The Edmonton Brickmen were next to take up the city's professional soccer

banner. Playing in the Western Alliance, an outdoor league in Western Canada and the United States, the team was again owned by Peter Pocklington, but took its name from the Brick Warehouse, the national chain of furniture stores that began in Edmonton.

The team played in the Canadian Soccer League beginning in the 1987 season, but never achieved the same level of success as it predecessors. The league folded in 1991.

The Eagles (above) and the original Drillers (below). (Photographs courtesy Ross Ongaro)

Edmonton Trappers

Edmonton's current professional baseball team is the Trappers, which has been playing in the city since 1981. The Trappers was the province's first Triple-A professional team, as well as the most successful.

The team is currently affiliated with the Anaheim Angels. The team was affiliated with the Oakland Athletics from 1995 to 1998, the Florida Marlins in 1993 and 1994, the California Angels between 1983 and 1992, and originally was the farm club for the Chicago White Sox, in 1981 and 1982.

In less than 20 years, the team has managed to post several major awards and records. Most notably, it won the Pacific Coast League championship in 1997, 1996, and 1984.

The team also won the 1983 first-half northern division title, and the 1990 second-half northern division title. The team was named the Minor League Team of the Year in 1996 by *Baseball America* newspaper.

Baseball America has also handed out awards to individual Trappers as Minor League Player of the Year: Ron Kittle in 1982, Tim Salmon in 1992, and Eric Chavez in 1998.

Trappers players have also gone on to American League Rookie of the Year awards after moving up to the majors.

Kittle won the title in 1983, Salmon won in 1993, and most recently Ben Grieve took the award in 1998.

Baseball has a long history in Edmonton. Semi-pro, fully amateur and recreational baseball teams have been a regular sight almost since the city's inception. Indeed, in the 1920s

Edmonton was the busiest baseball town west of Toronto.

Perhaps no one in Edmonton's baseball history is as well-known as John Ducey.

As a player, umpire, coach and general manager, Ducey spent his life promoting the game in Edmonton, and as such was one of the first six people - and the only Western Canadian - named to the Canadian Baseball Hall of Fame when it was established in 1983. The award came just weeks before his death.

Two players for the Edmonton Eskimo baseball team (the forerunner of the Trappers) were named to the Baseball Hall of Fame: Heine Manush and Leon Day. The Eskimos were part of the Western International League, and started operations in 1953.

One of the city's firsts in baseball came with the installation of floodlights at Renfrew Park ball diamond after the Second World War.

The new lights were fired up August 15, 1947 - Canada's first ever night game.

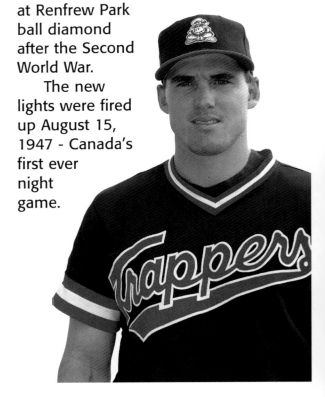

Tim Salmon is just one of the major-league baseball stars who once called themselves Trappers.
(Photo courtesy Edmonton Trappers)

Rodeo

Major cities don't often have people competing in rodeo events, but Edmonton has a strong connection to the sport.

Roger Lacasse is the 1998 Canadian Bareback Champion, and the first Edmontonian to win a major rodeo championship. Leading up to his title, Lacasse won the Calgary Stampede's $50,000 bareback riding bonus (the richest event in Canada), the most prestigious U.S. title at the Cheyenne Frontier Days Rodeo, and the international bareback event in Barretos, Brazil.

The most recent local winner is Tyler Helmig, who won the 1999 Klondike Chuckwagon Derby championship heat (although he came second for the overall title).

Edmonton's main connection to the sport comes from its position as host of the Canadian Finals Rodeo (CFR) each year. The CFR is the largest annual indoor sporting event in Western Canada, second-largest in the nation, and has the biggest rodeo purse in Canada.

With a budget of $1.2 million and prize money of more than $500,000, the event takes place in Skyreach Centre.

The CFR is produced by Northlands Park in cooperation with the Canadian Professional Rodeo Association, and runs in mid-November.

The event has seen an increase in attendance for five straight years, culminating in attendance of more than 91,000 fans in 1998 - the CFR's silver anniversary.

The CFR sees the Canada's top ten season money winners in each of professional rodeo's six premier events compete for national titles in bull riding, bareback riding, saddle bronc riding, calf roping, steer wrestling and ladies barrel racing.

With such a large following, the CFR attracts all sorts of side events.

One noteworthy attraction is Farmfair International, Canada's largest purebred cattle show-and-sale. The event began in 1974, and features more than 5,000 farm animals,

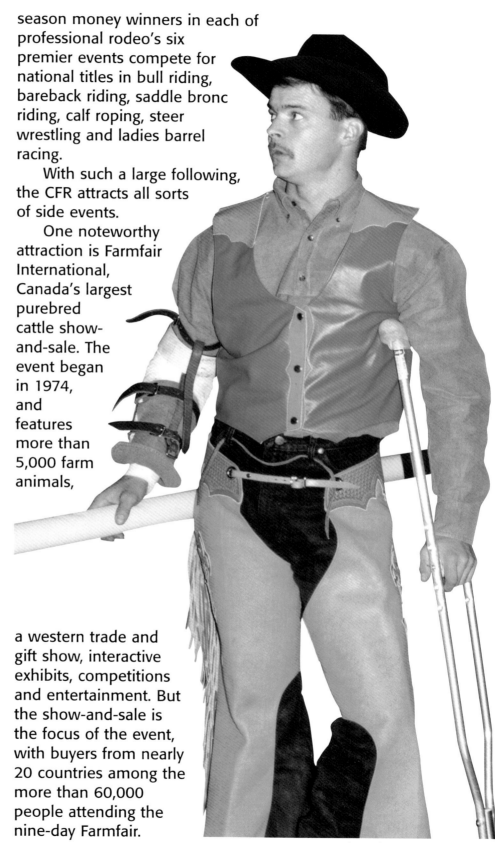

a western trade and gift show, interactive exhibits, competitions and entertainment. But the show-and-sale is the focus of the event, with buyers from nearly 20 countries among the more than 60,000 people attending the nine-day Farmfair.

Rodeo champion Roger Lacasse. (Photo courtesy Edmonton Northlands)

Amateur Sports

Without the legacy of championship amateur sports Edmontonians have created, it's doubtful the city would have today's crop of elite pro sports teams.

From Edmonton's earliest days, people have been active athletic participants. There have been literally hundreds of teams and thousands of individual athletes over the decades who have made their mark in sports ranging from traditional to off-beat. They've covered the gamut from school-age athletes to masters, international elite to the purest recreational sportsmen. And in all of these, Edmonton athletes have proven themselves to be among the best in the world.

While all the athletes have made their mark, one team deserves special attention, as arguably the best sporting team in history: The Edmonton Grads.

(Photo courtesy The Brick)

Amateur Sports

In any discussion of great Edmonton sports champions, mention must first be made of the Edmonton Grads women's basketball team. Arguably the best sports team of all time, it is generally recognized as the most successful basketball team ever assembled.

Commercial Graduates Basketball Club

The history of the team began in the fall of 1914, when teacher J. Percy Page was at McDougall School, overseeing typing and bookkeeping classes for young women. Since physical education was mandated for the girls, Page decided to organize a basketball team. He would later say he knew little of the game when he started, but reviewed as much material and learned as much as possible about the sport.

Coming from nowhere, the team won the 1914/15 city championship in its first try. But that was just the beginning. The team would go on to beat the Camrose Normal School for the Alberta championship that same year.

The girls had graduated after their first year together, but Page decided to keep the team going and created the Commercial Graduates Basketball Club.

The team continued its winning ways, dominating almost every team it played. Between 1915 and 1940, the team amassed an amazing record of 502-20 in official play. Winning streaks were long and decisive. At one point, the team won 147 games in a row, a record for consecutive sports wins that still stands.

The team's first international title came in 1923, when it won the Underwood Trophy against Cleveland (the first international tournament for women's basketball). Over the next 17 years, the Grads would win the title every year. The last title came when it was decided not to hold another tournament. Organizers that last year awarded the trophy to the Grads in perpetuity.

The year 1924 saw another first for the Grads. Challenging all comers in order to claim recognition as the best women's basketball team in Canada, the team went on to the Olympics (women's basketball was a demonstration sport). The team won the Olympic title in each of the four years it competed. In those four Olympiads, the Grads did not lose a single game of the 27 the team played.

Despite the fact they were all amateurs who supported themselves with outside jobs, the Grads could not be dismissed as a strong group in a weak sport. Although women's basketball has never received the recognition or popular support of men's basketball, the Grads proved they were the best no matter the competition.

The Grads practised with men's teams because they could not find any women's teams of their own calibre. In actual games, the Grads would play men's teams nine times, winning seven. In all the time the team existed, the Grads only lost one title attempt. The University of Alberta women's basketball team won the provincial title in 1921.

Although players would come and go over the years, some would be recognized for their outstanding contributions to the team's record. The

Grads' scoring leader was Margaret MacBurney, who ended her 10-year career with 2,079 points, averaging 12.6 points a game. MacBurney also held the world free-thrown record of 61 consecutive baskets in official play. The highest career scoring average on the team was 13.8 points per game, held by Noel MacDonald.

The team was inducted as a group into the Alberta Sports Hall of Fame, in 1974 (see the *Citations* chapter for the full players roster).

Although there were many players over the team's history, the one constant was Page, who was known affectionately as 'Papa Page' by the players. He was a strict disciplinarian who protected his players, but demanded both total commitment to the game, and proper ladylike behaviour. With a combination of athletic conditioning, constant practice and the groundbreaking innovation of having the players use hand signals during a game, Page turned the group of women into continual champions.

The Grads were even recognized by Dr. James Naismith, the Canadian-born inventor of basketball. Naismith was quoted as saying:

"The Grads have the greatest team that ever stepped out on a

Dot Johnson was one of the many standout players who made the Grads such a success.
(Photo courtesy City of Edmonton Archives)

basketball floor. Your record is without parallel in the history of basketball. There is no team I mention more frequently in talking about the game. My admiration is not only for your remarkable record of games won, but also your record of clean play, versatility in meeting teams at their own style, and especially for your unbroken record of good sportsmanship. My admiration and respect go to you also because you have remained unspoiled by your success and have retained the womanly graces notwithstanding your participation in a strenuous game. You are not only an inspiration to basketball players throughout the world, but the model for all girls teams. The message would not be complete without a reference to my good friend Mr. Percy Page, who of course is chiefly responsible for your success. You are indeed fortunate in having a man like Mr. Page as your coach, for I regard him as the greatest coach and the most superb sportsman it has ever been my good fortune to meet."

Archery

Murray Hipkin is Edmonton's leading competitive archery figure, with many championships and national records to his credit. Hipkin holds the 1999 Canadian Target Championship and Open Record in the Master Male Unlimited Division. He also won both the 3D Canadian and provincial championships in 1997. In 1989, Hipkin set the Canadian Indoor Championship record with the first-ever perfect score in Canada. In 1987, he won the Canadian Fita Championship. Hipkin won provincial titles in 1999 (indoor target-male master unlimited), 1988 (indoor target-male master unlimited) and 1987 (indoor target-senior male bowhunter unlimited).

More recently, teen Sean O'Neill has won a total of seven national and Alberta championships. Competing as a junior, O'Neill shot two perfect rounds to become the youngest-ever winner of the men's open event at the prestigious Vegas Open.

Badminton

The Royal Glenora Club in Edmonton's river valley is a hotbed of badminton champions. In the masters-level competition, Keith Spencer won the 1998 Masters Games gold medal for 55+ Men's Singles. Ken Grierson has also won masters titles. Those achievements are covered in the *Tennis* section of this chapter.

A number of young badminton players have also been successful in recent years (where no partner is noted for doubles titles, the second player was from outside Edmonton).

Bobby Milroy was on the team which won the 1996 Under-19 mixed doubles national championship, and with brother William Milroy won both

Dot Johnson and Connie Smith show off their aggressive winning style.
(Photo courtesy City of Edmonton Archives)

the 1996 and 1997 Under-19 Boys doubles Pan Am Gold. Also in 1996, Bobby won the Under-19 boy's singles national championship.

In 1998, William Milroy won the Under-19 national championships for boys singles, singles Pan Am Gold, and boy's doubles Pan Am Gold. In 1999, he won the Under-19 boy's doubles national championship.

Sunil Bhambhani won the 1994 Under-16 boys doubles national title, and the 1995 under-16 boy's singles title

Caroline Spiers and Lindy Vanriper combined to take the 1997 Under-16 girls' doubles national championship. Vanriper alone won the 1998 Under-16 girls single title and with a different partner took that year's Under-16 girls doubles championship.

Spiers also won the 1997 Under-16 mixed doubles national championship.

Wang Wen won the men's singles national championship in 1990, 1994 and 1997.

William Milroy and Lindy Vanriper played together to take the Under-17 mixed doubles junior Pan Am Gold in 1996/97, and the national title in 1997/98.

Duncan Milroy won the 1998/99 Under-16 boy's singles national championship, and the Under-16 boys doubles title. In 1999, he also won the Under-16 mixed doubles national title.

Baseball

One of the successful amateur baseball teams to play in Edmonton was the Edmonton Tigers, which won the 1999 and 1974 Senior Canadian Baseball championship (1974 was the

first time for any Alberta team). The team has won many provincial titles and western Canadian titles since, and has won two national silver awards and one national bronze.

The Edmonton Burns Shamrocks won the 1969 Alberta senior baseball championships, and the Western Canada Championships.

During a period when there was precious little professional sporting activity in Edmonton, the Edmonton Campion Pipe Liners baseball team carried the city's name in championship play.

The late 1950s saw the Pipe Liners unequalled in the west, partly because it was the only junior team in Northern Alberta. During the summer months, the

*Champion archer
Murray Hipkin.
(Photo courtesy
Murray Hipkin)*

1960 Campion Pipe Liners
Back Row, left to right:
Lefty Mack, Rod Elgert, Wally Waddle, Lyle Rosseneau, Ron Babiuk, John Dosen, Bill Wiese, Dennis Johanson, Gene Kinasawich, Casey Monahan.
Front Row, left to right:
Larry Grekul, Fred MacDonald, Herb Sewers, Elmer Campion, Joe Hartwell, Al Craig, Don Podgurney, Ed Howoroko, bat boy: Marty Babiuk.
(Photo courtesy Lefty Mack)

Pipe Liners played intermediate teams, but switched to junior teams from across the prairies for title games. Coached by Lefty Mack and starring Bill Wiese, it took the Western Canada Junior Baseball championship three years in a row: 1956, 1957 and 1958, as well as numerous tournament wins.

One notable achievement came when the Eskimos baseball team carrying the Edmonton name all the way to the Global World Series in 1957, after winning its league championship. The team, however, lost to the Japanese entry.

Biathlon

The sport which combines cross-country skiing and rifle marksmanship has seen several Edmontonians achieve championship status.

National champions are as follows. Jan Robinson: 1983 (women's individual and sprint). Shannon Mooney: 1989 (girls' individual and girls' sprint), 1990 and 1991 (jr. women's individual). Gerhardt Klann: 1993 (boys' individual), 1999 (men's individual). Greg Hunter: 1993 (men's 40+ individual and men's 40+ sprint), 1994 (men's 40+ sprint), 1997 (men's 40+ sprint). David Manning: 1994 (boys' individual and boys' sprint), 1997 (jr. men's sprint). Kristin Viddal: 1994 (girls' sprint). Kathy Brodeur-Robb: 1999 (women's 35+ individual.

Provincial champions from Edmonton are as follows. 1983: Jan Robinson (women's individual and women's sprint). 1985: Jan Robinson (women's individual and women's sprint). 1986: Jan Robinson (women's individual). 1987: Jane Isakson (women's individual and women's sprint), Ole Madsen (men's 35+ individual). 1988: Jane Isakson (women's individual and women's sprint), Jan Robinson (women's 30+ individual and women's 30+ sprint), Ole Madsen (men's 40+ sprint). 1989: Shannon Mooney (girls' sprint), Steen Madsen (jr. men's sprint), Jane Isakson (women's individual and women's sprint). 1990: Shannon Mooney (jr. women's individual). 1991: David Manning (juvenile boys' individual). 1992: Carlos Settle (boys' individual and boys' sprint), Greg Hunter (men's 40+ individual). 1993: Colleen Mooney (juvenile girls' individual), Heidi Parent (juvenile girls' sprint), Gerhardt Klann (boys' individual), Jan Robinson (women's 30+ individual), Roger Tetrault (men's 30+ individual), Greg Hunter (men's 40+ individual). 1994: Jessica Klikach (juvenile girls' individual), David Manning (boys' sprint), Morwenna Lane (jr. women's sprint), Roger Tetrault (men's 30+ sprint), Greg Hunter (men's 40+ individual). 1995: Real Tetrault (midgets sprint), Colleen Mooney (girls' sprint), Jan Robinson (women's 30+

sprint), Paul Klann (men's individual). 1996: Real Tetrault (midgets individual and midgets sprint), Gerhardt Klann (jr. men's individual and jr. men's sprint), Kathy Brodeur-Robb (women's 30+ individual and women's 30+ sprint), Greg Hunter (men's 40+ individual), Mike Burke (men's 50+ individual). 1997: Cindy Templeman (girls' sprint) David Manning (jr. men's individual and jr. men's sprint), Jan Robinson (women's 30+ individual and women's 30+ sprint), Greg Hunter (men's 40+ individual), Roger Tetrault (men's 40+ sprint). 1998: Jaime Robb (juvenile boys' individual and sprint), Gerhardt Klann (men's individual), Kathy Brodeur-Robb (women's 30+ sprint), Greg Hunter (men's 40+ individual and men's 40+ sprint). 1999: Paul Manning-Hunter (midget boys' individual), Daniel Robb (midget boys' sprint), Jaime Robb (boys' individual and boys' sprint), Paul Klann (men's individual), Ron Reinhart (men's 50+ individual and men's 50+ sprint).

Alberta Summer Biathlon champions

The 1974 Tigers. Front row, left to right: Bruce Gullet, Brian Betts, Tim Young, Stu Henderson, Jules Owchar (coach), Dave Sowinski, Marv Chupka, John Elick, Al Symington (coach), and Glen Nelson. Back row, left to right: Wayne Commodore, Al McKee, Fred Cardwell, Dick Hazell, Ron Watamaniuk (field manager) Ken Ewasiuk, Doug Homme, Paul Sullivan and Murray Steeves. Absent are General Manager Joey Edwards and President John Sowinski. (Photo courtesy of Ron Watamaniuk)

Louis 'Kid' Scaler vs.
Freddie Welsh in a
1913 bout.
(Photo courtesy City of
Edmonton Archives)

from Edmonton are as follows. 1982: Mark McTavish (sr. men). 1986: Jane Isakson (women). 1988: Jane Isakson (women). 1993: Paul Klann (men). 1995: Gerhardt Klann (jr. men).

Several Edmontonians have been members of Canadian relay championship teams.

1983: Dave Blanchard, open 4x8km. 1984: Jan Robinson, women 3x6km; Ken Karpoff, men 4x7.5km.

1985 and 1987: Jan Robinson, women 3x5km.

1988: Ole Madsen, masters 3x7.5km. 1989: Ole Madsen; men 40+ 3x7.5km; Jane Isakson, women 3x7.5km.

1990: Shannon Mooney, jr. women 3x7.5km; Jane Isakson, women 3x7.5km; Ken Karpoff, men 4x7.5km. 1991: Shannon Mooney, jr. women 3x7.5km; Jane Isakson, women 3x7.5km.

1992: Kirsten Watt, jr. women 3x7.5km. 1993: Roger Tetrault and Greg Hunter, men 30+ 3x7.5km.

1994: Colleen Mooney, girls 3x5km; David Manning, boys 3x5km. 1995: Kristin Viddal and Heidi Parent, girls 3x5km; David Manning, jr. men 3x7.5km; Frank Weisner, men 30+ 3x7.5km. 1996: Heidi Parent and Kristin Viddal, jr. women 3x7.5km; David Manning and

Gerhardt Klann, jr. men 3x7.5km.

1997: Eric Lund, boys. 1998: Cindy Templeman, girls 3x6km. 1999: Greg Hunter, men 30+; Marcie Reinhart, jr. women 3x7.5km.

Billiards

Edmonton's Wal-Mac Pool League Championship is the largest pool event in Canada. The annual competition has 90 pool tables and thousands of competitors.

A team of eight Edmontonians won the title of best nine-ball team in America by winning the 1999 American Pool Players Association 9-ball Team Championship in Las Vegas. The players on the team were: Greg Dussome, Vince Sinclair, Tim Duhamel, Barry Mathiassen, Craig Nowell, Todd Phillips, Grahame Lovett and Tom Kuester.

Bobsleigh

Bobsleigh does not have the constant presence in Edmonton that many other sports enjoy, since there is no world-class facility for training or attracting young athletes. But athlete Pierre Lueders (with Charlottetown teammate Dave MacEachern) brought the city an Olympic gold medal in the two-man event in the 1998 games - the first Canadians to do so in 62 years. Lueders and MacEachern became the first Canadian bobsledders in history to capture any medal. Lueders earlier won a bronze medal in the Junior World Championships. Leuders took gold medals in races in all three World Cup categories (two-man, four-man and combined) in the 1994-95 season, a feat never before accomplished by any bobsledder. He also won the World Cup

Championship two seasons in a row, in 1996-97 and 1997-98.

Bowling

Sisters Shannon Foran-Lindenberg (bantam category) and Gail Foran-Woodward (junior) each won 1965 provincial 10-pin bowling championships.

Boxing

Edmonton has produced many top-quality boxers. The first Edmontonian to win a major title was Louis 'Kid' Scaler, who won the Canadian lightweight championship in the early 1910s. Originally from Spokane, Washington, Scaler was active in boxing for many years, fighting 287 times in his career.

Originally from Toronto, Canadian Heavywieght Champion Vern Escoe moved to Edmonton in 1953 and fought here for several years before he retired in the city.

The next title came 10 years later, when Doug Harper won the Canadian light-heavyweight title. And in 1958, Wilf Greaves won the Canadian middleweight title, and would later take the Commonwealth title.

The 1960s brought more championships for Edmonton boxers. Bill McGrandle won the Canadian featherweight title in 1966. And in 1968, 18-year-old Allan Ford won the Canadian lightweight title; the youngest boxer ever to capture a Canadian title. He would hold the title until 1972.

In recent years, the two most successful and best known have been Scotty Olson and Ken Lakusta.

Olson has held several titles, including being the Canadian amateur flyweight champion from 1984 on. He has held championship flyweight belts with both the USBA and the IBO.

Lakusta was Canadian heavyweight champion twice in seven attempts. The first time came in 1986, when he defeated Conroy Nelson. The second time was in 1990, when he beat Tony Morrison.

Willard Lewis won the title of Canadian Cruiserweight Champion in 1998, and Tony Bedea is the current Canadian super-welterweight champion, taking the title in 1999.

Car Racing

Drag racer Terry Capp began his racing career in the 1960s, and today has been called "Canada's fastest man," with a race speed of 298.98 miles per hour. He also set the quarter-mile world record for front-engine top-fuel car, at 245.66 miles per hour. Capp won the 1980 U.S. Nationals, the 1980 U.S.

Quick Facts

In one of the more obscure records, John Blatta and Wilf Patrie set the Canadian marathon bowling record in 1969. Blatta and Patrie (then 16 and 19 years old) bowled 170 straight games over 72 hours.

Terry Capp pilots the Ron Hodgson-owned Royal Canadian.
(Photo courtesy Ron Hodgson Pontiac Buick GMC)

These pictures show just some of Edmonton's curling champions. Below, Hec Gervais. Opposite page: top, the 1954 Matt Baldwin team. Middle: the 1979 Alberta Consuls representatives - John Hunter, Paul Devlin, Pat Ryan and Derek Devlin.

(Photos courtesy: Hec Gervais Jr., opposite courtesy Northern Alberta Curling Association)

Opposite, bottom photo shows the 1998 women's provincial and national champions. Left to right: Cathy Borst, Heather Godberson, Brenda Bohmer and Kate Horne.

(Photo courtesy Northern Alberta Curling Association)

National Championship, the 1981 Grand American Series, and the 1989 American Hot Rod Association World Championship.

Ron Hodgson Pontiac Buick GMC owns The Pacemaker Funny Car, which set the world speed record (245 miles per hour) for its class, in 1979. The car was campaigned between 1972 and 1980 on the National Hot Rod Association world circuit. The car won six major U.S. titles. The car won the Gatornationals in 1977, 1979 and 1981; the Winston World Finals in 1977 and 1979, and the U.S. Nationals Title in 1979. Hodgson is still actively involved in sprint-car racing, and has been nominated to the Canadian Motorsport Hall of Fame.

While it couldn't be confirmed as a record, Tommy Fox was believed to be the oldest race-car driver when he began his career in 1970, at the age of 60. Today's CASCAR stock-car event at the City Centre Airport is named the Tommy Fox Classic in honour of the

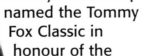

man who was also the first Edmontonian to fly his own home-made airplane.

Canoe and Kayak

David Ford won the gold medal in men's K-1 white water slalom at the 1999 world championships, and several national titles. Roy Sharplin took the national singles title five times since 1984. The pair has also won a national doubles title.

Meghan Thomas won 11 medals at the 1999 Western Canada Summer Games, including gold in the 200-metre, 500-metre and 6,000-metre doubles event, with Edmontonian Danielle Dubeta. The local pair also teamed up with Leduc's Vanesa Boudrau and Sherwood Park's Megan Oviatt to take the gold in both the 500-metre and 1,000-metre events for fours.

Cricket

Cricket is one of the oldest organized sports played in Edmonton. The Edmonton Cricket Club won the 1905 Osler Cup. Edmonton teams have also won

Western Canadian Club Championships. The Sportsmen Cricket Club won in 1977, the Strathcona Cricket Club won in 1991, and the Gujarat Cricket Club won in 1997.

Cross-Country Skiing

One of the most successful cross-country ski athletes in Canada today is Edmontonian Tara Whitten of the Edmonton Nordic Ski Club. Competing in the junior women's category, she won first overall national championship in both 1997 and 1999, and took first in the 5k national championship category in 1998.

Madeleine Williams of the Edmonton Nordic Ski Club took first overall in the juvenile girls category at the 1999 national championships. Other skiers to win junior championships out of Edmonton are sisters Amanda and Jaime Fortier.

Curling

Curling has been one of the most popular sports in Edmonton for decades, and the city's curlers have long been proving themselves to be of championship calibre. In fact, Edmonton teams have won more titles than those of any other Alberta town or city. Edmonton has had a total of 129 title-winning teams since 1928, while Calgary curlers have 77 titles. The winning teams (skip, third, second and lead) from the Metro Edmonton area are as follows.

Men's Champions

1929 - Arnold Johnson, Charles Cairns, Stewart Williams, J.K. Hays: provincial championship.

1930 - Robert Munro, A.W. Matthews, Donald Edwards, Jack Hall: provincial

Two of the many curling champions to come out of Edmonton: Kevin Martin, below, and Pat Ryan, opposite.
(Photo courtesy Northern Alberta Curling Association)

championship.

1933 - Clifford Manahan, Harold Deeton, Harold Wolfe, Bert Ross: Canadian and provincial championship.

1936 - George Wanless, William Rose, D.W. Ritchie, William Murray: provincial championship.

1937 - Clifford Manahan, Wesley Robinson, Ross Manahan, Lloyd McIntyre: Canadian and provincial championship.

1938 - Clifford Manahan, Wesley Robinson, Ross Manahan, Lloyd McIntyre: provincial championship.

1940 - Clifford Manahan, Wesley Robinson, Ross Manahan, Robert Manahan: provincial championship.

1941 - Howard Palmer, Jack Lebeau, Arthur Gooder, Clare Webb: Canadian and provincial championship.

1950 - Clifford Manahan, Ross Manahan, Gordon Haynes, William Bull: provincial championship.

1951 - William Gray, Glenn Gray, John Ferry, Warren Scott: provincial championship.

1954 - Matthew Baldwin, Glenn Gray, Pete Ferry, James Collins: Canadian and provincial championship.

1956 - Matthew Baldwin, Gordon Haynes, Arthur Kleinmeyer, William Henning: provincial championship.

1957 - Matthew Baldwin, Gordon Haynes, Arthur Kleinmeyer, William Price: Canadian and provincial championship.

1958 - Matthew Baldwin, Dr. Jack Geddes, Gordon Haynes, William Price: Canadian and provincial championship.

1959 - Herbert Olson, Barry Coleman, Mervin Dufresne, George Dufresne: provincial championship.

1961 - Hector Gervais, Ronald Anton, Raymond Werner, Wally Ursuliak: World, Canadian and provincial championship.

1962 - Hector Gervais, Ronald Anton, Raymond Werner, Wally Ursuliak: provincial championship.

1970 - Hector Gervais, William Mitchell, Wayne Saboe, William Tanish: provincial championship.

1971 - Matthew Baldwin, Thomas Kroeger, Richard Cust, Reg VanWassenhove: provincial championship.

1974 - Hector Gervais, Ronald Anton, Warren Hansen, Darrel Sutton: Canadian and provincial championship.

1975 - Thomas Reed, Kevin Byrne, Anthony Rankel, Lorne Reed: provincial championship.

1977 - Thomas Reed, Kevin Byrne, Anthony Rankel, Lorne Reed: provincial championship.

1979 - Paul Devlin, John Hunter, Patrick Ryan, Derek Devlin: provincial championship.

1985 - Patrick Ryan, Gordon Trenchie, Donald McKenzie, Donald Walchuk:

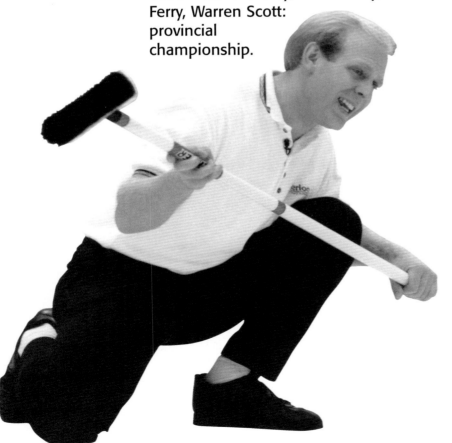

provincial championship.

1987 - Patrick Ryan, Randy Ferbey, Donald Walchuk, Roy Herbert: provincial championship.

1988 - Patrick Ryan, Randy Ferbey, Donald Walchuk, Donald McKenzie: Canadian and provincial championship.

1989 - Patrick Ryan, Randy Ferbey, Donald Walchuk, Donald McKenzie: World, Canadian and provincial championship.

1991 - Kevin Martin, Kevin Park, Daniel Petryk, Donald Bartlett: Canadian and provincial championship.

1992 - Kevin Martin, Kevin Park, Daniel Petryk, Donald Bartlett: provincial championship.

1995 - Kevin Martin, Kevin Park, James Pahl, Donald Bartlett: provincial championship.

1996 - Kevin Martin, Donald Walchuk, Shawn Broda, Donald Bartlett: provincial championship.

1997 - Kevin Martin, Donald Walchuk, Rudy Ramcharan, Donald Bartlett: Canadian and provincial championship.

1998 - Thomas Reed, Warren Kushnir, Larry Gardeski, Garry Landry: provincial championship.

1999 - Ken Hunka, Brent MacDonald, Blake MacDonald, Wade Johnston: provincial championship.

Women's Champions

1961 - Dorothy Thompson, Ila Watson, Vivian Kortgaard, Ruth Hayes: provincial championship.

1965 - Dorothy Thompson, Vivian Kortgaard, Ruth Hayes, Ila Watson: provincial championship.

1966 - Gail Lee, Hazel Jamison, Sharon Harrington, June Coyle: Canadian and provincial championship.

1968 - Hazel Jamison, Gail Lee, Jackie

Spencer, June Coyle: Canadian and provincial championship.

1970 - Betty Cole, Doris Olsen, Betty Jamison, Bonnie Cessford: provincial championship.

1971 - Kay Baldwin, Joyce Bucholz, Shirley Mitchell, Gladys Tanish: provincial championship.

1973 - Betty Cole, Shirley Fisk, Bonnie Cessford, Sharon Grey: provincial championship.

1974 - Marilyn Johnston, Elaine Souness, Irene Fielder, Marie Schultheiss: provincial championship.

1976 - Gale Lee, Jackie Spenser, Anne McGarvey, Liz Gemmell: provincial championship.

1978 - Betty Cole, Liz Gemmell, Anne McGarvey, Shirley Fisk: provincial championship.

1982 - Catherine Shaw, Karen Jones, Sandra Rippel, Donna Martineau: provincial championship.

1983 - Catherine Shaw, Christine Jurgenson, Sandra Rippel, Penny Ryan: provincial championship.

1986 - Lil Werenka, Mabel Thompson, Karen Currey, Jean Slemko: provincial championship.

1988 - Lil Werenka, Simone Handefield, Beverly Karasek, Kathy Bacon: provincial championship.

1989 - Deborah Shermack, Penny Ryan, Diane Alexander, Twyla Pruden:

provincial championship.

1990 - Deborah Shermack, Jackie-Rae Greening, Diane Alexander, Leanne Usher: provincial championship.

1991 - Deborah Shermack, Jackie-Rae Greening, Diane Alexander, Leanne Usher: provincial championship.

1995 - Cathy Borst, Maureen Brown, Deanne Shields, Kate Horne: provincial championship.

1997 - Cathy Borst, Heather Godberson, Brenda Bohmer, Kate Horne: provincial championship.

1998 - Cathy Borst, Heather

1957 Canadian and provincial champion skip Matt Baldwin. (Photo courtesy City of Edmonton Archives)

Godberson, Brenda Bohmer, Kate Horne: Canadian and provincial championship.

Mixed-Team Champions

1964 - Glen Gray, Mae Norris, Bill Graham, Olwyn Graham: provincial championship.

1968 - Bucky Stochinsky, Hazel Stevenson, Garry Levine, Bernice Hunter: provincial championship.

1969 - Don Anderson, Bernie Hunter, William Tanish, Connie Reeve: Canadian and provincial championship.

1970 - Bill Mitchell, Hadie Manley, William Tanish, Connie Reeve: Canadian and provincial championship.

1973 - Ronald Anton, Gale Lee, Warren Hansen, Anne McGarvey: provincial championship.

1974 - Marv Porowski, Bunny Porowski, Roger Comeau, Darlene Clark: provincial championship.

1977 - Don Sutton, Donna Shantz, Allan Hackner, Kay Savil: provincial championship.

1978 - Gerry Wilson, Ruby Sowinski, Millard Evans, Dorothy Sutton: provincial championship.

1984 - Mark Johnson, Deborah Shermack, Lorne Reed, Bonnie Lane: provincial championship.

1985 - Randy Ferby, Michelle Solinger, Don Bartlett, Wendy Bain: provincial championship.

1986 - Randy Ferby, Penny Ryan, Pat Ryan, Wendy Bain: provincial championship.

1987 - Ken Ursuliak, Sandra Rippel, Millard Evans, Robin Pettit: provincial championship.

1988 - Ken Ursuliak, Cathy Borst, Millard Evans, Robin Pettit: provincial championship.

1990 - Marvin Wirth, Glenna Rubin, Millard Evans, Robin Pettit: Canadian and provincial championship.
1994 - Les Rogers, Cathy Borst, Warren Kushnir, Robin Pettit: Canadian and provincial championship.

Junior Men's Champions
1948 - Jim Harper, Bob Dunsworth, Jonn Reeves, Lorne Wood: provincial championship.
1955 - Ron Munro, Cyrus Little, Murray MacKay, Jack Vallens: provincial championship.
1959 - John Trout, Bruce Walker, David Woods, Allen Sharpe: Canadian and provincial championship.
1961 - John Williams, Gary Lawrence, Victor Anderson, Ken Stewart: provincial championship.
1962 - Brian Taylor, Ray Kent, Ed Poznasky, Doug Rattray: provincial championship.
1963 - Wayne Saboe, Ron Hampton, Rick Aldridge, Mick Adams: Canadian and provincial championship.
1967 - Stan Trout, Doug Dobry, Allan Kullay, Don Douglas: Canadian and provincial championship.
1972 - Lawrence Niven, Rick Niven, Jim Ross, Ted Poblawski: Canadian and provincial championship.
1974 - Robb King, Brad Hannah, Bill Fowlis, Chris King: Canadian and provincial championship.
1976 - Robb Williams, John Climenhaga, Jim Butler, Jeff Armstrong: provincial championship.
1978 - Darren Fish, Lorne Barker, Murray Ursulak, Barry Barker: provincial championship.
1979 - Darren Fish, Lorne Barker, Murray Ursulak, Barry Barker: provincial championship.

1980 - Curtis Monsebroten, Brian Beuerlein, Brad Monsebroten, Brad Thomas: provincial championship.
1982 - Steve Petryk, Dave Zabolotniuk, Lyle Horneland, Denis Krysalka: provincial championship.
1983 - Kevin Park, Scott Park, Allen Highet, Kevin Mills: provincial championship.
1984 - Scott Park, Kevin Park, Kevin Mills, Rob Maze: provincial championship.
1985 - Kevin Martin, Richard Feeney, Dan Petryk, Michael Berger: Canadian and provincial championship.
1989 - James Pahl, Shane Park, Troy Berreth, Jeff Davidson: provincial championship.
1990 - Robert Schlender, Jeff Wieschorster, Paul Sorenson, Jason Stone: provincial championship.
1991 - Robert Schlender, Jeff Wieschorster, Greg Lahti, Craig Waples: provincial championship.
1994 - Colin Davison, Kelly Mittlestadt, Scott Pfeifer, Sean Morris: World, Canadian and provincial championship.
1995 - Cameron Dechant, Blake MacDonald, Wade Johnston, Jason Lesmeister: provincial championship.
1997 - Ryan Keane, Scott Pfeifer, Blayne Iskiw, Peter Heck: Canadian and provincial championship.
1998 - Carter Rycroft, Glen Kennedy, Marc Kennedy, Jason Lesmeister: provincial championship.
1999 - Jeff Erickson, Marc Kennedy, Kevin Skarban, Kevin McNee: provincial championship.

Junior Women's Champions
1975 - Debbie Sass, Brenda Lintz, Charlene Callies, Joyce Kintz: provincial championship.

1977 - Cathy King, Robin Ursuliak, Maureen Olsen, Mary Kay James: Canadian and provincial championship.

1978 - Cathy King, Brenda Oko, Maureen Olsen, Diane Bowes: Canadian and provincial championship.

1980 - Jackie-Rae Anderson, Gwyneth Buchanan, Diane St. Claire, Janet MacKenzie: provincial championship.

1981 - Leanne Usher, Amanda Graves, Patty Ursulak, Jacqueline Burch: provincial championship.

1982 - Jennifer Buchanan, Janice Hawkins, Lori McLennan, Alison Tibbs: provincial championship.

1983 - Jennifer Buchanan, Janice Hawkins, Debra Cutler, Alison Tibbs: provincial championship.

1985 - Lindsey Graves, Sandy Symyrozum, Twyla Pruden, Colleen Burden: provincial championship.

1987 - LaDawn Funk, Raylene Jones, Marcy Strong, Laurelle Funk: provincial championship.

1988 - LaDawn Funk, Sandy Symyrozum, Cindy Larsen, Laurelle Funk: World, Canadian and provincial championship.

1989 - Renee Handfield, Nicole Handfield, Joanne Goudreau, Renee Bussiere: provincial championship.

1990 - Renee Handfield, Nicole Handfield, Joanne Goudreau, Renee Bussiere: provincial championship.

1991 - Tara Brandt, Nicole Handfield, Shannon Hall, Nicole Lamb: provincial championship.

1993 - Irene Chamczuk, Carmen Whyte, Holly Bobier, Shannon Bredin: provincial championship.

1997 - Kristie Moore, Lori Olsen, Lesley Ewoniak, Diane Lee: provincial championship.

Senior Men's Champions

1965 - Gordon Walker, Bert Wright, M.W. Williamson, George Bissett: provincial championship.

1966 - Connie Ferguson, Walter Sharplin, Seve Hrudey, Len Wilson: provincial championship.

1969 - Gordon Walker, Craig Ross, Wilf Harrington, Joe Magnuss: provincial championship.

1971 - Stu Pearce, Bert Palmer, Sam Stevenson, Bob Robertson: provincial championship.

1974 - Ralph Shirley, Wilf Carrington, Walter Boddy, Fred Allison: provincial championship.

1975 - Del McIntyre, Roy Schumaker, Ray Gerlitz, Mike Grycan: provincial championship.

1976 - Don Killips, Ralph Shirley, Gerry Meyer, George Hipkin: provincial championship.

1977 - Don Killips, Ralph Shirley, Gerry Meyer, George Hipkin: provincial championship.

1993 - Len Erickson, Merl Brown, Bernie Desjarlais, Nelson Caron: Canadian and provincial championship.

1994 - Al Pankowski, Bert Proskiw, Mitch Hansuk, Herb Zmurchuk: provincial championship.

Senior Women's Champions:

1971 - Winnie Reid, Betty Jamison, Margaret Collier, Muriel Skidmore: provincial championship.

1972 - Ruth Elliot, Sal Embelton, Teresa Duffield, Dorothy Roberts: provincial championship.

1976 - Hadie Manley, Bernice Durward, Anna Kasting, Gladys Baptist: Canadian and provincial championship.

1977 - Hadie Manely, Bernice Durward, Dee MacIntyre, Anna Kasting: provincial championship.

1978 - Hadie Manely, Bernice Durward, Dee MacIntyre, Anna Kasting: Canadian and provincial championship.
1980 - Betty Jamison, Doris Olsen, Muriel Gablehouse, Muriel Skidmore: provincial championship.
1986 - Lorriane Elgie, Dorothy McKenzie, Catherine Acheson, Bobbie Hougen: provincial championship.
1991 - Shirley Tucker, Betty Jean Buchanan, Ruth Kimmitt, Lorna Priddle: provincial championship.
1995 - Dorothy Goulet, Lori Kosh, Jenny Pollard, Jackie Reid: provincial championship.
Women's Masters
1998 - Shirley Innes, Audrey Connor, Bev Forbes, Sandy Ramsley Way: provincial championship.
1999 - Dorothy Goulet, Irene Kenyon, Ulan Hazel, Shirley Rebus: provincial championship.

Cycling

Kelly-Ann Carter Erdman has been the preeminent cyclist to come out of Edmonton. Carter Erdman has won 12 national titles, in different cycling track events, between 1985 and 1992. Carter Erdman was on the national team from 1985 to 1992, and competed in many world-class events.

Colin Davidson won the 1990 National Road Race championship. Davidson also won the overall title in the 1992 Canadian Tire Series, in which a series of road races was held in cities across Canada.

Diving

Edmonton's best contemporary diver is Eryn Bulmer, who won the gold medal in three-metre springboard at the 1999 Pan Am Games, and a gold at the 1998 Commonwealth Games. In 1997, Bulmer became the first Canadian to ever win a three-metre diving world championship. Bulmer also won the national one-metre and three-metre titles in 1999 (summer), 1998 (summer and winter), 1997 (one-metre, summer and world trials), and in 1996 (one-metre, winter).

Other Edmonton divers have won national titles.

Igor Kopecky won the national titles in 1998 (one-metre summer and winter), and in 1996 (one-metre and three-metre, summer).

Lee Jay Strifler won the men's one-metre national title in winter 1996, both summer and winter in 1995, and in winter 1992.

Larry Flewwelling won the 1990 World Aquatic Trials on both the one-metre and three-metre springboard, 1989 (one-metre and three-metre, winter), 1988 (one-metre, winter) and 1987 (one-metre, winter).

Barbara Bush has won the three-metre Olympic Trials title. In 1988, she won the three-metre summer title. In

Two of Edmonton's best-known champions, Kurt Browning and Kristy Yamaguchi, at the unveiling of a painting of them at the Royal Glenora Club.
(Photo courtesy Royal Glenora Club)

1987, she won the summer one-metre title. In 1984, Bush won the one-metre and three-metre summer titles, in 1982 the winter three-metre, and in 1981 the summer three-metre.

In tower diving, Anna Dacyshyn has won national championships in winter 1990, summer 1989, winter 1988 and winter 1986. Dacyshyn also won the Commonwealth Games Trial in 1989.

Fastpitch

The Edmonton Express won the 1999 Senior Men's Canadian Fastball Championship.

Figure Skating

Edmonton has a long history of championship figure skaters. The best known is Kurt Browning, who grew up in southern Alberta but trained at the city's Royal Glenora Club. Browning won the Canadian novice men's championship in 1983 and the Canadian junior men's championship in 1985.

But it was Browning's remarkable string of Canadian and world men's championships that made him arguably the best Canadian figure skater of all time. Browning won the national men's title in 1989, 1990, 1991 and 1993, and the world men's championship in 1990, 1991 and 1993.

Michael Slipchuk also brought championships to Edmonton. He won the Canadian junior men's title in 1986, and the Canadian senior men's title in 1992. The junior men's title in 1992 went to Edmonton's Ravi Walia.

Lisa Sargeant-Driscoll won the 1990 Canadian senior ladies title. Susan Humphreys won the Canadian senior women's title in 1996.

Pairs skaters Jamie Sale and Jason Turner won the 1992 Canadian junior title. Sarah Schmidek won two national titles: the 1994 novice ladies championship, and the 1997 junior ladies championship.

While not an Edmontonian, U.S. figure skater Kristy Yamaguchi trained at Edmonton's Royal Glenora Club when she won her 1992 World and Olympic Championships.

Allison MacLean and Konrad Schaub were Edmontonians who competed as ice dancers early on for Canada, but for Austria after 1992. As Austrians, they won that country's national championship in 1995 and 1996, as well as the Sofia Cup in Bulgaria.

Ben Ferreira won the Orex Cup in 1996. He was also provincial novice champion in 1995, junior champion 1996, and senior champion in 1997.

Golf

Betty Stanhope-Cole is one of Canada's premier golfers and curlers, dominating Edmonton's ladies golf with

One of Edmonton's more recent champion figure skaters, Ben Ferreira.
(Photo courtesy Ben Ferreira)

25 city amateur championships and nine senior ladies titles. Over the years, she has won 17 provincial golf championships, the 1956 Canadian junior crown and the 1957 Canadian Ladies' Open.

One of the best-known names in Edmonton golf history is Henry Martell. He won many local and regional titles during his career from the 1940s on, including the Dominion Amateur Golf Championship of 1946, and the CPGA title in 1953 and 1958. He was the first Albertan to be named to the Canadian Golf Hall of Fame.

Later an MLA for Edmonton-Whitemud (1982-85), Keith Alexander was an outstanding amateur golfer beginning in the 1950s. During that time, he won many tournaments across the province, the Canadian Amateur title, and the Guadalajara International. He also won

Tracy Trueman (photo right) won the provincial all-around gymnastics championship for her age group in both 1982 and 1983. Keith Alexander (photo left) has won golf tournaments around the world.
(Right photo courtesy Deanna Trueman. Left photo courtesy Keith Alexander)

tournaments at Colorado College (where he was twice named as an all-star). He was inducted into the Canadian Golf Hall of Fame in 1986.

Ray Reid of the Edmonton Country Club won the Canadian Senior Golfing Championship in 1995.

Laurie Scott of the Mayfair Golf and Country Club won the 1998 Alberta senior championship.

Gymnastics

The Ortona Gymnastics Club has produced many champions.

Sherwood Park's Damien Miller is a recent young winner, taking the 1999 Alberta Provincial Championship by coming first all-around in the Class II, Under 12 category. He also won the

1999 Chinook Classic and the the 1999 Jurassic Classic. Justin Quach won the 1999 provincial floor championship. Rowan Bayne was the 1999 provincial ring champion, and the all-around champion at both the 1998 Macho Man competition and the 1998 Chinook Classic. Chase Richer won the all-around 1999 Alberta provincial championship in the Class III Under-13 category, and at the 1999 Chinook Classic.

Marleen Lavoie won the 1996 Olympic Games trials, first all-round in compulsory exercises. 1997 - Naomi Mitchell - provincial champion all-around in the national novice category. 1998 - Heather Foisy - provincial champion all-around in national novice category. Naomi Mitchel - all round provincial champion in national open category.

Capital City Gymnastics has also produced many champions.

Nicki Johnson was first on bars at the 1999 provincials (class 2, Pre-Argo). Ashlee Kadatz was first on beam at the 1999 trials to westerns. Lena Kawanami was first on bars at the 1999 provincial (class 3 open category). Kara Kawanami was first on bars at the 1997 provincials (class 3 Argo).

Chantelle Lutic was first on bars at the 1999 trials to westerns, first all-around at the 1998 provincials (class 3, Tyro), and first on vault at the 1997 provincials (class 2, Tyro)

Miranda Maley was first all-around provincial champion (class 3, Tyro).

Janelle McLean was first on beam and vault, at the 1997 provincials (class 3, Argo).

Brandon O'Neill was first all-around at the 1998 westerns and provincials, and was 1999 national champion for

Members of the Edmonton Monarchs pose with some of their trophies, about 1930.
(Photo courtesy City of Edmonton Archives)

both rings and vault.

Jennie Payne was first trials for the western championship on the bars in 1998 (open category).

Elissa C. Slemko was first all-around at the 1998 provincials (class 2, Argo).

Jared Walls was first all-around at both the 1999 and 1998 national championship (under 17), at the 1999 and 1998 western championship, and the 1999 and 1998 provincials. He was also first all-around at the 1995 westerns and provincials (under 12).

Cassandra A. Wells was first all-around at the 1998 provincial champion (class 2, Pre. Argo).

Hockey (Men's and Underage)

Many people may know Edmonton's hockey accomplishments only in terms of the Oilers and other professional clubs. But the city has a long history of accomplishments in amateur hockey that established the reputation of top-level competition and championship achievements.

There had been amateur and recreational hockey teams in Edmonton in the late 1800s, but the city's first attempt at greatness came when the Edmonton Hockey Club of the 1900s and 1910s decided to try for the Stanley Cup. The first team in Alberta to make the attempt, the club played two sets of challenge matches for the Stanley Cup. In 1908, the Edmonton Thistles played the Montreal Wanderers in a two-game, total-goal series. Despite replacing all but three of the Thistle players with high-priced pros, the team lost. In 1910, the Thistles (without the so-called

mercenary players) again challenged for the cup, losing to Ottawa.

There were many other amateur teams that had varying degrees of success representing Edmonton, including The Edmonton Hustlers in the 1910s and 1920s.

The Edmonton Bearcats was one of the most successful of the earlier teams. The team's best season was 1915-1916, when it won every game it played, including taking the Alberta championship.

The city's first real claim to hockey glory came in 1923, when the Edmonton Eskimos won the Western Canadian Hockey League championship by beating Regina. The win elevated the Eskimos to the Stanley Cup finals, again playing (and losing) Ottawa.

The Edmonton Superiors played in the 1930s. Although details of the team's achievements are sketchy, they were the 1930/31 Alberta and B.C. Senior Champions. There are unconfirmed references to the Superiors winning the 1932 World Hockey Championship.

The Edmonton Athletic Club had its best year in 1934. After winning the Alberta Junior Hockey Championship, the team took the Abbott Cup for the Western Canadian Junior Hockey title. A crowd estimated at more than 6,000 welcomed the team back from that victory.

Despite being competitive on a local and provincial level, and even with the western title, Edmonton's hockey teams had never achieved world-class greatness. That all changed with a team called the Edmonton Waterloo Mercurys.

The Mercurys (named after the team

sponsor, a local car dealership which later gained more fame as the employer of world-champion curler Kevin Martin), won the Olympic gold medal at the 1952 games in Oslo, Norway. The Mercurys was the fifth Canadian team in six winter Olympics to win the gold medal, but the last team to do so.

Another hockey achievement came in the Alberta Junior Hockey League, when the Edmonton Western Movers won the league championship in 1968.

The Edmonton Western Movers won the championship by beating the Red Deer Rustlers 6-3 in the fourth game of the best of seven series.

Edmonton is today home to the biggest novice hockey tournament in the world. The Brick Super Novice Invitational Hockey Tournament is in its tenth year in 1999. It features 12 teams from across North America, with another 12 teams on a standby list. The host Edmonton Team Brick has won the tournament a record four times, in 1998, 1995, 1993 and 1992.

Hockey (Women's)

Although lesser-known than its male counterpart, women's hockey in Edmonton has a history almost as long and full of achievements. Strictly amateur, the various women's teams began as a recreational movement, but have come to bring the city many national and international championships.

The first women's hockey teams of note were the Strathcona Ladies Hockey Club in the late 1800s, and the Edmonton Ladies Hockey Club, in the 1900s.

The first championship team of note

was the Muttart's Blizzards, which won an Alberta Senior Ladies hockey championship.

More women's hockey greatness came with the play of the Edmonton Monarchs. Formed from the amalgamation of the Edmonton Victorias and the Nationals, the team had its best year in 1926. That year saw the Monarchs win the Alpine Cup, the Misener Cup and the Western Canadian championship. More championships came for the team in 1929, when it won both the Alberta and Western Canada championships.

The Edmonton Rustlers played during The Great Depression, but also achieved greatness. Originally called the Jasper Place Rustlers, the team won the 1933 Dominion Senior Women's Hockey championship, and in 1934 took the title of Western Canada Senior Women's Hockey champions.

But the most successful women's hockey team - and arguably the most successful Edmonton sports team since the Grads basketball organization - has been the Edmonton Chimos.

A breeding ground for Canada's international players, the Chimos have racked up many titles since coming into being in 1972.

It didn't take long for the team to establish a high standard of play. The Chimos won the Western Canada Women's Hockey championships in 1975, 1976, 1977 and 1978. And national titles have also come in waves. Playing in the finals most years, the Chimos have won the national championship in 1984, 1985, 1992 and 1997. No other team has won the national title as often in the modern era.

Junior Football

Junior football (community-based teams with players between 18 and 22 years old) has a history of success in Edmonton, with the Edmonton Huskies and Edmonton Wildcats battling for supremacy. Each team has won national titles, starting with the Huskies' string of victories in the early 1960s. It began with the 7-3 victory over Montreal in 1962. The Huskies also won the national championship in 1963 by beating Montreal 47-3, and the 1964 title with another win over Montreal, 48-27. The Wildcats didn't take long to pick up the winning tradition, taking the 1967 national championship with a 29-6 win over Burlington. It was another 10 years until the Wildcats' next championship, winning 28-0 over Hamilton. The last national championship came with the 1983 win by the Wildcats over Ottawa, by a 30-11 score.

Lacrosse

The Edmonton Lacrosse Club won the 1904 championship of the Canadian Northwest. More recently, the Edmonton Miners won the Western Canadian Championship in both 1987 and 1988. The Miners also won the First Nations Trophy for National Junior Field Lacrosse in 1998. The Miners' provincial titles came in 1998, in both the Senior and Junior divisions.

In 1975, the Fullers team won the Presidents Cup Senior B National Box Lacrosse Championship. The 1980 Founders Cup Junior B National Box Lacrosse Championship went to the

The 1998/99 University of Alberta Golden Bears hockey team, winners of the national championship.
(Photo courtesy University of Alberta)

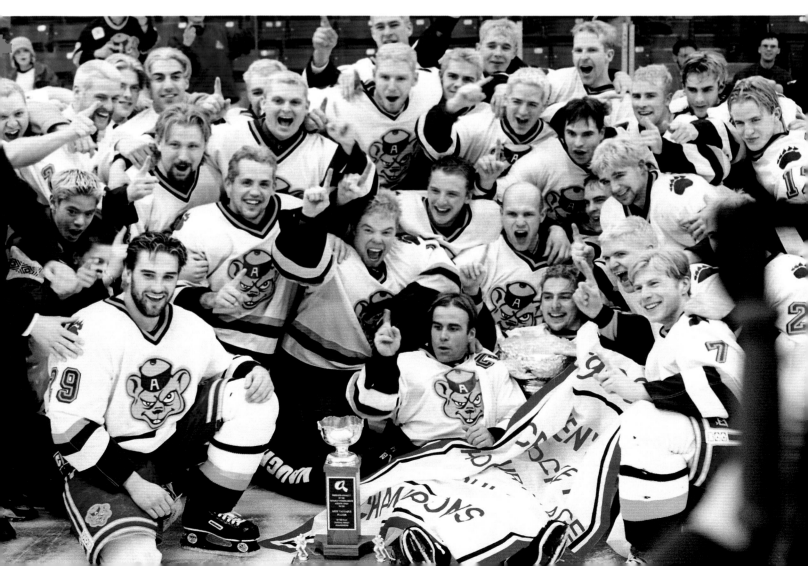

Tomahawks team. In terms of provincial championships, the Edmonton area has produced a steady stream of winners. The Sherwood Park Titans won Peewee titles in 1987, 1991 and 1993; and won Bantam titles in 1990 and 1992. The team from Devon won the 1987 Peewee C title, while the Bantam B title that year went to the Gold Bar Miners and the Bantam C championship was won by the South Whitemud team. South Whitemud also won the 1988 Bantam title.

The St. Albert Rams teams have won provincial titles in various divisions: Novice title in 1988, Peewee in 1990, Midget in 1992, Peewee in 1994, Novice in 1995, Bantam in 1996 and Novice in 1997. In 1998, Rams teams won both the Novice and Peewee titles, and the 1999 Peewee title went to one of the Rams teams.

The West Edmonton Blues won the provincial Midget title in 1990 and 1991. The South Edmonton Warriors won the provincial Bantam championship in 1993, 1994 and 1997, and an Edmonton Warriors team won the 1999 Bantam title. The South Edmonton Warriors shared the 1995 Midget title with the Sherwood Park Titans. The Edmonton Dragons won the 1996 Midget provincial title.

Lawn Bowling

Alf Wallace won the 1998 men's singles Canadian championship. Greg Dolsky won the same title in 1994. Together, they won the 1999 pairs title.

Lyle Adams has two major titles to his credit. He was a member of the team which won the 1994 men's pairs Canadian championship (with a bowler from Calgary), and a member of the team which won the 1993 men's fours Canadian championship. Also on the latter team were Edmontonians Wayne Sembaluk and John Barnes, and a bowler from Calgary.

Post-Secondary Athletics

University of Alberta

With its emphasis on higher education, Edmonton has benefitted by having many post-secondary institutions with winning athletes.

The University of Alberta men's (Golden Bears) and women's (Pandas) teams and individual athletes have won dozens of national championships since the Canadian Interuniversity Athletics Union (CIAU) began 1962-63.

The 1998-1999 University of Alberta athletic season was the most successful ever, producing the most national medals and attracting the most national recognition (as expressed through medals and national television exposure) in its 91-season history.

Over five consecutive Sundays in late February and early March, University of Alberta teams played for the CIAU championship, winning three of five big final games. Each of these events was televised on The Sports Network (TSN). It was as if the Golden Bears and Pandas had their own channel in the competitive world of sports television.

In all, 16 of 18 University of Alberta interuniversity teams in 1998-1999 appeared in the CIAU tournament. The Golden Bears and Pandas finished with eight national medals: three gold, four silver, one bronze.

The women's basketball team won

the CIAU national championship, while the men's basketball team won the CWUAA title and ended the season ranked at number one. The Golden Bears men's hockey team won the national championship, while the Pandas hockey team and the field hockey team each won their conference championship The men's soccer team also won the conference title. The men's volleyball team ended the season with the number-one national ranking, and the conference championship. (The University of Alberta has not earned three national championship programs since 1980-1981, when Golden Bears cross-country,

volleyball and football were tops).

Individual titles also came to University of Alberta athletes in 1998/99. Jenny Cartmell, of the women's volleyball team, was the CIAU women's volleyball Player of the Year, while Murray Grapentine of the Golden Bears volleyball team took the men's honour. This marked the second time in three seasons the University of Alberta swept the CIAU Player of the Year award in that sport. Individual honours also went to the following. Terry Danyluk (men's volleyball) was named CIAU Coach of the Year. Pascal Cardinal (men's volleyball)

Three of the University of Alberta's many championship wrestlers, left to right: Blake Dermott, John Barry, and Mike Payette.
(Photo courtesy University of Alberta)

was named CIAU Rookie of the Year. Four athletes were named CWUAA most valuable player in their sport: Sarah Joly, soccer; Jenny Cartmell, volleyball; Mike Thompson, hockey; and Murray Grapentine, volleyball. There were also four conference most valuable player awards, five conference coaches of the year, 52 conference all stars, and 21 CIAU All-Canadians.

Before 1998/99, male athletes and teams won a total of 26 national championships. Basketball championships were won twice in a row, in 1993/94, and in 1994/95.

Men's hockey teams have long been a standout at University of Alberta, with head coach Clare Drake leading many of the teams. The U of A took the national championship in: 1963/64, 1967/68, 1974/75, 1977/78, 1978/79, 1979/80, 1985/86, 1991/92, and most recently in 1998/99.

Men's gymnastics teams have been successful, also, winning national championships four years in a row, from 1966 to 1970. The program was ended in 1973.

The 1998/99 University of Alberta Pandas celebrate their national volleyball championship.
(Photo courtesy University of Alberta)

The University of Alberta football team has taken three national titles: in 1967/68, 1972/73, and lastly in 1980/81.

Wrestling has a long history at the university, and has produced several national amateur champions. Larry Shelton won the 1955 national title in the 125.5 lb. class.

But the 1970s were a boom time for U of A wrestling. The university team came out on top three times in a row at the national level, from 1969 to 1972.

In 1973, John Barry won the 125.5-lb. class championship and Ole Sorensen won the 149.5-lb. title. In 1981, Sid Thorowsky won the national heavyweight crown. Gord Bertie was a standout wrestler in the early 70s. He took the 1971, 1972, 1974 and 1975 national amateur titles in the 114.5-lb. class. In 1973, Dave Cummings won the 198-lb. class championship, and came back the next year to win the 180.5-lb. class title. Sid Thorowsky took the 1981 title in the over-100-kg weight class.

CIAU titles have also figured largely for U of A wrestlers.

Gord Bertie won the 118-lb. CIAU title three years in a row; 1969/70, 1970/71, and 1971/72. Serge Gauthier won the 134-lb. title in 1969/70, and the 158-lb. class in 1971/72. Tadamichi Tanaka won the 134-lb. title in both 1970/71 and 1971/72. Other winners in 1969/70 were Dave Duniec (158-lb.) and Brian Heffel (167-lb.). Dennis Glover won the 150-lb. class in 1970/71.

In the 1972/73 CIAU championships, William Dowbiggin won the 150-lb. class and Ole Sorensen won the 158-lb. title. John Barry won the 126-lb. championship in 1973/74, while Russ Pawlyk won the 134-lb. title in both 1975/76 and 1976/77. Another double winner was Pierre Pomerleau, who took the 158-lb. title in 1977/78, and the 167-lb. title in 1979/80. In the latter season, Scott Tate won the 118-lb. championship.

Mike Payette won the 54-kg title in 1982/83, and the 57-kg class in both 1984/85 and 1985/86. Phile Spile won the 54-kg title in 1984/85. Blake Dermott won the heavyweight title in 1982/83. Todd Graham won the 57-kg class in 1990/91, the same year Wayne Diduck won the 76-kg title. In 1993/94, Glenn Allen won the 52-kg title and Wade Wishloff won the 90-kg class. The most recent wrestler to win a championship was Shannon Mathie, who took the 1999 CIAU title for women in the 65 kg class.

Other members of the U of A Women's Wrestling Club have won senior national championships: Christine Grimble in 1992, Christine Nordhagen in 1992, 93 and 94, Alrette Malcolm in 1993 and Karen Tally in 1994. Nordhagen has even higher achievements as a member of the Edmonton Wrestling Club (listed in this chapter's wrestling section).

The Pandas wrestling team began in 1998/99, and has immediately shown results. Shannon Mathie was the 1999 CIAU champion, while Melissa Hillaby (50kg) and Theresa Vladicka (63kg) were the 1999 Canadian Junior Champions.

The Rawson Trophy, for Canada West Universities Athletic Associaion wrestling champions, has been won by the U of A more times (18) than any other university. The U of A has taken the title

The 1998/99 University of Alberta Pandas hockey rookie of the year, Lori Shupak.
(Photo courtesy University of Alberta)

in 1951, 52, 53, 57, 58, 59, 63, 64, 68, 70, 71, 73, 77, 79, 80, 81, and 83.

Colbie Bell has been a dominant force in Greco-Roman wrestling. He has won the senior national championship in 1996 (100kg), 1997, 1998 and 1999 (97kg).

Men's soccer teams won the national title in 1972/73, and again in 1979/80. The men's volleyball team has the same record, winning in 1980/81 and again in 1996/97.

Women's teams at the University of Alberta have also created a record of national achievement, winning a total of 15 championships.

The women's basketball team won the national title in 1998/99.

Women's gymnastics teams from the University of Alberta have won six national titles, in 1978/79, 1984/85, 1987/88, 1988/89, 1989/90, and in 1990/91.

The U of A track and field program has also produced many national winners. The Golden Bears cross-country team won the national title in 1980/81, while the Pandas took the title in 1984/85.

Individual track and field champions from the university have also excelled. Ian Newhouse won the 300-metre and 600-metre titles in 1981, and the 600-metre title in 1982. Dan Lanovaz took the triple jump championship in both 1984 and 1986. Nancy Gillis won long jump in 1986 and 1987; Jane Cox took the same title in 1990 and 1991. Oral O'Gilvie won the triple jump championship in 1991 and 1992. Rob Swartz won the 1,000-metre title in 1992, and 1993, and was part of the winning 4x800-metre relay team in 1993. Ron Huget won long jump in 1994, and the triple jump in 1996. Rohan Neil won both the 300-metre title and was a member of the 4x400-metre championship team in 1996.

Iraklis Kollias won the shot put in 1981. Brian Rhodes won the 10,000-metre and cross-country titles in 1983. Sue Kallal, Maureen Cush, Mary Burzminski and Birgit Otto won the women's 4x800-metre relay in 1983. Brian Monaghan, Roger Carl, Roy Riege and Kent Timanson took the men's

4x400-metre relay in 1993. The same race championship was won in 1996 by Kevin Olson, Garcia Brightly, Russ Kocuper and Rohan Neil. Noella Lee Pong won the 60-metre sprint title in 1986. David Lee Pong was the men's winner of the same event that year. Jonathan Moyle won the long jump title in 1993 (setting a CIAU record of 7.47 metres). Murray Heber took the weight throw championship in 1999 (setting the CIAU record of 19.56 metres).

Women's soccer produced national champions in 1989/90 and 1997/98.

A dynasty has emerged with the university's women's volleyball program. The teams have won national championships in every year since 1994, making it a series of five straight titles.

Northern Alberta Institute of Technology

The Northern Alberta Institute of Technology (NAIT) has a long history of winning teams and individual athletes.

At the national (Canadian College Athletic Conference) level, NAIT teams have won the following gold medals: badminton mixed doubles (1993), men's basketball (1989), women's curling (1988 and 1983), with the most national-level success coming in hockey (1996, 1992, 1990, 1989, 1986, 1985 and 1982), and in men's soccer (1987). In 1989, the hockey and basketball titles came as NAIT hosted both tournaments simultaneously. The championship games were won within one hour of each other.

Since its inception in 1964, the Alberta Colleges Athletic Conference has handed out dozens of gold medal awards to NAIT athletes.

Badminton team championships came to NAIT in 1992/93, 1991/92, 1989/90, 1981/82, 1980/81, 1970/71 and 1965/66. Mens' badminton champions from NAIT were: Les Peterson in 1983/84, Grant Pittman in 1981/82, Darrel Wood in 1977/78, and J. Chu in 1970/71. Women's badminton titles were won by: Noreen Humble in 1980/81, Lyn Nickel in 1973/74, and 1970/71.

Mixed doubles badminton champions from NAIT were: Karen Marner and Corey Morse in 1992/93, Barb Fehaiu and Ron Clarkson in 1981/82, and Janice Roman and Val Palm in 1980/81. Men's doubles champions were: William Clarkson and Rick Kosowan in 1987/88, Keith De Sousa and Jim Wu in 1985/86, Les Peterson and Grant Pittman in 1980/81, Les Peterson and Pryce Alderson in 1979/80, Ken Kosak and Byron Gray in both 1974/75 and in 1973/74. Women's doubles champions were: Shirley Mah and Karen Marner in 1991/92, Lynne Courchesne and Shirley Mah won in both 1989/90 and 1988/89, Noreen Humble and Janice Romans in 1981/82, and Chris Brower and Jackie Hailes in 1977/78.

The canoeing provincial team championship was won by NAIT in 1974/75. Men's relay teams won in 1975/76, 1974/75, 1973/74, and in 1972/73. Women's relay teams won in 1974/75, 1973/74, 1972/73, and in 1971/72. Mixed relay championships were won in 1980/81 and in 1973/74. War canoe championships came in 1974/75 and in 1971/72.

The cross-country running team has won seven men's team provincial titles

(1986/87, 1982/83, 1980/81 1978/79, 1972/73, 1969/70 and in 1968/69. The women's team won the ACAC championship in 1989/90. Men's individual championships came to: Shane Rush (1992/93), Ken Nowasiad in both 1980/81 and 1979/80, Murray Hunt (1977/78) Bevan Becker (1976/77), and Gary Cassidy (1975/76). Women's individual champions were: Rose Martin (1992/93), Denise Mitchell (1989/90), Joan Groothysen (1983/84), and Julie MacDonald in both 1979/80 and 1978/79.

Cross-country skier Joan Groothuysen won the individual ACAC championship in both 1983/84 and 1982/83. There was also a women's team title in 1982/83. John Gibson won the men's title in 1986/87.

In curling, there have been nine men's team provincial champions from NAIT: 1994/95, 1988/9, 1986/87, 1983/84, 1979/80, 1977/78, 1972/73, 1967/68 and in 1966/67. The women's team won in the following years: 1996/97, 1991/92, 1990/91, 1989/90, 1987/88, 1983/84, 1982/83, and in 1977/78. Mixed team championships came in: 1990/91, 1983/84, 1980/81, 1979/80, 1973/74, 1972/73 and 1965/66.

Golf saw men's ACAC team championships in: 1994/95, 1993/94, 1989/90, 1988/89, 1983/84, 1978/79, 1974/75, and in 1967/68. There were six men's individual provincial golf champions from NAIT: Gary Smith in 1994/95, Kevin Trefanenko in 1990/91 and in 1988/89, Jamie McSporan in 1978/79, Larry Maclise in 1974/75, and Darwin Sturko in 1973/74. Jana Kolot won the women's individual golf ACAC

Grant MacEwan Community College's basketball team won the 1998/99 ACAC title, and team members also hold records.
(Photo courtesy Grant MacEwan Community College)

championship in 1994/95.

NAIT hockey teams have won 13 provincial championships: 1995/96, 1991/92, 1990/91, 1989/90, 1986/87, 1985/86, 1984/85, 1983/84, 1975/76, 1971/72, 1970/71, 1967/68 and in 1966/67.

The Ooks hockey team holds the team scoring record for most points in a season (565 in 1984/85), most assists in a season (341 in 1984/85) most goals in a season (222 in 1984/85) and most short-handed goals in a game (three in 1986/87). It also holds the record for most short-handed goals in a season (15 in 1986/87), most shutouts in a season (five in 1991/92), and for having the only undefeated season in ACAC play, going 25-0 in 1984/85.

Ooks hockey players have won the ACAC scoring title eight times: Jamie Barnes in 1994/95, Greg Geldart in 1991/92, Ivan Krook in 1989/90, J.C. MacEwan in 1988/89, Sid Cranston in 1984/85, Dave McAmmond in 1974/75, Jack Braun in 1971/72, and Dale Evans in 1966/67. Ron Amyotte holds the ACAC career scoring title, with 151 points between 1984 and 1987. Jack Braun (1970/71) holds the record for most points in a single game, with 12. Most assists in a single game is held by Doug Buchta (1970/71), with eight. Dave McAmmond (1974/75) holds the record for most goals in a season, with 36. Robin Dube (1988/89) holds the record for most power play goals in a season, with 14. Don Davidge (1991/92) has the ACAC record for lowest goals-against average, at 1.63, and most shutouts in a season, at four.

NAIT men's soccer teams have won five provincial titles: 1989/90, 1988/89,

1987/88, 1984/85, and 1983/84. The women won the ACAC title in 1993/94 and 1992/93.

Swimmers have brought NAIT four men's provincial titles (1993/94, 1991/92, 1990/91 and in 1989/90) and two women's titles (1991/92 and in 1989/90). Behr Saretsky set the ACAC record in the 220m freestyle in 1991.

Men's volleyball players at NAIT have won the provincial crown four times: 1976/77, 1972/73, 1969/70 and in 1967/68. Mark Holowaychuk (1994/95) holds the record for the most stuffs in one match, with 12. Team records are held by NAIT for best kills per game average (16.81 in 1997/98), most kills in one match (91 in 1994/95), most kills in a season (1,261 in 1997/98), and for most stuffs in one match (33 in 1997/98). Although the women's volleyball team at NAIT hasn't won an ACAC championship, Daina Koska (1990 to 1994) holds the career records for both kills (1,041) and stuffs (198).

The NAIT men's basketball team won the ACAC provincial championship in 1988/89. NAIT player Rick Gawlick won the ACAC men's basketball scoring championship in 1974/75, with 404 points. Ron Hansuk of the Ooks (1991/92) holds the ACAC reccord for most three-point conversions in a single game, with 10.

While the NAIT women's basketball team has never won an ACAC championship, player Kathy Prochnau won the scoring title in 1986/87, with 354 points.

Grant MacEwan Community College

Grant MacEwan Community College

is a relative newcomer, but has quickly made its mark with provincial championships in many sports.

GMCC's women's swim team won the ACAC title in 1994/95 and in 1993/94. The men's team won in 1994/95, and that same year saw the overall team provincial title taken by GMCC swimmers.

ACAC swimming records are held by GMCC athletes. Colin Sood set the record for the 100-metre backstroke in 1994. Susan Murray set the record for the 200-metre butterfly in 1999. The women's 4x50-metre medley relay team from GMCC set the ACAC record in 1995.

The college has produced Canadian Colleges Athletic Association (CCAA) national championships in badminton. These have come in 1996 (men's doubles), 1994 (men's doubles), 1993 (men's singles), 1992 (men's singles), 1991 (men's singles), 1990 (men's singles), 1989 (men's singles and women's doubles) and 1988 (women's singles).

Badminton competitors at GMCC took the provincial team championship in 1998/99, 1990/91 and 1988/89. Men's singles ACAC titles went to Tim Rostrup (1997/98), Brad Alton (1992/93), Mark Lee (1991/92), Wang Wen (1990/91, 1989/90 and 1988/89), and

Andrew Ng (1984/85). Women's singles ACAC titles went to Adele Friess (1994/95), Kim Nelson (1993/94), Deng Sian (1988/89) and Aine Humble (1987/88). Men's doubles titles went to Steve Wong and Peter Chen (1996/97), Lionel Chong and Iain Fulford (1995/96), Mark Lee and Lionel Chong (1993/94), Tomoaki Meikari and Mark Lee (1992/93), Brad Alton and Trent McNeil (1991/92), and Wang Wen and Trent McNeil (1988/89). Women's doubles ACAC titles went to Kristina Polziegn and Jennifer Fong (1998/99), and to Rhonda Mackay and Julianne Cummin (1992/93). Mixed doubles titles were won by Eric Thai and Pam Bolton (1998/99), Peter Chen and Mandy Copeman (1997/98) and by Deng Sian and Wang Wen (1988/89).

Men's basketball ACAC titles went to the college in 1998/99, 1990/91 and in 1987/88. The Griffins, as the team is called, also hold two scoring titles. They scored the most points in a single game (172 during the 1988/89 season), and the most assists in a season (428 in the 1998/99 season). Darren Ross (1987 to 1993) holds the career scoring title in ACAC men's basketball play, with 1,350 points. GMCC players also hold down second, eighth and eleventh place on the all-time career scoring list. Dannis Farn (1998/99 season) holds the all-time individual ACAC records for most

Todd Pawlenchuk is a standout champion runner from Concordia University College of Alberta.
(Photo courtesy Concordia University College of Alberta)

points in a single game (75), most free throws in a single game (22) and most assists in a season (113).

Women's basketball player Rhonda Wolfram holds two all-time ACAC records for her play in the 1983/84 season: most free throws in a single game (17), and most free throws in a season (154). The women's team (also called the Griffins) set the record for most points in a season (1,791), most three-point conversions in a season (107) and most free throws in a single game (41), all during the 1997/98 season.

Cross-country running ACAC titles went to Jason Reist in 1996/97, Dave Corbet in 1993/94 and Brian Countryman in 1981/82.

Golf has been a successful sport for GMCC athletes at the ACAC level. The men's team won titles in 1996/97 and in 1995/96. The women 's team won in 1997/98, 1996/97 and in 1995/96. Scott Wenger won the individual ACAC golf title in 1996/97. Women's individual championships went to Shari Humbke (1997/98), Jeannette Passmore (1996/67), Jeanette Anderson (1995/96), and Sue Wright (1993/94).

The provincial championship in mixed curling was won by GMCC in 1995/96 and in 1991/92. Men's titles came in 1989/90. A woman's title was won in 1992/93.

The GMCC women's volleyball team won the provincial title in both the 1996/97 and 1997/98 seasons. The women's soccer team at GMCC took the provincial championship in 1997/98.

The college also began playing hockey in the Alberta Colleges Athletic Conference for the first time in 1998/99.

Although the team didn't come close to a championship, goalie Scott Reid was named the CCAA hockey player of the year, as well as receiving all-star honours from both the national and provincial athletics associations. He was cited for stopping the most shots of any goaltender.

The men's soccer team at GMCC won the ACAC championship in 1998/99, and in 1986/87. Jon Pino (1996/97) holds the ACAC record for most goals in a single game (seven) and most goals in a season (29).

The women's soccer team at GMCC won the ACAC title in 1997/98. Kristen Johnson (1997/97) holds the record for most goals in a single game (seven). Mandy Crawford (1997/98) has the record for most shutouts in a season (nine), and is tied with fellow Griffin Sandra Bonneville (1996/97) for the record for lowest goals-against average (.20). The team also holds the record for most goals in a single game (13, in the 1997/98 season), most goals in a season (62, in 1997/98), least goals against in a season (two, in both the 1996/97 and 1997/98 seasons), and for most shut-outs in a season (nine, in 1997/98). Patty Patallas holds the ACAC career scoring title, with 34 goals over three seasons (1993 to 1997).

The men's volleyball team won the ACAC title in 1983/84. Griffin player Travis Horiachka holds the ACAC record for most stuffs in a match (12). Women's volleyball championships went to GMCC in 1997/98 and 1996/97.

Concordia University College of Alberta

This small school has only been in

the university sports system for a few years, there has been one champion from Concordia. Todd Pawlenchuk won the Alberta Colleges Athletic Conference men's cross-country running championship in 1994/95.

King's University College

Peter Buwalda of the King's men's basketball team won the All-College Conference Player of the Year Award in 1998.

Rhythmic Gymnastics

A sport that combines physical and artistic goals, Edmonton has a growing list of junior- and senior- and novice-level champions. The following individual athletes come from Edmonton.

1999: Sara Al-Adra, senior provincial champion. Michelle Gunn, junior provincial champion. Judit Berecz, novice provincial champion.

1998: Alyssa Louw, junior provincial champion. Judit Berecz, novice provincial champion.

1997: Jody Miller, senior provincial champion. Kelli Kachur, junior provincial champion. Alyssa Louw, novice provincial champion.

1996: Ginny Lee, senior provincial champion. Cassy Smale, junior provincial champion. Alyssa Louw, novice provincial champion.

1995: Cassy Smale, junior provincial champion.

1994: Heather Halpern, senior provincial champion. Janine Durand, junior provincial champion. Cassy Smale, novice provincial champion.

1993: Esther Kim, senior provincial champion. Ginny Lee, junior provincial champion. Sara Al-Adra, novice provincial champion.

1992: Jody Miller, junior provincial champion.

1991: Jody Miller, novice provincial champion.

1990: Jody Miller, novice provincial champion.

1988: Chantal Labonte, senior provincial champion.

1987: June Sasano senior provincial champion. Chantal Labonte, junior provincial champion.

1981 through 1984: Janet Darwish, senior provincial champion.

*Sara Al-Adra is one of the many recent champions who have made Edmonton a centre of excellence in rhythmic gymnastics.
(Photo courtesy The Al-Adra family)*

Teams from Edmonton have also performed well.

1996: Sara Al-Adra, Lisel Burns, Kelli Kachur, Michelle Lee and Cassy Smale won the Canadian National Junior Group Championship.

1995: Sara Al-Adra, Lisel Burns, Teresa Hinsz, Kelli Kachur and Cassy Smale won the Provincial Junior Group Championship.

1994: Sara Al-Adra, Lisel Burns, Teresa Hinsz, Kelli Kachur, Michelle Lee, Ayssa Louw, Cassy Smale and Sarah Stauffer won both the Canadian and Provincial Novice Group Championship.

1993: Sara Al-Adra, Lisel Burns, Teresa Hinsz, Kelli Kachur, Michelle Lee, Alyssa Louw, Cassy Smale and Sarah Stauffer won both the Canadian and Provincial Novice Group Championship.

1981: Karen Alisio, Janet Darwish, Nancy Forrester, Tracy Kurchinsky, Ruth Samide and Scarlet Sharun won the Provincial Senior Group Championship. Jill Berrigan, Karen Davidson, Sherry Dobbler, Tanya Dobbler, Natalie Mousseau and Lynn Ulesky won the Provincial Junior Group Championship.

Ringette

Edmonton teams have excelled at ringette, bringing home many national and provincial titles. The Edmonton Ringette Club won the Canadian Ringette Championship Title in the following years: 1999 (Intermediate), 1998 (Deb division), 1997 (Belle and Intermediate divisions), 1996 (Junior, Belle and Deb divisions), 1995 (Junior), and 1988 (Belle).

Edmonton ringette teams have also won many provincial championships. In 1999, Inferno won Belle AA, Virus won Deb AA, Misfits won Intermediate B and Scorch won Intermediate AA. In 1998, Chaos won Belle AA and Flash won Deb AA. In 1997, Homesteader Hornets won Tween B, Rage won Junior AA, Blitz won Belle AA, Impact won Deb AA and Misfits won Intermediate B.

In 1996, Misfits Intermediate B, Siege won Junior AA, Greased Lightning won Belle AA, and Flyers won Deb AA. In 1995, Thunder won Tween AA,

Edmonton ringette teams have a long history of championships.
(Photo courtesy Ringette Alberta)

Double-world champion trapshooter John Primrose wasn't just good at aiming a gun. In 1960, he won the Alberta Junior Golf Championship.

Sabotage won Junior AA, Mavericks won Belle AA, and Flyers won Deb AA.

In 1995, Thunder won Tween AA, Sabotage won Junior AA, Mavericks won Belle AA, and Flyers won Deb AA. In 1994, Edmonton teams won Tween AA, Junior AA, Belle AA and Deb AA. In 1993, Edmonton Edge won Tween AA, and other Edmonton teams won Belle AA and Deb AA. In 1991, Stingers won Petite A, Blades won Tween A, and Kilkenny won Tween B. In 1990, Stingers won Petite A, and Kilkenny Cougars won Tween B. In 1989, Kilkenny won Petite A, and Caernarvon won Deb B. In 1988, Edmonton teams won Belle A and Belle AA.

Rowing

The Edmonton Rowing Club began in 1974, and has a solid list of winners.

Andrew Hoskins is one of the most recent champions, winning the 1998 intermediate and association single at the prestigious Royal Canadian Henley Regatta (RCHR), and the single at the Canada Cup regatta.

Pauline VanRoessel won the intermediate and senior 2- at the 1998 RCHR along with fellow Edmontonian Theresa Rivalin (they were competing for the Western Rowing Club after being cut from the national team). The pair also won the women's 2- at the Canada Cup.

Edmonton Police Service officer Malcolm Allan won the 200-metre and 1000-metre indoor rowing race at the World Police and Fire Games in 1997.

In 1995, Ken Attwood and Thomas Auer won the 140-lb. 2- at the RCHR. Thomas also won the 145-lb.1x that year. Attwood won the 1991 135-lb. 1x at the RCHR and the 2- with Bill Sabey.

Megan Delahanty was a member of the 1992 Canadian Women's 8+ that won the gold medal at the Barcelona Olympics.

Seniors Games

The Edmonton team has won the Alberta Seniors games for seven years in a row (to 1999). The event is a mixture of sporting and recreational events for Alberta seniors. The 1999 gold-medal winners from Edmonton were as follows.

Five-pin bowling: Marian Fulmore. Bridge: Helen Jesse and Ole Oleson. Carpet Bowling: John Berbey, Milke Kulba, Walter Cikaluk and Sam Dytiuk, gold (70+). Cycling (sprint) Inge Telzerow. Floor curling: Sames Burke, Henry Jurykovsky, George Kokotailo and Doug Mackenzie (55+). Frisbee golf: Josephine Kuster. Golf (low scores): Betty Gegolick, Miles Daigneault. Horseshoes: Henry Dewald (55A+), David Chambers (55B+). Shuffleboard: Earl Hillman and Orville Stemmler. Slow pitch: Edmonton team won gold in 65+. Swimming: Vinus Van Baalen (two - 55+), Jackie Scott (two - 55+), Rudy Jarosch (two - 70+), Harold Johnston (two - 75+). Track events: Bruce Selby (1,500 meters and 800 meters), Dora Bilko (100 metres and 400 metres). Visual arts and crafts: Mary Dolynchuk and Josie Kulba were each winners.

Although there were no medals handed out for triathlon, the Edmonton ladies' team and men's team each took first place. The ladies' team members were: Jackie Scott, Inge Telzerow and Dora Bilko. The men's team members were: Vinus Van Baalen, Tom Molenaar and Bruce Selby.

Shooting

When it comes to champions in shooting sports, John Primrose rises to the top on sheer longevity and number of awards. Primrose was at the pinnacle of International-Style Trapshooting for almost two decades. One of his first major prizes was the gold medal at the 1974 Commonwealth Games. The next year, he won the world championship - a feat he would repeat in 1983. The 1978 Commonwealth Games in Edmonton saw Primrose win a second gold medal.

Although Olympic gold eluded his many attempts, Primrose won medals and trophies in international competition throughout his career. In 1993, he won his fourteenth Canadian national championship. That came almost 10 years after his career performance saw him receive the Order of Canada in 1986.

Another legendary name from Edmonton in the shooting world is Ed Shaske - both senior and junior.

Ed Shaske Sr. won nine Canadian trapshooting championships and has been instrumental in promoting the sport for several decades, including development of the Strathcona Shooting Range, generally considered the top competitive-shooting facility in Canada.

Ed Shaske Jr. was a champion from

One of Edmonton's great international champions, Susan Nattrass brought the city fame in the shooting sports.
(Photo courtesy Strathcona Shooting Range)

a young age, winning the Alberta Sub-Junior or Junior Championship in Olympic Trapshooting (a style of shooting competition, not the Olympic Games) every year from 1969 to 1974. In 1977, he won the Pacific Coast United States Championship. Shaske Jr. won the non-resident category of the U.S. National Championship the next year, and again in 1980. Also in 1980, he tied for first place in the British Grand Prix trapshooting event.

Destined to become a true world star, Shaske Jr. was known for his lightening-fast reflexes. He was being sponsored by a British ammunition maker, who custom-made 30,000 rounds for him, each engraved with his name.

Shaske Jr. was playing hockey in 1982, when he died of a heart attack at age 25.

Another legendary name in the shooting world is Susan Nattrass. Considered the best female shooter in the world, she won the women's section of trapshooting at the 1988 Seoul Olympics. This came after a remarkable career, where she won the world championship in 1974, 1975, 1977, 1978 and 1979.

Showjumping

Gail Greenough brought the sport of showjumping to national attention in 1986 when, aboard her horse Mr. T, she became the first non-European (and the first woman) to win the World Showjumping Championship.

Greenough also won many national and international events, including: the 1984 Gold Medal at the Nations Cup at the New York National Horse Show; first at the 1986 International Grand Prix in Stuttgart, Germany; and the 1987 Loblaws Classic in Toronto.

Other awards and titles won by Greenough include: Sports Federation of Canada International Achievement Award, 1984; Alberta's Top Female Amateur Athlete of the Year in 1986; and being named to the Alberta Sports Hall of Fame.

Greenough was named to the Order of Canada in 1990. She continued to compete and show well, but would never take another world title before retiring in 1992. Mr. T was put down after becoming ill in 1991.

Skiing & Snowboarding

Although not blessed with nearby mountains, Edmonton has produced some world-class skiers in several different events.

The biggest success in skiing came when Edi Podivinsky of the Snow Valley Ski Club won a World Cup downhill event in Austria. He would also win an Olympic bronze medal in downhill skiing in the 1994 Games in Lillehammer, Norway. His earlier successes were highlighted by winning the World Junior Downhill Championship. Snow Valley Ski Club was also named the provincial club champion in 1999

Snowboarding, with its exploding popularity, has also contributed to Edmonton's list of champions. In 1995, Brad Zapisocky won the gold medal in downhill at a World Cup event at Canada Olympic Park in Calgary.

Cross-country skiing gave Edmonton two gold medal winners in 1999. Claire Critchley and Tara Whitten won the medals at the Canadian junior championships.

Even ski jumping has a history in Edmonton. In the early part of the century, a ski jump hill was located on Connors Hill. The popularity of the sport was boosted when John Hougan set a Canadian ski jump record at the facility in 1913.

Slow Pitch

Teams playing in the St. Albert Men's Slow Pitch League have won several national and provincial competitive championships.

The national champions from the league are: White Sox in the 55+ category (1999,1995 and 1994), Alta Auto Antiques in the 60+ category (1998), the Poor Boys in the 55+ category (1997 and 1992), and the Accords in the 40+ category (1991).

Provincial champions from the league are: Bennys in the 40+ category (1999), White Sox in the 55+ category (1998 and 1997), Old Buzzards in the

50+ category (1998), Accords in the 40+ category (1992 and 1991), and Poor Boys in the 55+ category (1991).

Softball

Softball is one of Edmonton's most popular sports. In competitive play, there have been several Canadian championship teams.

In 1981, the Ardrossan Hen House Coiffures won the Midget Women title. In 1981, the Edmonton Crown Well Oilers won the Senior Men's title. The Edmonton Jolane Transport team won the 1982 Junior Women's championship. The Edmonton/Calahoo Erins won the Senior Women's championship in both 1988 and 1990. The Edmonton Bandits won the 1999 Alberta Amateur Softball Association junior women's championship.

Speedskating

Gail Foran-Woodward won national and provincial age-group championships in 1958, 1960, 1962, 1963 and 1964. Her sister Shannon Foran-Lindenberg won provincial and national age-group championships in 1957, 1959, 1961 and 1963.

Swimming

Edmonton has a history of winners when it comes to competitive swimming. The most successful group of swimmers is the Smith family. Known as "The Swimming Smiths," the eight children of Dr. Don and Gwen Smith (George, Susan, Lewis, Sandra (Sam), Graham, Allison, Scott and Becky) reaped numerous titles and records during the 1960s, 70s and 80s. In 1968

alone, Smith family members would hold 15 of 24 individual Alberta records.

In all their years swimming, the Smiths would win 13 gold medals, 12 silver medals, and eight bronze medals.

The first of the eight children to receive recognition was 10-year-old George, who became the first Albertan to set a national swimming record, in 1960, and who won a gold medal in the 100-metre freestyle. By 1962, he would set a total of nine national records. George would compete on Canada's national all-star team in 1963, 1964 and 1967.

In 1966, George set Canadian and Commonwealth records for both the 200- and 400-metre individual medley, and 200-metre butterfly. He would also set the Canadian record for the 800-yard freestyle in 1968. George competed for Canada in the 1967 Pan Am Games, the

Glenn Anderson,
Gail Greenough,
horse, Stanley Cup.
(Photo courtesy
Deanna Trueman)

Becky and Graham Smith smile at their father, who was in the crowd during a swim meet. It was the last time Don Smith would be at his childrens' swim meets before passing away.
(Photo courtesy Gwen Smith)

1968 Olympics, and won two gold medals at the 1970 Commonwealth Games. He would win six gold medals in meets that year.

George retired from competitive swimming in 1971 after a near-fatal motorcycle accident. But perhaps his greatest achievement came in 1975. After spending years recuperating from his severe injuries, he had picked up swimming once again, as a therapy. He was persuaded to swim for University of British Columbia, and won races in 1974, and was named that year's CIAU outstanding male swimmer. The next year, he won UBC's Bobby Gaul Trophy as the university's outstanding athlete - the first time the honour was awarded to a swimmer.

Born in 1950, Susan Smith set her first national age group record in 1963. She was named to the Canadian All-Star Team in 1965, 1966, 1967, 1968, and 1969. Also in 1969, Sandra was the national champion in the 100-metre butterfly, after winning medals in meets throughout the late 1960s.

Sandra began setting records in 1962, when she set three national age group marks in the breaststroke. She set Canadian records in both the 200-metre and 400-metre freestyle in 1966. Susan was a member of the Canadian All-Star Team in 1963, 1965, 1967, 1968 and 1969.

The most successful of the Smiths was Graham.

In the 1970s, Graham Smith set and smashed many records and took home many medals and trophies. He set his first national age group record in 1968, in the 100-metre breaststroke. He was named to the Canadian All-Star Team in 1969, 1972 and 1973. Winning many races and setting more national age group records in the early 1970s, Graham took first place in both the 100-metre and 200-metre breaststroke at the World Aquatic Games Trials in 1975.

Graham posted three Canadian records in 1976. His first world record came in 1977, when he set the standard for the 200-metre individual medley. In 1977, as a student athlete at the University of California Berkeley, Graham won championships and set U.S. records in the 100- and 200-metre breaststroke.

But Graham's finest year was in 1978, competing in the XI Commonwealth Games in Edmonton. Graham won six gold medals in the competition - the most by a single athlete in Commonwealth Games history. Alone, he would have ranked fifth among the nation standings. That same year, Graham won both a gold and a silver medal at the World Aquatics Championships in Berlin.

He won the first World Cup Gold in the 100-metre breaststroke in 1979, and at that year's NCAA championship, Graham won four gold medals. It was the first time a swimmer from Berkeley won the NCAA championship.

Graham Smith was given the Lou Marsh Award as Canadian Male Athlete of the Year for 1978 and the Lionel Conacher Award from Canadian Press as Canadian Male Athlete of the Year. He was named a Member of the Order of Canada in 1978. Other awards include being made a member of the Alberta Sports Hall of Fame (1978).

Rebecca Smith set national age group records in both the 100-metre butterfly and the 200-metre breaststroke in 1972. She set records again in 1973, for backstroke and 100-metre butterfly, and was a member of the Canada-America All-Star Team in 1972-73. Rebecca won gold at the 1974 Commonwealth Games, in the 400-metre freestyle relay. She won silver and bronze medals in individual races at that event.

Rebecca won golds in meets around the world in the early 1970s (and came just behind steroid-assisted East Germany swimmers at the 1976 Olympics), and she set more national records in the 200-metre and 400-metre individual medley at the 1974 national championships. After winning national titles in the 200- and 400-metre individual medley races in 1977, she swam for another year before retiring with acute tendonitis.

Other Edmonton-based swimmers have turned in great performances, setting records and winning championships.

Chris Bowie set Canadian records in the 800-metre freestyle in 1980 and 1989. He was national champion in the 400-metre freestyle in 1989, in the 800-metre freestyle in 1990, and in the 1500-metre freestyle in both 1988 and 1990.

Keltie Byrne won the national championship in the 200-metre individual medley in 1986.

Derek Cathro won the national championship in the 100-metre butterfly in 1978.

Keltie Duggan won the 100-metre breaststroke title at the 1987 Pan Am Games and the 1990 Commonwealth Games. She also won the national championship for the event in 1989, 1990 and 1992.

Scott Flowers was national champion in the 400-metre freestyle in 1986. Rob Fox won the national championship in the 100-metre breaststroke in 1992.

Cheryl Gibson won the

Graham Smith shows off one of his Canadian championship trophies for the breaststroke.
(Photo courtesy Gwen Smith)

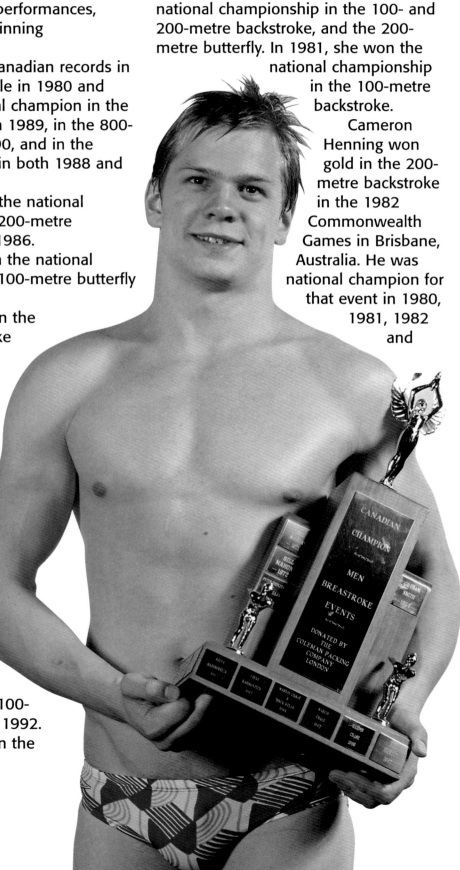

1978 Australian swimming championship title in the 100-metre breaststroke and 200-metre individual medley. In 1977, Gibson won the national championship in the 100- and 200-metre backstroke, and the 200-metre butterfly. In 1981, she won the national championship in the 100-metre backstroke.

Cameron Henning won gold in the 200-metre backstroke in the 1982 Commonwealth Games in Brisbane, Australia. He was national champion for that event in 1980, 1981, 1982 and

1983, and set Canadian records for the race two times in 1980.

Wendy Hogg won the 1978 national championship in the 100-metre backstroke.

Morgan Knabe is the most recent champion Edmonton has produced in the pool. He won the 1999 Pan American Games gold medal in the 200-metre breaststroke, setting a games record. Donna McGinnis was national champion in the 200-metre butterfly in 1987, and national champion in the 400-metre individual medley in 1984, 1985, 1986 and 1987.

George Nagy set the Canadian record for the 200-metre butterfly, and won the national championship in the event, both in 1980.

Jason Pratt won the national championship in the 200-metre individual medley in 1992.

Wendy Quirk set the Canadian record in the 200-metre freestyle, and the 200-metre butterfly (three times for each event), in 1980. She also won the national championship in the 400-metre freestyle (in both 1979 and 1980), and the 100- and 200-metre butterfly in 1980. Tara Seymour won the 1992 national championship in the 1500-metre freestyle.

Peter Szmidt's highlight came when he set the world record for the 400-metre freestyle in 1980. In the 100-metre freestyle, he won the national championship in 1983. In the 200-metre freestyle, he won the national championship in 1980, 1982, 1983 and 1984. Szmidt set the national record for the 200-metre freestyle twice in 1980.

In the 400-metre freestyle (along with his world record) Szmidt won the national championship in 1980, 1981, 1982, 1983 and 1984. He set records in the 800-metre freestyle in 1980 and 1983.

Michael Scarth set Canadian records in the 200-metre backstroke twice in 1976, and was national champion of the event in both 1976 and 1978. The 1500-metre freestyle was another showcase event for Szmidt. He was national champion of that event in 1978, 1980, 1981 and 1982. He also set Canadian records for that event in 1980 (two times) and 1983.

Harry Taylor held Canadian records in the 800-metre freestyle in 1987 and 1988, and Canadian records in the 1500-metre freestyle in 1988 and 1990. Taylor won the national championship in the 1500-metre freestyle in 1986, 1987, 1988, 1989 and 1990.

Megan Watson was national champion in the 100-metre breaststroke in 1980. Debbie Wurzburger won the 1989 national championship in the 1500-metre freestyle.

National masters-level titles have been won by the following athletes.1997: Harold Johnston, Karen Fradette, Leigh Garvie, Aart Looye. 1998: Deborah Gaudin, Cheryl Gibson, Mary Henning, Loreen McKellar, Annalee Woollam, Grant Andruchow, David Ellis, Harold Johnston, Larry Judge, Aart Looye, Karen Fradette, Jim McDonald, Bob McRory, Kurt Miller, Richard Roberts, Barry Saretsky, David Stoneblake, John Sutton, Kim Howland, Andrea Helten, Lori Ingram, Janice Kalyta, Terry Dewhurst, Kevin Golightly, Vinus Van Baalen and Tim Wuetherick. 1999: Karen Fradette, Barry Saretsky and Harold Johnston.

Synchronized Swimming

Swimming titles haven't been limited to the traditional speed events. The Edmonton Aquadettes won the 1961 Canadian synchronized swimming championship. The Aquadettes also won the 1988 and 1989 world masters titles.

The Edmonton Auroras won the 1999 Western Canadian senior team championship. Team members Janet and Lisa Burrows, swimming as a pair, won the Western Canadian senior championship.

Team Handball

A distinct and growing sport, which at first appears to be similar to waterpolo on dry land, team handball has produced Edmonton-based champions.

The Alberta senior men's team is based in Edmonton and has only two non-Edmonton players. It won the national championship in 1998, and the Western Canadian and national championship in 1999.

The Alberta senior women's team, also based in Edmonton, won the Western Canadian championship in 1999.

Tennis

Edmonton's earliest tennis champion was Simone Marie Coupez Starkey. Born in Belgium, she arrived in Edmonton via Winnipeg in 1910. After spending time back in Winnipeg and and Seattle, she returned to Edmonton and won the 1926 Dominion doubles tennis championship with a Vancouver woman. Starkey (who was married to local winning athlete Jack Starkey), also won regional titles in badminton and golf.

The most successful tennis player to come out of Edmonton is Erik Dmytruk. As well as winning three tournaments in 1998, Dmytruk won the Provincial Open championship at the Royal Glenora. In 1997, Dmytruk won the boys singles at the Canadian Junior International Championships.

That came after Dmytruk's banner year of 1994, when he won four championship titles in the under-14-years-old category: singles national outdoor, doubles national outdoor, singles national indoor, and doubles national indoor.

Ken Grierson is one of Edmonton's most accomplished racquet-sports athletes. He won numerous city, provincial and national championships, playing both badminton and tennis. He won three gold medals in badminton at the World Masters Games.

Sisters Gail Foran-Woodward and Shannon Foran-Lindenberg won the provincial doubles championship in 1964 and 1965.

Shannon Foran-Lindenberg went on to win provincial doubles titles (with different partners) in 1966, 1967, 1968 and 1969.

She also won provincial and prairie regional singles tennis titles in 1965, 1966, 1967, 1968 and 1969.

Track and Field

Being a winter city, Edmonton has not produced an abundance of track and field champions, but there have been some. The earliest was James Buster Brown, who was on the winning 440-yard relay team at the 1930 British Empire Games.

Tim Berrett is a race walker who has

been competing at the top international level for several years. He has been ranked first in the Commonwealth in the five-kilometre race in 1993, and in the 50-km race in 1992, 1993, 1995 and 1996. Berrett holds the Commonwealth and North American record in the five-kilometre indoor, 20-km track, and 50-km track. He also holds the Canadian record in the 30-km road race, three-kilometre track, one-mile indoor and 1500-metre indoor. Berrett won the national championship in the following events: 20-km (1992, 1993, 1994, 1997 and 1998), 10-km (1994), indoor five-kilometre (1991 and 1993), and the United States' national title in the five-kilometre indoor (1990). He has also been ranked number one in Canada in several race walking events in the 1990s: 50-km (1991, 1992, 1995, 1998 and 1999); 20-km (1990, 1991, 1993, 1996 and 1997); 10-km (1990, 1991 and 1994).

Although originally from Saskatoon, Diane Jones Konihowski has been associated with Edmonton for many years. Her greatest triumph came in Edmonton, when she won the women's pentathlon at the 1978 Commonwealth Games.

More recent champions have included Tanya Wright of Leduc, who won the Canadian Junior Championship in the 800-metre in 1997, 1998 and 1999.

Vicky Lynch-Pounds, also of Leduc, won the Canadian Senior Championship in the 800-metre in 1999.

Triathlon

Heather Fuhr, of the metro Edmonton town of Stony Plain, has been Canada's best success in the sport that mixes cycling, running and swimming. Fuhr has won four triathlon titles around the world, including the 1997 Hawaii Ironman competition.

Twins Christine and Karen McEvoy, of St. Albert, are two of the rising stars in triathlon.
(Photo courtesy The McEvoy family)

Identical twins Christine and Karen McEvoy are two St. Albert triathletes who are coming to the top of the sport's junior elite level.

Christine won the 1999 Canadian junior women's title at the national championships in Edmonton, as well as the provincial title and the 1999 women's duathlon championship. Christine also won the junior title in 1998, along with the female provincial title.

Karen tied for first at the 1998 provincials, and was named national junior triathlete of the year in 1996 and in 1998.

St. Albert has produced several championship triathletes. Kevin Shopland won the under-20 age group in the 1999 Western Duathlon. Sarah Cary-Barnard took first in her age group at the 1997 Alberta Summer Games.

St. Albert's Laurie Murray was first in her age group at the 1998 national and provincial championships, and at the 1999 provincials. Cathy Dixon was first in her age group at the 1998 national championships.

Wietski Eikelenboom won her age group at the Provincial Long Course championship in 1997 and 1998, and her age group at the provincial championship in 1996, 1997 and 1999.

Mark Fewster was first in his age group at the 1997 Alberta provincial championships.

Wrestling

Edmonton wrestlers have been winning national championships for decades.

In 1935, Pat Meehan won the heavywieght championship, while Jack Garry won the 145-lb. class title. Two years later, Lawrence Jacobson won the 174-lb. class.

There were two national titles in the 1940s: John Lindsay's 1947 championship in the 123-lb. class, and H. Evans 114.5-lb. title in 1949.

The Edmonton Wrestling Club took five consecutive national women's championship titles, from 1993 to 1997. Team member Christine Nordhagen won four women's world championships (1994, 1995, 1997 and 1998).

The club has also produced many national age-group champions this decade. Robert Grozic won in 1990 and 1991 and Ryan Ebner and Carlo Panaro in 1991. In 1993, the club's age-group winners were: Carmen Hage, Melissa Brooke, Erin Walker, Athena Collins, Elyssa Jensen, and Terri Tyson. Tyson won again in 1995. Theresa Vladicka won her age group in 1995, 96, and 97. Shannon Mathie won her age group in 1996, while Melissa Hillaby won hers in both 1997 and 1998.

The late 1960s and early 1970s were a time of great success for wrestlers in Edmonton.

The 1969 national junior champions from Edmonton were: Karl Stark (114.5-lb. class, also the Canadian senior champion that year); Len Langner (154-lb. class); and Joe Worobec (super heavyweight class, he was also named national junior athlete of the year, and was a success in both track and football).

Tom Towns, later a successful Edmonton Eskimo player, won the national junior wrestling championship in the 191-lb. weight class.

The 1967 national senior champions

from Edmonton were Larry Speers (177-lb. class) and Brian Heffel (136-lb. class).

Russ Paulyk (136-lb. class) was the national champion for several years in the early 1970s.

Ronn Lappage was the 1969 national senior champion in Greco-Roman (191-lb. class). Ole Sorenson also won several national championships for Greco-Roman wrestling in the early 1970s.

Sporting Championships

Edmonton has been home to many sporting championship events over the years, several of which have set records of their own. The two largest events were the 1978 Commonwealth Games and the 1983 World University Games.

Running from Aug. 3 to 12, The Commonwealth Games was Edmonton's first time on the world stage. The city did not disappoint, setting its own records as Canada's athletes proved themselves to be among the best in the world.

The biggest Commonwealth Games ever featured athletes from 46 countries. It was estimated that more than 100,000 people took in the sports spectacular. Although the $80-million cost would lead to a last-minute civic plebiscite, the games left behind $36 million worth of sporting facilities, such as Commonwealth Stadium and the Commonweath Aquatic Centre, which have been key in attracting more world-class events. Commonwealth Stadium remains one of the largest and best sporting complexes in the country. It is now Canada's biggest natural-grass stadium, and home to the national soccer team. One of the records set by

the event itself was the fact the games included a cultural festival - the first time such a project was included. The cultural event brought more than 300 artists and entertainers from all over the Commonwealth to Edmonton, entertaining visitors and showcasing culture. One of the lasting legacies was the installation of several statues and other works of art throughout the city.

Another record was that Canadian athletes won 45 medals in the games,

The World Figure Skating Championships came to Edmonton in 1996. The city has hosted many world-calibre events, and more are soon to come.

(Photo courtesy Northlands)

the most ever won by a single country in any Commonwealth Games.

Sports observers had expected Canada to come in third behind the English and Australian teams, but they dominated most of the major events.

One of the more obscure records set was for the world's most expensive portable toilet. When it was discovered that Queen Elizabeth would not have a private facility when she opened the games in Commonwealth Stadium, organizers spent about $50,000 on a royal commode.

The World University Games - or Universiade - was the first time the games had ever been held in Canada. Coming in 1983, it made use of many Commonwealth Games facilities, and added a few more in the University of Alberta area. The games saw more athletes, more records and more attention than any Universiade before or since.

The games brought China back into world athletic competition for the first time since the 1932 Olympics.

The Edmonton games set two important athletic precedents: it included the first women's marathon and the first cycling competitions in World University Games. Edmonton was also responsible for bringing in the largest television viewing audience the World University Games had ever seen.

Many individual sports have also held their world or national championships in Edmonton.

1970
World Amateur Senior Wrestling.
North American Water Polo.
1977
Canadian Intercollegiate Athletic Union

Hockey Championships.
Canadian Junior Basketball Championships.
Canadian Weightlifting Association National competitions.
World Lawn Bowling Championships.
1978
Western Divisional Figure Skating Championships.
Pacific Rim gymnastics competition.
Can-Am-Mex waterpolo competition.
Canada Cup International Diving
Canada Cup Swimming Championship.
Canadian track trials.
North American Volleyball Tournament.
1979
Pacific Gymnastics.
1980
Canadian Ladies Curling Association national bonspiel.
Canadian Amateur Hockey Association.
1981
Canadian Badminton Association Senior.
Intercontinental Cup baseball.
1982
Shell Cup Senior Cross-Country Skiing.
Canadian National Cycling.
World Amateur Senior Wrestling.
Canada Cup volleyball tournament.
1983
CWUAA Gymnastics.
CIAU National Basketball.
Winter National Diving.
International Swim Meet.
National Fencing.
National Weightlifting.
World Moving-Target Shooting.
Canadian National Archery.
Commonwealth Ladies Golf.
1984
Canadian National Squash.
National Pistol Shooting competition.
Canadian National Arabian Horse Show.

Canadian Fastball Senior B.
Canada Cup hockey series.
Breeder's Crown Harness Racing.
1985
Intercontinental Cup Baseball.
1987
Labatt Brier Canadian Curling.
1989
National Hockey League All-Star Game.
1990
Edmonton International Law
Enforcement Games.
World Senior Baseball.
World Senior Basketball.
1991
Pan Pacific Swimming.
World Junior Basketball.
1993
World Arm Wrestling.
1994
Royal Bank Canadian Figure Skating.
World Cup Soccer - Canada vs. Brazil
World Wheelchair Basketball.
1995
Americas Baseball Challenge.
1996
World Figure Skating.
Davis Cup tennis qualifier.
CONCACAF Olympic Qualifying Event in
soccer.
Firefighters World Games
Du Maurier Classic Ladies Professional
Golf Association Tournament.
World Junior Water-skiing.
1998
World Cup Swimming event.
Canadian Open Taekwondo.
Canadian National Taekwondo.
1998 Canadian National Rhythmic
Gymnastics.
Canadian National Table Tennis.
1999
Labatt Brier Canadian Curling.

Canadian
Triathalon.
World
Taekwondo
Championships.
World Junior
Women's
Volleyball.

The coming years
will see more
worldwide championships
in Edmonton.

The biggest is the 2001 World Track
and Field Championships, the third-
largest athletic competition in the world
next to the World Cup Soccer and the
summer Olympics. The biggest single-
sport event ever in Western Canada will
attract more than 3,000 athletes from
209 countries, and 3,000 media people.
The event will be watched on television
by an estimated audience of 3.9 billion
people.

The games will have an economic
impact of $385 million in Northern
Alberta. One of the benefits of the
games will be a major overhaul and
upgrade of the Commonwealth Stadium
complex and the adjoining Clarke Park.
The first upgrade was the installation of
the world's largest Jumbotron wide-
screen colour video display, in the
summer of 1999. The $6.2-million
scoreboard includes a 12.5-metre (41-
foot) by seven-metre (24-foot) video
board, and a nine-metre (28-foot) by
seven-metre (24-foot) dot matrix board,
and is so bright and crisp that its picture
is clear, even in direct sunlight.

Other events coming are the 2000
World Youth AAA Baseball
Championship, and the 2001 World
Triathalon Championships.

*One of
the more
unusual
championship events
to take place in
Edmonton was the
Millennium World
Championships of
Musical Whistling.
The event took place
in September 1999,
with more than 20
participants from
around the world at
the Francis Winspear
Centre for Music.*

Festivals

With a shorter summer than in more southerly cities, Edmontonians have learned to make the most of their leisure time. Almost all year through, there are parties and events designed to bring local residents out of doors - especially in warmer weather.

Many of the festivals were invented here. Others, after picking up on an idea from another city, have become the biggest of their kind (such as the Edmonton Folk Music Festival, in this photograph, with a sunset performance by Emmylou Harris seen both on stage and projection screen). The end result is that Edmonton has earned worldwide recognition as Canada's Festival City.

It's all part of that championship spirit that has Edmonton leading the way.

(Photograph by Thomas Turner, courtesy Edmonton Folk Music Festival)

Festivals

There are 19 major festivals in Metro Edmonton, most of them in the summer. Events compete for attention, boosting the fun and making Edmonton one of the most vibrant cities anywhere.

Animethon

Begun in 1993, this celebration of Japanese animation in early summer is the biggest animation festival in Western Canada. The 1999 version attracted more than 3,000 people to see nearly 200 hours of video and film screenings, as well as animation art displays, trading and sales areas.

The Birkebeiner is the only event of its kind in Canada. (Photo courtesy Birkebeiner Festival)

Birkebeiner Ski Festival

The largest classic cross-country ski festival in North America and the only Birkebeiner in Canada, this event is held about 35 km east of Edmonton each February. The festival celebrates the legend of two Norwegian Birkebeiner warriors who rescued the crown prince of Norway in 1206 during a civil war. They saved the infant prince by carrying him - while skiing - over two mountain ranges.

Started in 1985, the Birkebeiner attracts close to 2,500 registrants and 650 volunteers. The event is held in conjunction with an evening presentation, a Viking's feast and a Nordic Fair. It features two 55-km races, one involving the carrying of a 5.5-kg (12-pound) pack (the equivalent weight of the infant crown prince), one without the weight, and four shorter distances.

Blueberry Bluegrass and Country Music Festival

Started in 1986, Stony Plain's Blueberry Bluegrass and Country Music Festival was founded by local musician Chuck Skinner.

Now the premier festival of its kind in Canada, the event features the best bluegrass musicians in North America - those who are taking bluegrass to the forefront of country and roots music.

The event on the August long weekend attracts an audience of up to 3,000 people from across the western United States and Canada, making it the biggest such festival in Canada in terms of both attendance and the number of performers. The festival has been the jumping-off point for local bluegrass musicians who have gone on to international acclaim.

Cariwest

In its fifteenth year in 1999, this three-day Caribbean carnival combines the elements of Mardi Gras with the celebration of Caribbean culture. Held in August, it's the most northerly festival of its kind. The colourful carnival features parades, Caribbean food and crafts and

CariWest is always a colourful favourite.
(Photo by Allyson Quince)

First Night has become a right of passage in Edmonton. Below, a costumed performer greets one of the thousands of younger visitors to the family-oriented blast-off to the New Year.

(Photo by Richard Bouley, courtesy First Night)

a beer garden. More than 50,000 people enjoyed the 1998 parade alone.

Edmonton Sports Festival

The first and largest of its kind in Canada, the Edmonton Sports Festival is a 10-day summer event which attracted about 10,000 athletes and volunteers in its first year. Begun in 1997, it includes 19 athletic events such as tennis, sailing and triathlon.

First Night

The oldest and largest event of its kind in Canada, First Night features performances and activities staged throughout the downtown on New Year's Eve. The

celebration culminates in a midnight finale and an elaborate rooftop fireworks display at Churchill Square. The family-oriented and alcohol-free event has music, theatre, dance, visual arts, storytelling, clowning and interactive activities. Following the long-standing success of the First Night Festival in Boston, Massachusetts, Canadian cities began to take up the idea and Edmonton hosted its initial year-end First Night in 1988. Now up to 40,000 participants enjoy the festival that features performers on 23 stages. With 95 per cent of the activities held indoors, the venues are accessible through city pedways.

Folk Music Festival

Considered the best attended (and among the most influential) folk music events in North America, the Edmonton Folk Music Festival is an annual four-day event featuring folk, blues, Celtic, bluegrass, gospel and world music. Held outdoors at Gallagher Park with a spectacular cityscape as a backdrop, the festival hosts as many as 300 musicians on eight stages in early August.

With the help of more than 1,700 volunteers, the event entertains an audience of more than 80,000 people. The influence of the 20-year-old festival can be seen in the fact that others have modeled themselves after the Edmonton event, and many top-quality performers (including some of the most concert-shy), make a point of taking part. These include such internationally known artists as

Emmylou Harris, Lyle Lovett, k.d. lang, Bruce Cockburn, Randy Newman, Long John Baldry, and Joni Mitchell (who came out of performance retirement to play the festival).

Fringe Theatre Festival

The largest festival of alternative theatre in North America, the International Fringe Theatre Festival is an eleven-day extravaganza held in Old Strathcona in mid-August. Modeled after Scotland's Edinburgh Fringe Festival in its attempt to provide simple and inexpensive access to a variety of theatre, the event showcases new and old plays, as well as dance, music, mime, and street entertainment.

With an attendance of 450,000 and performances by over 120 theatre companies, the Fringe has grown from its beginnings in 1982 with 7,500 spectators to one of Edmonton's most popular summer events. Founded by producer/director Brian Paisley, the Fringe attracts local, North American and

Edmonton's biggest single theatre event, the Fringe is a mecca for off-the-wall performers. Even at the casual outdoor venues, backstage is sometimes the only place to get a break from the crowds.
(Photo by Peiter de Vos, courtesy Fringe Theatre Adventures)

Heritage Days at Hawrelak Park celebrates the city's cultural diversity. (Photo courtesy Heritage Festival)

international performers who are selected on a non-jury basis of either first-come first-serve, or by lottery. Each group creates its own work and receives 100 per cent of its ticket revenues. Shows take place at the 11 indoor theatres, three outdoor stages and several of the more casual bring-your-own-venue sites.

The KidsFringe, a free area focused on theatre-based play, has also become a favorite of young theatre enthusiasts. Every August the Old Strathcona area becomes a riotous scene of the colourful and bizzare as patrons take in any of the more than 100 daily performances, ongoing street performances, and booths of exotic foods and arts and crafts.

Heritage Festival

The largest one-site multicultural festival in the world, Edmonton's Heritage Festival features three days of non-stop ethnic food, music, dancing, crafts and games at Hawrelak Park.

Designated as one of 1999's top 100 events in North America by the American Business Association, the festival showcases up to 60 local cultural groups in 48 pavilions.

Following the Alberta government's decision in 1974 to set the first Monday in August as Heritage Day, a cultural concert was held at Fort Edmonton Park in 1975.

Recognizing the enthusiasm for a multicultural event of this kind in Edmonton, then-Minister of Culture and Multiculturalism Dr. Horst Schmid encouraged the development of a heritage celebration.

In 1976, the first Edmonton Heritage Festival was held, involving 11 local cultural groups. Attended by 20,000 people that first year, the Heritage Festival has grown into an annual multicultural celebration with average attendance of 300,000.

Held during the August long weekend, the free festival is a tribute to Edmonton's cultural mosaic.

Jazz City International Music Festival

A showcase of the best local, North American and international jazz musicians at clubs, outdoor concerts and workshops, Edmonton's Jazz City International Music Festival is the longest continuously running international jazz festival in Canada. The festival, which runs each year in June and July, attracts an annual audience of approximately 150,000 and is also broadcast on the radio. Jazz City began in 1980 and now takes place in 30 venues with more than 120 shows featuring a range of music from bebop to blues and European new music to traditional jazz.

Kiwanis Festival

The oldest music festival in Canada and still one of the largest, the Edmonton Kiwanis Music Festival began in 1908. Held at Alberta College and McDougall Church each spring, the festival annually attracts approximately 3,000 competitors from throughout Northern Alberta and involves 18 judges from across Canada and the United States. Originally a choral-vocal festival known as the Edmonton Festival, it was started by British musicians Vernon

Quick Facts

Edmonton's Klondike Days has had colourful ambassadors in its history. Klondike Mike is a gold miner, accompanied by his mule. Bob Breen - with his mule Chico - is the only person who ever brought Klondike Mike to life. Although Breen and Chico have passed away, Mike lives on as a cartoon logo. Klondike Kate is a character modeled on saloon singers of the Klondike era. Different singers have portrayed her over the years.

Barford, Howard Stutchbury, and Jackson Hanby after they settled in Edmonton. Run by the downtown Kiwanis Club since 1963, the festival has gradually expanded to include competitions in piano, strings, woodwinds, brass, speech, classical guitar, chamber groups and voice.

Following the festival each year is the Shean Competition, established by and named after long-time local music teachers Ranald and Vera Shean. With piano and violin competitions in alternate years, the Shean competition involves entrants from the four western provinces with the first-prize winner receiving a $5,000 award and the opportunity to perform with the Edmonton Symphony Orchestra.

Many alumni of the Edmonton Kiwanis Festival have gone on to international fame, including Angela Cheng (award-winning pianist), Robert Goulet (Broadway singer), and Jens Linderman (a member of the Canadian Brass).

Klondike Days

Edmonton's largest annual celebration is a 10-day party built around the theme of Edmonton's connection to the 1890s gold rush. Organized by Northlands Park, Edmonton Pride Events and the Sourdough Raft Race Association and held at Northlands Park and downtown

sites, Klondike Days was awarded the Major Fair of the Year Award for 1997 by the Canadian Association of Fairs and Expositions. Affectionately known as K-Days, the fair has won the prestigious award four times.

Alberta's original fair was hosted by the Edmonton Agricultural Society in 1879. In 1962, the fair was given the theme of Klondike Days to celebrate the euphoria felt in a booming Edmonton during the 1890s. Attracting crowds of more than 700,000 people annually, the $6 million July fair employs 3,000 people and has an annual economic impact of approximately $52 million.

One of the unique events during the fair is the Sourdough Raft Race which runs through the centre of Edmonton down the historic North Saskatchewan River. The race is a tribute to the sourdough adventurers who embarked by raft to the Yukon gold fields from Fort Edmonton.

As much an event for spectators as participants, the Sourdough Raft Race features home-made rafts being paddled down the river and battling each other with water cannons as onlookers line bridges to pelt the rafts with water balloons.

Local Heroes International Screen Festival

Since its beginning in 1985, Edmonton's Local Heroes International Screen Festival has developed a global reputation as one of the best non-competitive festivals of its kind. Giving the 9,500 audience members a chance to see innovative new films and meet with the people who make them, Edmonton's Local Heroes showcases approximately 20 Canadian short films and 50 feature films from across the country and the world.

The festival also attracts hundreds of filmmakers to Edmonton who attend workshops and seminars on the making of films.

Past guests have included filmmakers John Landis, Julia Sweeny, Edmontonian Arthur Hiller, Costa Gravas and Werner Herzog.

Medieval Festival

When it was selecting a theme for a fundraising event in the Hamlet of Sherwood Park, the Kinsmen Club there chose a medieval festival to complement the already popular local theme, based on the English legend.

The festival recreates the days of Robin Hood and Sherwood Forest and transforms the community into a medieval carnival with a parade, pancake breakfast, midway, beerfest and re-enactments of medieval sword fighting and warfare.

First held in 1979, the Sherwood Park festival is unique in Alberta and is held annually in late spring.

Edmonton's title of Canada's Festival City owes much to Klondike Days. One of the unique attractions is the Promenade, when Edmontonians put on their full Klondike regalia and stroll the downtown. (Photo courtesy Northlands)

Northern Alberta Children's Festival

Held in the suburban city of St. Albert on Edmonton's northern border, the Northern Alberta International Children's Festival is the second oldest and the third largest of its kind in Canada.

Begun in 1981, the festival is held in early summer. It has grown into a showcase of music, dance, theatre, storytelling and entertainment to delight children over five days.

A stilt-assisted performer wows a young patron of the Northern Alberta Children's Festival.
(Photo courtesy Northern Alberta Children's Festival)

With as many as 174 local and international artists performing (many of them at no charge) and many free games and hands-on visual arts activities, the festival attracts audiences of as many as 50,000 a year.

rESOund Festival of Contemporary Music

Begun in 1999, the rESOund Festival of Contemporary Music celebrates this century's music.

The February event is hosted by the Edmonton Symphony Orchestra and complements the symphony's regular concert series by showcasing contemporary music.

The event featured 18 groups and ensembles performing the works of over 50 composers, and attracted an overall audience of 4,200.

Highlights included the Canadian Concerto Competition that required competitors to perform a Canadian concerto written in the twentieth century. The competition was the first of its kind in Canada.

Street Performers Festival

Comics, musicians, jugglers, mime artists, clowns and magicians from around the world transform Sir Winston Churchill Square into a live stage leaving audiences bursting with smiles for 10 days each July.

The first such festival in North America, the Edmonton International Street Performers Festival has become world renowned and performers line up to be invited to take part.

Co-founded in 1985 and produced for many years by Dick Finkel, the festival today presents more than 50 of the world's best street performers in over 1,000 shows with an attendance annually of more than 200,000.

The vast majority of performances are by buskers in Sir Winston Churchill Square, where the only cost is what patrons are willing to put into a hat passed through the crowd.

Symphony Under the Sky

Symphony Under the Sky is a five-day extravaganza of musical entertainment, festivities, and symphonic music presented by the Edmonton Symphony Orchestra.

What would a Prairie city be without its fair? Klondike Days has always been known for the crowd-pleasing midway rides.
(Photo courtesy Northlands)

Held outdoors each Labour Day weekend at the Heritage Amphitheatre at Hawrelak Park, the event features recitals, concerts, Pub in the Park and children's entertainment.

The elaborate fireworks display on opening night and the festival's closing performance of Tchaikovsky's 1812 Overture, complete with cannon blasts, are favorite Symphony Under the Sky traditions.

The Works

This festival is the largest festival of the visual arts in North America, and is unique for its use of alternative venues such as empty office spaces, street corners and parks.

The Works spotlights the visual arts such as painting, photography and sculpture.

The Works has more than 70 exhibits and 200 events in 30 art galleries, parks and buildings throughout the city (most in the downtown core). Featuring anywhere from 500 to 1,000 artists, the festival was initiated by a small group of Edmonton visual artists. The Works now attracts audiences of up to 250,000 people.

As part of the 1999 edition of The Works, the largest cartoon exhibition ever in Western Canada was held.

The exhibit had 200 pieces of original Canadian comic strip and editorial cartoon art, in what organizers say was the most diverse collection of such work anywhere.

The Works attracts all kinds of visual artists, including performance artists.
(Photo by Jill Watamaniuk, courtesy The Works)

Sir Winston Churchill Square is the focal point for buskers from around the world at the Street Performers' Festival. (Photo by Allyson Quince)

Arts & Leisure

Almost from its very beginnings, Edmonton has shown an affinity for the arts. From the early theatre and visual arts scene, to today's bustling creative community, there have been many artists and artistic groups (such as the Cheremosh Ensemble seen here) which have set records or been at the forefront of their craft.

Leisure activity is also one of the areas where Edmonton has nurtured a history of achievements and firsts. The quality and quantity of arts and leisure activities and groups in Edmonton show the city is second to none.

(Photography courtesy Cheremosh Ensemble)

Arts & Leisure

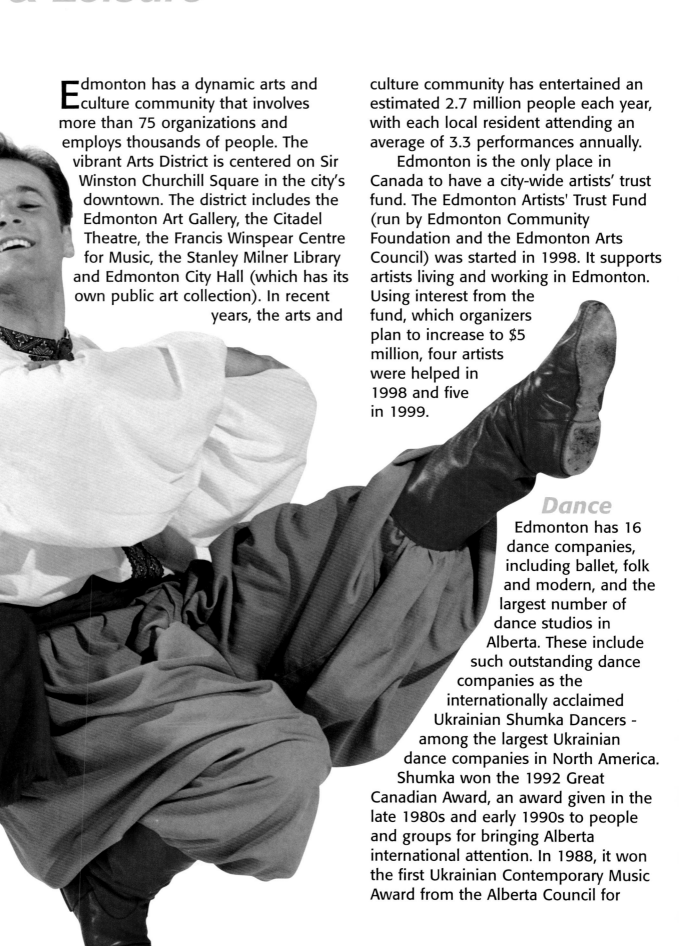

Edmonton has a dynamic arts and culture community that involves more than 75 organizations and employs thousands of people. The vibrant Arts District is centered on Sir Winston Churchill Square in the city's downtown. The district includes the Edmonton Art Gallery, the Citadel Theatre, the Francis Winspear Centre for Music, the Stanley Milner Library and Edmonton City Hall (which has its own public art collection). In recent years, the arts and culture community has entertained an estimated 2.7 million people each year, with each local resident attending an average of 3.3 performances annually.

Edmonton is the only place in Canada to have a city-wide artists' trust fund. The Edmonton Artists' Trust Fund (run by Edmonton Community Foundation and the Edmonton Arts Council) was started in 1998. It supports artists living and working in Edmonton. Using interest from the fund, which organizers plan to increase to $5 million, four artists were helped in 1998 and five in 1999.

Dance

Edmonton has 16 dance companies, including ballet, folk and modern, and the largest number of dance studios in Alberta. These include such outstanding dance companies as the internationally acclaimed Ukrainian Shumka Dancers - among the largest Ukrainian dance companies in North America. Shumka won the 1992 Great Canadian Award, an award given in the late 1980s and early 1990s to people and groups for bringing Alberta international attention. In 1988, it won the first Ukrainian Contemporary Music Award from the Alberta Council for

Ukranian Arts for favorite dance repertoire album. In 1987, it was awarded the Federation Award by the Ukrainian Canadian Professional Business Association in recognition of its contribution in the field of culture.

Another internationally recognized Ukrainian dance group in the city is the Cheremosh Ensemble. Celebrating its thirtieth anniversary in 1999, the ensemble has toured throughout the world, and was chosen in 1996 as Canada's sole artistic representative to the prestigious Aberdeen International Youth Festival in Scotland. In 1996, Cheremosh won the award for artistic excellence from the Alberta Council for Ukrainian Arts. The group produced the first Ukrainian music compact disc in the world after a successful 1988 tour.

The Polonez Polish Folk Arts Ensemble dance group was founded by Dr. Walenty Michalik. He was awarded the Order of Poland in 1998 for his work with the group. As well, the Polish Ministry of Fine Arts and Culture presented the group with the Order of Cultural Merit in 1997.

Vinok, the only group of its kind in Western Canada, presents folk music and dances from around the world. Formed in 1988, the company has a repertoire of dances from 24 countries and five continents.

An award-winning contemporary dance group, the Brian Webb Dance Company began in 1979, and is company in residence at Grant MacEwan Community College. Webb won the 1995 Syncrude Canada Award for Innovation in Artistic Direction. The company's work, *Project Desire: the mountains and the plains*, was

presented in New York at the prestigious Performance Space 122 in 1999.

Film

Recognized around the world, Edmonton filmmakers are consistently invited to show their films at international festivals.

One of the most recognizable names in the Edmonton film business is Anne Wheeler. During the 1980s, Wheeler was the most successful of the local filmmakers, winning a Genie Award for her 1986 film *Loyalites*. That came after her 1983 film *A War Story* was named Best Feature-Length Documentary at the American Film Festival in New York. Wheeler's work has won many awards in Alberta, and she was named an Officer of the Order of Canada in 1995.

Among other award-winning Edmonton producer/directors is Joe Viszmeg, whose 1995 film *In My Own*

Dance (such as the world-famous Shumka, photo left) has been an integral part of the Edmonton arts scene for years. Arthur Hiller (photo below, with Alan Arkin and Peter Falk) has been one of Edmonton's most successful and famous filmmakers.
(Photos courtesy Shumka and Gold Quill Productions)

Time: Diary of a Cancer Patient, won awards that year such as the Best Biography prize at the Houston International Film Festival, and the Best Educational title at the Columbus International Film and Video Festival. Viszmeg also won the 1997 Gemini Award for best documentary director. Vizmeg died June 21, 1999. A cinema in the Princess Theatre was named in his memory as a Fringe Festival venue.

Edmonton director and writer Gil Cardinal has won numerous awards, including a National Aboriginal Achievement Award in 1997, and the Prix du Public in 1991 from Nyon International Du Film Documentaire for *Tikinagan*. Cardinal's film *Foster Child* won a Gemini award for direction, a special jury award at the Banff Television

Festival in 1988, and a Gold Apple Award from the National Educational Film and Video Festival in 1989. His film *Discussions in Bioethics: The Courage of One's Convictions*, won The Chris Award in the Health and Medicine category at the 1987 Columbus International Film Festival.

Producer Jerry Krepakevich has been honoured at film festivals around the world. His film *Foster Child* has collected nine awards since its release in 1987. *The Spirit Within* won a Wilbur Award, and the educational video *Unsuitable Actions* won the 1998 Canadian Educational Association Achievement Award at the Amtec Media Festival.

Marty Chan's TV pilot *The Orange Seed Myth and Other Lies Mothers Tell* won the 1997 Gold Award at the Charleston International Film Festival. Chan wrote the pilot, which was produced by Edmonton's Great North Productions.

In 1998, Eva Colmers won the Prix Telebec Award at the festival du cinema international en Abitibi-Temiscamingue in Quebec, for her film *No Problem*.

Dave Cunningham won Best Instructional/Educational Program at the Yorkton Short Film and Video Festival in 1991, for *Great Expectations*. The Children's Broadcasting Institute gave him the 1990 Award of Merit for *Solving the Harmony Puzzle (You're Part)*. He also won Best Visual Presentation at the 1984 World Conference on Education in New Delhi, India, for *To Call An Eagle*.

Karvonen Films' *Stories from the Seventh Fire* (with partners Scorched Wood Comunications and Dinosaur Soup) took the 1999 Best Animation Award from CanPro (the National

Canadian Broadcasters). The same work won Best Aboriginal Program at the Banff International Television Festival, and the Best Communication to a Young Audience Award at the International Wildlife Film Festival in Missoula, Montana.

Edmonton has been the birthplace of several actors who went on to award-winning careers (such as Michael J. Fox and Robert Goulet), but one of the best-known to remain connected to the city is Kenneth Welsh. A graduate of the drama school of the University of Alberta, he received an honorary Doctorate of Law in 1998. His awards for acting include a 1998 Gemini Award for best lead actor as President Harry Truman in *Hiroshima*. In the same year, he won the Earl Grey Award for lifetime

body of work. Welsh won a 1991 Gemini Award for his supporting role in *Journey Into Darkness: The Bruce Curtis Story*. He has also won a best actor Gemini award in 1988, and a best actor from ACTRA in 1983. But Welsh is best-known in Canada for his role in the CBC/NBC miniseries *Love and Hate*, for which he won the best actor Gemini for his portrayal of convicted murderer, politician Colin Thatcher.

Another award-winning Edmonton actor is Tom Peacocke, who was a faculty member at the University of Alberta drama department. He won the 1981 Genie Award for Best Actor, for his portrayal of Father Athol Murray in *The Hounds of Notre Dame*. He was named to the Order of Canada in 1996.

Literature

Edmontonians read more books per capita than people in any other city in Canada. The city is home to more than 75 published authors, including Governor General Award winners Rudy Wiebe (1994 for *A Discovery of Strangers,* and 1973 for *The Temptations of Big Bear*), Greg Hollingshead (1995 for *The Roaring Girl*) and Ted Blodgett (1996 for *Apostrophes: Woman at a Piano*).

Edmonton has two of the largest independent bookstores in Canada, Audreys Books and Greenwoods Bookshoppe.

The Writers Guild of Alberta has 750 members, and is believed to be the largest writers association of its kind in Canada. It was established in 1980 to provide a meeting ground and collective voice for Alberta writers, and has its main office in Edmonton.

Greg Hollingshead is one of Edmonton's many award-winning writers. (Photo by Geoff McMaster, courtesy of University of Alberta)

Edmonton was the first city in Canada to have a city-sponsored book prize. Administered by the Alberta Writers Guild and co-sponsored by Audreys and the city of Edmonton, it was introduced in 1995. The largest book fair in Alberta is also held in Edmonton. Established 15 years ago, it attracted almost 3,000 people in 1998.

Edmonton writers have won many of the Guild's annual awards, including the following.

The Georges Bugnet Award for Fiction: Mary Walters Riskin (1987 for *The Woman Upstairs*), Greg Hollingshead (1991 for *Spin Dry* and 1998 for *The Healer*).

The Howard O'Hagan Award for Short Fiction: Merna Summers (1982 for *Calling Home* and 1988 for *North of the Battle*), Greg Hollingshead (1992 for *White Buick* and 1995 for *The Roaring Girl*) and Sally Ito (1998 for *Floating Shore*).

The R. Ross Annett Award for Children's Literature: Monica Hughes (1982 for *Hunter in the Dark*, 1983 for *Space Trap*, 1986 for *Blaine's Way* and 1992 for *The Crystal Drop*), and Tololwa M. Mollel (1995 for *Big Boy*).

Tommy Banks is a composer, musician and actor who is one of Edmonton's most-loved award winners.
(Photo courtesy Tommy Banks)

The Stephan G. Stephannson Award for Poetry: E.D. Blodgett (1983 for *Arche/Elegies*), Douglas Barbour (1984 for *Visible Visions*), and Tim Bowling (1997 for *Dying Scarlet*).

The Wilfred Eggleston Award for non-fiction: Myrna Kostash (1987 for *No Kidding*, 1993 for *Bloodlines*), Judy Schultz (1997 for *Mamie's Children*), and Rudy Weibe and Yvonne Johnson (1998 for *Stolen Life*).

The Henry Kreisel Award for the best first book: Curtis Gillespie (1997 for *The Progress of an Object in Motion*).

Alice Major won the fourth Alberta Writing for Youth Award in 1988 for *The Chinese Mirror*. Cora Taylor won three awards for her work *Julie*: the 1985 Canadian Library Association Book of the Year Award, the 1985 W.G.A.R. Ross Annett Award, and the Canada Council award in 1986. Taylor also won the Ruth Schwartz award in 1988 for *The Doll*, and the Canadian Library Association Book of the Year award in 1995 for *Summer of the Mad Monk*.

Edmonton publisher Mel Hurtig has been awarded Book Publisher of the Year awards several times. Both the printed and multimedia versions of *The Canadian Encyclopedia* were produced by his Hurtig Press in Edmonton. Hurtig has been named to the Order of Canada. Editor-In-Chief James Marsh was also named to the Order of Canada.

The University of Alberta Press has won many publishing awards. In 1997, it won First Prize for Excellence in Book Design from the national Alcuin Book Society Citation, and the Graphic Designers of Canada's Design Award. In 1995, it won the Typographic Book Award from the Association of American University Presses (AAUP). In 1992 it was awarded the Illustrated Book Award from the AAUP and the Award of Excellence in Concept, Design & Manufacture from the AAUP in 1990.

Edmonton's annual Stroll of Poets has become a popular literary event. The first event of its kind in Canada, Stroll of Poets began in 1991 as an October afternoon event in coffeehouses, bookstores and showrooms along Whyte Avenue. It has expanded to include up to 130 poets reading their work. After the October event, a poetry anthology is published based on the readings. Judges choose 11 winning poets who then go on to read during the Twelve Days of Poetry event held in December and January. Audiences at this event select five winning poets from that group to read in the grand finale on the last day.

Edmonton's main library, the Stanley A. Milner Library on Sir Winston Churchill Square, has the highest per-capita circulation of any major municipal library in Canada. In 1998, more than seven million items were borrowed from the total library system, and more than 4.1 million visits were recorded. The total collection has approximately 1.5 million items. More than 50 per cent of Edmontonians own valid library cards and, on average, someone visits one of Edmonton's 15 public libraries every eight seconds.

In 1941, the library and the Edmonton Radial Railway (which became the Edmonton Transit System in 1947) introduced the first traveling library in a streetcar. In 1951, when streetcars were discontinued, the library service was continued with bookmobile buses. In 1979, Edmonton's Public

Library became the first computerized library system in Canada.

Music

Music has always been a big part of Edmonton. The city has 24 music organizations, including the Edmonton Symphony Orchestra (ESO).

Edmonton's 56-member symphony has an annual overall attendance of 165,000 patrons and over 12,000 subscribers.

The ESO has an award-winning history, including performances with internationally known artists such as Itzhak Perlman, YoYo Ma, Frederica von Stade, Ben Heppner and Marvin Hamlisch. The ESO holds more than 100 performances each year.

Formed in 1920 as an amateur group, the ESO became a non-profit professional orchestra by 1952. The ESO's 1959 concert in Yellowknife was the first ever performed by a symphony orchestra in the Northwest Territories. Its recording of an album with British rock group Procol Harum in 1971 was the first recording with a symphony orchestra to reach gold-level sales of 500,000. In 1982, the same album reached platinum (over one million copies sold) status, also a record for an orchestral recording.

The ESO's 1985 recording, *Orchestral Suites of the British Isles*, was awarded the Canadian Music Council's prestigious Grande prix du Disque that honours the best Canadian orchestral recording. In recognition of imaginative programming of contemporary music, the orchestra won the Award of Merit from the Performing Arts Organization of Canada in 1986 - the fourth year in a row it won the award.

The ESO received a Gemini Award in 1992 for Best Television Variety Performance for its presentation with k.d. lang and Tommy Banks.

The home to Edmonton's Symphony Orchestra, the Francis Winspear Centre for Music is a $40-million, world-class concert hall. It was named 1999 Performing Arts Centre of the Year (in the more than 1,500 capacity category) by the Canadian Session and Touring Industry.

Among the contributors to the hall was Dr. Francis Winspear, whose $6-million donation was the largest single private donation ever made to an arts organization in Canada.

Classical violinists Juliette Kang and Judy Kang are not related, but each has attained recognition.

Juliette began playing violin at age four. At age nine, she was the youngest student ever accepted by the Curtis Institute of Music, in Philadelphia. In 1993, at 17, she was the youngest student to receive a Master's Degree in the history of the Julliard School of Music. The same year, she won the Sylvia Gerber Foundation award as the best classical musician under 30. She has also won several first-place awards at the Canadian National Music Competition. In 1992, she won a gold medal at the Yehudi Menuhin Competition in Paris. In 1994, she won the overall top prize at the Indiannapolis International Violin Competition.

Judy Kang, also a child prodigy, won overall first place at the 1989 and 1990 Canadian National Music Competitions. In 1997, she was first at the CBC Radio Competition for Young Performers.

Pro Coro Canada, one of three professional chamber choirs in Canada, has won the Canada Council's Healey Willan Award. A former principal conductor of Pro Coro, Agnes Grossmann, later became the first woman conductor to direct the Vienna Boys Choir.

Edmonton Opera produces four operas and at least one recital per season. Established in 1963, the company today is recognized as a leader in production and promotion of innovative opera. Among the famous performers to have performed with Edmonton Opera, award-winners Beverly Sills (1969), Anna Moffo and Jose Carreras (1974) and Carol Neblett (1978) each made their Canadian operatic debut in Edmonton. CBC broadcasts of Edmonton Opera productions in 1977, 1978, and 1980, won awards for the best opera broadcast in Canada.

The University of Alberta's Madrigal Singers has won the first-prize Bord Gais Fleischmann International Trophy at the prestigious Cork International Choral Festival in Ireland. The group also won CBC Choral Competition first prizes in 1992, 1996 and 1998, and the Schumann International Competition in Germany in 1995.

In 1992, the Hammerhead Consort, a four-member piano/percussion ensemble of students and alumni from the University of Alberta, received the Chamber Ensemble Award from the Sir Ernest MacMillan Memorial Foundation. In 1991, the group won the CIBC National Chamber Music Competition.

Consort leader Corey Hamm (teacher and chamber music coach at Alberta College) won the 1994 prize for

best Dutilleux performance at the French Piano Institute in Paris, and the 1998 Debut Atlantic Award as solo pianist.

Fellow Alberta college instructor Edward Connell won the Royal Canadian College of Organists Healey Willan Prize in 1997.

Edmonton's Cosmopolitan Music Society has a number of awards, including first place in the 1967 Federation of Canadian Music Festivals at the Centenary Festival of Music, St. John, New Brunswick. It also won the Government of Alberta Centennial Award in 1967. In 1978, director Harry Pinchin was awarded both the Alberta Achievement Award of Excellence, and the National Music Award from the Canadian Band Association.

Grant MacEwan Community College has one of only three music programs in Canada devoted solely to popular and commercial music, and Alberta College's Conservatory of Music is the second largest conservatory of music in Canada.

One of the most successful singers to come out of Edmonton in recent years is opera tenor Anthony Flynn. In 1996, Flynn placed first overall, and received the award for Most Outstanding Performance Overall at the National Association of Singing competition in Montreal. He has won feature roles in operas and concerts around the world, including San Francisco Merola Opera Program's role of Don Jose in *Carmen* in

1997, and performed with the Stichting Pagliacci's European tour of *I Pagliacci*.

Edmonton is also home to composer Malcolm Forsyth, winner of three Juno Awards: 1987, 1996 and 1998. Juno Awards have also been won by Edmonton musicians P.J. Perry and Tommy Banks. One of the other performers to boost Edmonton's musical profile was blues and big band legend Clarence (Big) Miller. He was the vocalist on Tommy Banks' Juno Award winning-record *Live at Montreaux*. Miller's best-known legacy is the Edmonton Jazz Festival.

Jazz music is also popular in Edmonton, and the city is home to the longest-running jazz club in Canada - the Yardbird Suite. The Edmonton Jazz society presents a regular series of local and international jazz artists at the Yardbird Suite.

Country music has been a favourite of Edmontonians for years, and one of the most successful musicians has been fiddle player Alfie Myhre. Now the owner of a respected music shop, Myhre won the Grand North American Fiddle Championship in 1984 and 1987. The latter year was when he also won the prestigious Carrot River (Saskatchewan) Fiddle Contest. Myhre took the Western Canadian Fiddle Championship in 1959 and 1960. One indication of his talent was his winning the CFAC radio fiddle title nine years in a row, from 1974 to 1983. The station ended the contest that year, and in 1984 decided to give Myhre the trophy, since his was the only name ever engraved on it.

Myhre's son Byron has also won the Grand North American Fiddle Championship twice, in 1989 and 1997.

One of the world-famous country musicians to come out of Edmonton is Hank Smith, along with his Wild Rose Country band. He was named to the Order of Canada in 1994.

The Emeralds are one of the world's most famous old-time dance bands. The original members were: Dave Hnatiuk, Wallis Petruk, Don Remeika, Allan Broder and Al Oswald. Jerry Huck later replaced Hnatiuk. Formed in 1970, the group sold more than one million records by 1983. Numerous gold- and platinum-selling albums have been recorded by The Emeralds. Propelled by its hit title song, the album *The Bird Dance* received a double-platinum award.

Visual Arts

There are many outstanding artists in Edmonton. These are the individuals and groups which are consistently recognized by a variety of arts groups in the city.

Edmonton is home to Alberta's longest-running cultural institution and largest art museum, the Edmonton Art Gallery. Celebrating its seventy-fifth anniversary in 1999, the gallery houses nearly 5,000 works of art by Alberta, Canadian and international artists and mounts more than 30 exhibitions a year.

The Latitude 53 Gallery was the first artist-run co-operative in Alberta. It was founded in 1973 by nationally renown artists Sylvain Voyer and Harry Savage.

Edmonton also has about 70 other art galleries and dealers. A popular art event in the city is the Gallery Walk that is held three times a year in the 124 Street district. The first of its kind in a major Western Canadian city, the event

The Moon's Lair (1995/96) is by Edmonton artist Graham Peacock. The acrylic painting, with glass and glitter pigments on canvas, is an example of the award-winning artist's work.

(Image courtesy Graham Peacock)

was initially held in 1982. It now involves eight local galleries within a six block radius that feature crafts, jewelry, aboriginal, contemporary, and historical art by local and international artists.

Abstract painter Doug Haynes has exhibited his works internationally, and he has pieces in the National Gallery of Canada, Art Gallery of Ontario and the Vancouver Art Gallery. In 1967, he won the Senior Arts Award from the Canada Council.

Painter Graham Peacock won first prize for painting at the Stanford Festival of Arts in Connecticut, in 1990. A professor at the University of Alberta's Department of Art and Design, his work is in permanent collections around the world, including the Museum of Modern Art in Vienna, the Museum of Fine Arts Boston, and the British Embassy in Rome. A member of the internationally acclaimed New New Painting Group, his work has been shown around the world, including at the inaugural exhibition of the Musee D'Art Modern et D'Art Comtemporain, in Nice, France.

Painter and installation artist Amy Loewan won first prize at the 1999 Tyndale College and Seminary National Art Competition in Toronto with her piece *A Cruciform*. She also won the 1998 Canadian Artists and Producers Professional Relations Tribunal Award for Excellence in the Arts. Entitled *Mandala 2*, Loewan's piece illustrates the integration of her Chinese heritage with western postmodernist art practices. In 1977, Loewan won first prize in watercolour at the Royal Melbourne Show, and her work is in collections such as the Asian American Arts Centre in New York and the Ministry of Art in Singapore.

Known for his landscapes of Western Canada, Doug Barry has his work in collections across North America and Europe, including Calgary's Horseman's Hall of Fame and government collections. Barry helped to establish both rural art classes throughout Alberta, and the art program at the University of Alberta's extension department.

Edmonton is sometimes referred to in the art world as 'Sculpture City'

because it is an international centre for sculpture.

Sculptor Peter Hide is recognized for his abstract steel sculptures. One of his most recent large sculptures, *Full House*, stands in front of the Francis Winspear Centre for Music. A member of the faculty of the University of Alberta's Department of Art and Design, Peter Hide has two sculptures in the Tate Gallery in London. He also has pieces in numerous international collections such as the Museum of Modern Art in Barcelona, the Arts Council of Great Britain and the University of California.

Edmonton sculptor Danek Mozdzenski is recognized nationally for his life-size bronze sculpture of former Prime Minister Lester Pearson on Parliament Hill. His tribute sculpture to Ukrainian settlement in Canada on the Alberta Legislature grounds was chosen following an international competition.

Abstract sculptor Catherine Burgess has pieces in galleries and collections across Canada, including the Art Gallery of Hamilton, and the Kitchener-Waterloo Art Gallery. Burgess is best known locally for her *Big Rock* sculpture (at Rice Howard Way in downtown Edmonton), which was made in collaboration with local sculptor Sandra Bromley. Bromley won the 1978 Esso Petroleum Arts Award.

Another recognized Edmonton artist is sculptor Barbara Paterson whose collections and public commissions include the Famous Five Foundation monument to be installed in 1999 and 2000 in Calgary and Ottawa.

Recognized as one of the best in the country, the University of Alberta's Department of Art and Design was the first fine art department in Alberta and the first to offer a graduate program in fine art and design in Canada. The Fine Arts Building Gallery offers a venue for students' works.

Award-winning print and installation artist Lyndal Osborne has her work in museums and collections in Germany, Argentina and Hong Kong, as well in the National Gallery in Ottawa. Her many scholarships and prizes include the Jurors Award at both the 1990 Prints International competition in Connecticut and the North American Print competition the same year, and the 1992 Sponsor's Prize in the Sapporo, Japan, International Print Biennial.

Print artist and book and poster designer Walter Jule won the 1996 Superior Prize at the International Print Biennale in Seoul, Korea, and the 1996 International Purchase Award at the Portland Art Museum's International Print Exhibition. Jule also won the Tallinn City Prize at the 1998 Tallinn Print Triennial in Estonia, and the 1992 Award of Great Distinction from the Graphic Design Association of Canada. Jule has his work in the National Gallery of Canada, the Tochigi Prefectural Museum of Art in Japan, the Museum of Modern Art in Lodz, Poland and the Israel Museum in Jerusalem.

Print artist Liz Ingram won the Award of Excellence at the International Exhibition of Miniature Prints in Seoul, Korea in 1994, the Honorary Award at the Cabo Frio International Print Biennale in Brazil in 1985, and the Diploma Award at the Tallinn International Print Triennial in Estonia, in 1998. Ingram's pieces are in such international collections as the Portland Art Museum, National Center of Fine Arts in Egypt, and the Suchting International Museum in Holland.

Osborne, Ingram and Jule are all faculty members in the internationally recognized Division of Printmaking at the University of Alberta's Department of Art and Design and were all inducted into the prestigious Royal Canadian Academy of Art in 1999.

Steven Dixon, a technician/print artist in the University of Alberta's Printmaking Division, won the Juror's Award at the 1996 North American Printmaking Exhibition in Los Angeles and the Grand Prize at the Pacific States Biennial Print Exhibition in Hawaii in 1994.

Also located in the city is the Society of Northern Alberta Print Artists (SNAP), the first artist-run non-profit printmaking society in Alberta.

Among its award-winning members are the following artists. Marna Bunnell won a first prize at Mexico City's Second International Biennale of the Poster in 1994, and the Grand Prize at the Seoul International Biennale in 1984. Sean Caulfield won the second Great Canadian Printmaking Competition Award in 1996 and the 1995 Grand Prize Twenty-First Century Print Grand Prix Exhibition in Tokyo. Print artist Karen Dugas won the Jury Prize at the International Biennale of Graphic Art in Yugoslavia, 1985, and the Superior Class Prize Award at the Seoul International Biennale in 1986, and a 1999 award from the Boston Printmakers North American Print Exhibition.

New media artist and marketer Steven Csorba won numerous Benny Awards in 1997-98, the premier print awards in the worldwide Printing Industries of North America competition. Csorba won the awards in categories such as innovation, four-colour digital printing and poster and fine arts prints. In his work, Csorba had combined traditional methods of printmaking with new digital imaging. In 1997 he was given the ComputerWorld Smithsonian

The intricate and detailed work of Tracy and Eric Tremblay has brought them the prestigious Booker Award.
(Photo courtesy Tracy and Eric Tremblay)

Danek Mozdzenski was chosen to create this work, honouring slain Edmonton police officer Ezio Faraone. This piece is in a prominent space in a park near the Alberta Legislature. Mozdzenski has also been commissioned for other prestigious public works in Canada.

(Photo by Danek Mozdzenski)

Institute Award for his innovative work and his development of this process for marketing. He is also well known for his outstanding sports artwork.

Among the award-winning Edmonton craft artists are Tracy and Eric Tremblay, who recently won the Canadian Doll Guild's prestigious Booker Award for Originality for their character doll *Annabelle's Treasure*.

Well-known metal artist Karen Anderson Cantine has pieces in exhibitions and collections across North America including in the Museum of Civilization in Hull, Quebec and the University of Iowa. Her pieces include silver jewelry boxes, bowls, chalices and tea sets and her commissions have included the Papal Chalice to commemorate the visit of Pope John Paul II in 1984.

Ceramics artists Carol and Richard Selfridge have their artistic stoneware pieces in prestigious collections throughout North America, including those of Prime Minister Jean Chretien, and the Bronfman Foundation.

Local artist Sam Uhlick has participated in international exhibitions in Japan, Australia, France and England and his creative functional-pottery pieces have been purchased for prestigious collections at locations such as Rideau Hall (home of Canada's Governor General), and at the National Museum of History in Taiwan.

Edmonton stained glass artist Brenda Malkinson has been commissioned to do work for buildings throughout Western Canada. One piece of her work, a life-size, 300 glass-piece rendition of a fuchsia plant, was selected by the Massey Foundation in 1980 as one of 106 craft works from across Canada to be included in the permanent collection at the Canadian Museum of Civilization in Hull.

Theatre and Cinema

Edmonton has more professional theatres per capita than any other Canadian city. There are 19 theatre companies, four dinner theatres, and numerous heritage theatre organizations in the city. Edmonton's theatre community began as early as 1896 when the first Edmonton-based professional theatre company, La Cigale, was formed.

The Citadel Theatre is Canada's largest theatrical complex, and was Edmonton's first permanent professional theatre. Covering a full city block, it houses five theatres and is the largest non-commercial theatre in Canada. The building won the 1978 Stelco Design Award, for innovative and imaginative use of structural steel. It was founded in 1965 by Joseph Shoctor, a prominent Edmonton lawyer. Among its unique programs was Citadel on Wheels/Wings. The program, which ran between 1969 and 1985, was a school outreach program which brought theatre to people who might not otherwise have had such an experience. The program saw the theatre travel across Alberta, the Northwest Territories and the Yukon (The Citadel was the first Canadian professional theatre to fly into the Arctic).

Other venues include the New Varscona Theatre, home to award-winning theatre companies Shadow Theatre and Teatro la Quindicina. It is the busiest small theatre in Canada.

Free Will Players is a professional theatre company which is devoted to producing Shakespeare-in-the-Park (expanded and renamed The River City Shakespeare Festival in 1998). The event featuring productions of Shakespeare's works has been held annually at Hawrelak Park since 1989. In 1990, the company was presented with the Guthrie Award for artistic excellence from the Tyrone Guthrie Committee of the Stratford Festival for its production of *Twelfth Night*.

Edmonton's Theatre Network, a contemporary theatre company founded in 1975 and operating out of the Roxy Theatre, became the first Edmonton professional theatre to have a play produced in New York during a tour there in 1978.

Edmonton's Catalyst Theatre, committed to creating original Canadian work and unique in its exploration of the Western Canadian experience, won the prestigious Fringe First Award for Outstanding New Work at the Edinburgh Fringe Festival for its *Elephant Wake* in 1997.

Edmonton also has numerous cinema complexes. Famous Player's Silver City West Edmonton Mall complex sold more tickets than any movie house in Canada for *Star Wars Episode One: The Phantom Menace* the first

Internationally known actors such as Megan Follows (seated) and Jane Spidell (standing) regularly perform at The Citadel Theatre because of its reputation for excellence.
(Photo by David Cooper, courtesy The Citadel Theatre)

weekend the complex opened. From its opening, it was immediately the top-grossing cinema in Canada.

In 1949, Edmonton's first drive-in movie theatre and what was considered to be the largest in North America, the Starlight Drive-In, was opened. With the opening of the Belmont Drive-In theatre in 1954, Edmonton introduced the first curved screen to Alberta. By 1977, Edmonton had 10 open-air movie theatres, more than any other Canadian city.

Parks

As the city with the most parkland per capita of any major centre in Canada, Edmonton offers year-round recreational activities for all ages.

The spectacular North Saskatchewan River valley is the largest stretch of urban parkland in North America. Covering 7,425 hectares (18,348 acres) of land, the river valley winds for 48 km

(30 miles) from the city's southwest to northeast edges to create a scenic natural corridor that is visited each year by an estimated 3.5 million people (close to 10,000 people daily). The river valley is home to tourist attractions such as the Valley Zoo, golf courses, ski hills, swimming pools, lakes, outdoor rinks, nature trails and approximately 122 kilometres (76 miles) of trails for activities such as cycling, jogging, walking, rollerblading and cross-country skiing. Walking for pleasure has consistently taken the number-one spot for recreation activities in Edmonton, according to provincial surveys. Trails through the river valley are extensive. In total there are 58 km (36 miles) of paved trail, 67 km (42 miles) of gravel trail, 48 km (30 miles) of ski trail and 6.7 km (4.2 miles) of horseback riding trail.

With three major ravines and 19 secondary ravines, the river valley makes

Rollerblading, cycling, jogging and walking are the major activities on Edmonton's river valley trail system. In winter, cross-country skiing becomes a popular pastime.

(Photo by Allyson Quince)

up approximately 67 per cent of the city's 11,086 hectares (27,400 acres) of parkland. In total, the city has 896 parks. There are almost 18 hectares (44 acres) of park for every 1,000 people.

Almost 22 times larger than New York City's Central Park, the river valley system is not only one of Edmonton's greatest attractions and leisure areas, it is also an undisturbed natural preserve. The system is home to a multitude of wildlife, including whitetail and mule deer, coyotes, beavers and, on occasion, moose and black bear.

For more than 90 years the river valley has been carefully protected from development, and that has led to at least one award. In 1975, Edmonton was the first Canadian city to be declared a Green Survival City by the American Association of Nurserymen.

William Hawrelak Park is Edmonton's most popular family park. Located in the river valley, the 62-hectare (153-acre) park is home to the Heritage Amphitheatre, Western Canada's largest outdoor performance facility. Architecturally designed to resemble a giant leaf, the amphitheatre adds an artistic dimension to the cityscape and provides a summer venue for a number of Edmonton's performing arts groups including the award-winning Edmonton Symphony Orchestra. Hawrelak Park's artificial lake offers a summer spot for picnics, walking, and paddling. In winter it becomes an outdoor ice rink, and there is an adjacent skating pavilion.

In the early 1970s, the designers of Hawrelak Park (then called Mayfair Park) won the national Vincent Massey Award for Park Planning in the open space classification. The park, located on what

had been a gravel pit, opened in 1967 after six years of construction and development.

As well as the Hawrelak Park facilities, the valley parks system has many feature attractions.

The Whitemud Equine Centre was the site where Canada's World Champion Showjumper, Gail Greenough, trained in the 1960s and 70s.

Just west of the equestrian complex is the John Janzen Nature Centre, the first municipally owned nature centre in North America and the first urban nature centre in Canada. Opened in 1976, the centre offers hands-on exhibits, interpretive programs, information on the environment, and birch tree and river loop nature trails with information posted about the area. Exhibits are regularly changed.

The John Janzen Centre was recently awarded the Alberta Emerald Award for sustained excellence in Environmental Education, a provincial award which was established in 1991 to celebrate and promote environmental excellence. The centre attracts up to 100,000 visitors a year and has become a model for nature centres in almost every major city in Canada. It is situated next to Fort Edmonton Park.

The 50,000 square-metre (538,200 square feet) Kinsmen Sports Centre, in the valley, encompasses the Kinsmen Fieldhouse and Commonwealth Aquatic Centre. The facilities include four swimming pools, two indoor tracks, racquet and net-sport facilities, and more than 400 pieces of the newest weight-training and aerobic equipment. The Kinsmen Fieldhouse, opened in

1968 and used as a multi-use facility for sports as well as social events, was the first municipally operated facility of its type in North America.

The $1.3-million building was funded in part by the Kinsmen Club and featured a stadium covering an area of 0.6 hectares (1.5 acres) with a 11.3-metre ceiling (37 feet) and a playing area the size of an NFL football field.

In December, 1977, the $8.1-million Commonwealth Aquatic Centre was opened as one of the facilities to host the 1978 Commonwealth Games. The complex has added other facilities including the Keltie Byrne Fitness Centre in 1993. In 1994, the Kinsmen Sports Centre won the Facility Excellence Award from the Canadian Recreation and Parks Association. Its Kin-Kids Fitness Centre was the first fitness centre ever designed for children ages six to 15 years old.

Covering almost 50 hectares (123 acres), Kinsmen Park has been developed over the past 30 years through the support and financial assistance of the Kinsmen Club of Edmonton, and now includes outdoor tennis courts, a Pitch and Putt par three, 18-hole golf course and a large outdoor playground.

The river valley is also home to six golf courses (three municipally owned). Located on the north bank of the river, Victoria Golf Course was the first municipal golf course to open in Canada (in 1907) and it is today one of the busiest municipal golf courses in the country.

Expanded in 1947, the course became the only 27-hole municipal golf course in the British Empire. When Groat Road was constructed in 1953-54, nine of the holes were removed.

Improvements to the Victoria Driving Range in 1989 included the addition of an upper deck, making it the first two-

The Edmonton Space and Science Centre was designed by internationally acclaimed Edmonton architect Douglas Cardinal. It is one of the most popular attractions in the city.
(Photo courtesy City of Edmonton Archives)

tiered range in Alberta. The driving range was originally a 50-tee range when it was constructed in 1961.

As well as a par-three 18-hole golf course, Rundle Park in Edmonton's northeast end has mini-golf and Frisbee-golf courses.

Initial development at Rundle Park involved the construction of the A.C.T. Aquatic and Recreation Centre in 1977. The first recreation centre complex for the handicapped to be constructed in Canada, the centre was built and originally operated by the Associated Canadian Travellers. Rundle Park was later expanded to include the golf courses, outside tennis courts, and man-made ponds that are used for outdoor skating in winter and paddleboat rides in summer.

Recreation activities and areas outside the river valley system have also set precedents or hold records.

The demand for golf here is higher than almost anywhere in the world, and there are more than 40 courses in the immediate area. There are more than 70 courses within a 60-km radius.

The Mill Woods Recreation Centre had the first indoor wave pool in North America when it opened in 1983.

Coronation Park is home to several firsts and record-setters. Originally, the 40-hectare (100-acre) park was called West End Park, and 2.5 hectares (six acres) of it were used as a city nursery containing a quarter of a million seedlings.

In 1953, the largely undeveloped park was renamed Coronation Park when Mayor Hawrelak planted an elm tree to commemorate the coronation of Queen Elizabeth II. The Queen officially

opened the park with the planting of an oak tree on the planetarium grounds in 1959. It became home to the first municipal planetarium in Canada when that opened in 1960. In 1970, Coronation Pool was opened - the first 50-metre indoor pool in Alberta.

In 1977, the Coronation Bowling Greens were added in preparation for the Commonwealth Games, and in 1984 the Edmonton Space and Science Centre was built in the park.

A haven for birds, the Edmonton region holds world records for the number of recorded Black-capped Chickadees, Black-billed Magpies, Bohemian Waxwings and Merlins. Edmonton's annual Christmas Bird Count attracted an unsurpassed record of 1,288 local birdwatchers in 1987 - the biggest turnout of the 1,800 bird counts around the world that day.

Elk Island National Park, just outside Metro Edmonton's eastern border, is the oldest wildlife sanctuary in Canada. It is the only park in the world with free-roaming herds of both plains and wood bison.

Elk Island's herd of plains bison is the largest in Canada and it has the purest genetics of any plains bison in the world. The wildlife park is also home to elk, beaver, moose, deer and coyotes, archaeological sites, and 100 km (62 miles) of trails.

With 60,000 of them forming decorative stands and picturesque archways over many older streets, Edmonton boasts the largest number of healthy elm trees of any city in the world. The trees have an estimated value of more than $420 million.

West Edmonton Mall

When the Ghermezian family members announced they were going to create the world's biggest shopping and entertainment centre in Edmonton, there were some who thought the project was doomed to failure. But the project has flourished, expanded and been a gigantic ambassador for the city.

West Edmonton Mall is now one of Canada's most successful tourist attractions, and holds many world records. Plus, it's still growing.

(Photo courtesy West Edmonton Mall)

West Edmonton Mall

Ask people in other countries about Edmonton, and often the only thing they'll know about the city is West Edmonton Mall. Along with the Edmonton Oilers, the mall is one of Edmonton's truly world-famous attractions.

Spreading out impressively from the corner of 87th Avenue and 170th Street, West Edmonton Mall is the world's largest shopping and entertainment complex, covering approximately 492,000 square metres (5.3 million square feet). The Guinness Book of World Records has recognized it as the biggest of its kind in the world. It covers an area equivalent to 104 Canadian football fields (115 U.S. football fields).

The mall is a virtual city under one roof. Open every day of the year, there are more than 800 stores and services in the mall, including major department stores. One of the larger tenants is Red's Family Rec Room, a 9,290-square-metre (100,000-square-foot) family amusement centre featuring bowling, a restaurant, a video arcade, concerts and other live and televised events. The main section of the mall (not including the Phase Four section opening in stages in 1999) has 19 movie theaters, 100 restaurants and food court outlets, a bingo hall, a casino and a chapel. There are also tropical fish displays, fountains and works of art scattered throughout the mall. There are several nightclubs and bars in the mall, and the Jubilations Dinner Theatre.

The mall cost close to $1.2 billion to build. It has been constructed in four phases.

Phase One opened in 1981 at a cost of about $200 million, and covers 25 hectares (62 acres). It has a floor space of 106,000 square metres (1,140,560 square feet), and features major department stores, and 220 retail stores and services.

Phase Two opened in 1983. The 32-hectare (79-acre) extension added 105,000 square metres (1,129,800 square feet), including another department store and 240 new retail stores and services. At a cost of $250

Entertainment is one of West Edmonton Mall's drawing points. Emphasizing indoor rollercoasters and other rides was one of the mall's groundbreaking ideas.
(Photo courtesy West Edmonton Mall)

million, the project also saw the addition of the Galaxyland Amusement Park (then called Fantasyland) and the Ice Palace skating rink.

Phase Three was added in 1985, and at $650 million, was the most expensive section to date. A 48-hectare (119-acre) addition, it added major retail stores, hundreds of smaller retail and specialty shops, and the major attractions of World Waterpark, Deep Sea Adventure, Dolphin Lagoon, Sea Life Caverns and Professor Wem's Adventure Golf. It also houses the Europa Boulevard and Bourbon Street theme areas, where shopping areas are designed to look like streets in Europe and New Orleans. The Fantasyland Hotel was added the next year.

Phase Four is opening in stages throughout 1999. Although it is based on an expansion of what had been a department store area, the project is costing $85 million. Topped by a pyramid, it will cover 49 hectares (121 acres), and will include megastores such as Chapters, HMV and Starbucks. There are two main features of Phase Four. First is the Famous Players Silver City entertainment complex. It houses 12 movie theatres with a total of 3,400 high-back seats in a stadium design, plus an IMAX movie theatre (with 260 seats) that can play both traditional and 3-D IMAX films. The lobby area, dominated by animated characters such as a fire-breathing dragon, offers six national-brand fast-food outlets, plus an

One of the newest attractions is the fire-breathing dragon in the lobby of the Silver City cinema complex. The mega-movie house features some of the world's most advanced film and sound technology.
(Photo by Allyson Quince)

amusement centre and party rooms. The second major feature of Phase Four will be a Playdium entertainment complex. The cutting-edge interactive video amusement centre is one of only a handful in North America.

The mall has seven major attractions.

Galaxyland is the world's largest indoor amusement park, at 37,160 square metres (400,000 square feet). It houses 27 rides and attractions and 30 games of skill. The rides include the Mindbender roller coaster (the world's first and largest indoor triple-loop roller coaster) and the 13-story tall Drop of Doom free-fall ride.

The Mindbender was built in 1985. It has the highest gravity-force rating of any roller coaster in the world, creating a force of 6.4 times that of gravity, and is ranked number 12 in the world by the American Coaster Enthusiasts. The Mindbender is 1,285 metres in length (4,198 feet), and reaches more than 41.5 metres (145 feet) high at its tallest point.

Galaxyland is also home to the Xorbitor, a ride which uses film images and movement to simulate a trip on a spaceship. It is the first virtual reality motion-base pod of its type to be permanently installed in Western Canada.

World Waterpark is a two-hectare (five-acre) indoor water recreation area; the largest of its kind in the world. The size of five NFL football fields, the park's temperature is kept at 30C (86F). There is a massive wave pool, which holds 12.3 million litres (2.7 million gallons) of water. The park also has more than 20 waterslides (the tallest begins at a height of 26 metres, or 85 feet), tube

rides, three hot tubs and children's play areas. Overlooking the wave pool is the 34-metre (110-feet) bungy jump, the only permanent indoor bungy jump in the world, which opened in 1992.

Deep Sea Adventure in Phase Three is the world's largest indoor lake. It has four real submarines, complete with sonar and underwater cameras, which make a 35-minute tour through the lake. Each submarine holds 25 people. The trip takes visitors past coral reefs, displays of a sunken ship, and marine life from around the world.

The lake is 122 metres (400 feet) long and up to six metres (20 feet) deep. The lake is dominated by the Santa Maria, a full-size replica of the famous Spanish sailing ship used by Christopher Columbus. The ship's deck area is occasionally open to the general public, and can be booked for weddings and other events.

Dolphin Lagoon is home to four Atlantic Bottlenose Dolphins (two males and two females). The salt water is specially mixed at 34,500 kg (76,000 pounds) of salt for its 1.36 million litres (300,000 gallons) of water.

The lagoon consists of three tanks, two of which are not open to public view. The largest is in a public amphitheatre area, and is where the dolphins do shows throughout the day, including (on special request) educational presentations for schools and groups.

Sea Life Caverns, a walk-in attraction, has more than 200 species of exotic fish, sharks and penguins. There is a unique interactive touch pool exhibit. The newest addition to the caverns is Klinger, a Giant Pacific Octopus which can grow up to three metres (10 feet) long and weigh as much as 23 kg (50 pounds) when mature. There is also a Giant Sea Turtle, which weighs in at approximately 181 kg (400 pounds).

The Ice Palace is a regulation-size NHL rink, under a massive dome skylight. As well as public skating, the rink hosts practices for the Edmonton Oilers, and is the stage for figure skating events, and an annual international minor hockey tournament.

Professor Wem's Adventure Golf is an 18-hole miniature golf attraction winding through part of the mall, with cartoon-like characters and structures throughout.

The mall also has two theme street

The dolphin lagoon is one of the areas where crowds are always gathered.
(Photo courtesy West Edmonton Mall)

areas. Bourbon Street is designed to look like a New Orleans streetscape, with its own starry night sky. Bourbon Street is dominated by theme restaurants and bars serving everything from Cajun to English pub fare. Europa Boulevard is an upscale shopping area patterned after European streets, and covered with a glass archway.

The Fantasyland Hotel, which opened in 1986, is located in Phase Three of the mall. It features 354 rooms, including 118 theme rooms: Hollywood, Roman, Polynesian, Truck, Victorian, Coach, Arabian, Canadian Rail, Igloo, Western and African Safari. Along with the rooms, the hotel has more than 2,230 square metres (24,000 square feet) in convention and meeting space.

There is a public transportation station at West Edmonton Mall, as well as the world's largest parking lot (with parking for more than 20,000 vehicles, including trailers and recreational vehicles), and 58 entrances. The mall is lit by 325,000 fixtures, and employs

more than 23,500 people both in the mall and in spin-off jobs.

West Edmonton Mall has four life-size character mascots. Deep Sea Danny (an alligator pirate) entertains in the Deep Sea Adventure area, Sharkey (a shark) patrols the World Waterpark, Cosmo the alien watches over the Galaxyland Amusement Park as well as being the overall mall mascot, and Professor Wem represents the miniature golf course.

West Edmonton Mall has a significant economic impact on Edmonton. According to a consultant's report done for the provincial government, the mall contributes about $1.2 billion a year to the city's economy. In taxes, the mall contributes $235 million a year to the federal government, $74 million to the province, and $30 million to the City of Edmonton.

The total economic impact of the mall is enormous. The impact includes almost $400 million in goods imports to

World Waterpark is one of the most impressive attractions at West Edmonton Mall. This view shows the main slide area and wave pool. Other features include a bungee jump and tube ride.
(Photo courtesy West Edmonton Mall)

All year through, the Ice Palace draws skaters to its NHL-size rink. Even the Oilers sometimes use the surface as a practice rink.
(Photo courtesy West Edmonton Mall)

Alberta from outside the province.

With more than 20 million visits annually (including 10 million by people outside the Edmonton region) West Edmonton Mall is the city's top tourist attraction.

On an average weekend, there are 140,000 visitors to the mall, with that number jumping to 170,000 on a holiday weekend.

Almost 40 per cent of West Edmonton Mall visitors are from Edmonton, with more than 17 per cent from British Columbia, 21 per cent from other parts of Western Canada, almost 12 per cent from Central and Eastern Canada, and more than 10 per cent from outside Canada. Of every dollar spent in Edmonton by tourists, 47 cents is spent at the mall.

Visitors to West Edmonton Mall also contribute to the provincial economy by

seeing other Alberta attractions while visiting Edmonton. In total, it is estimated that $617 million of Albertans' income comes from mall-related tourism.

The principle months for retail activity are November/December and July/August. The attractions are busiest in the months of July/August, and then in the months of November and December.

Overall, the single largest group of people to visit West Edmonton Mall is women between the ages of 18 and 24. The second-largest group is teenagers. The attractions are mostly visited by families with school-age children, but teenagers and seniors are also frequent visitors.

The newest attraction to open at the mall is the Pro Golf driving range; the world's only rooftop driving range. The two-tiered, covered range is open year-round.

There are 24 tees on the rooftop driving range, which also features the world's first automatic ball retrieval system. The computer-controlled system kicks in when the balls roll to a conveyor belt. The belt brings the balls back to the players and tees them up automatically, through small holes on the tee-off area.

Future plans for the mall include a 94-room motel across 90 Ave., and a second major hotel near Galaxyland, next to Phase One. Although plans and cost have not been set, it is expected to be similar to the Fantasyland Hotel in size.

When West Edmonton Mall's Phase Three was opened, the event reportedly cost more than $1 million. The mall served a feast to more than 100,000 people, and the event included the world's largest mass launching of balloons. With more than 500,000 helium-filled balloons launched from the mall roof, airlines were forced to alter their flight plans.

Tourist Attractions

The Metro Edmonton area is a tourist mecca for many reasons. Some of the world's biggest, best and most innovative attractions are right here.

From the massive historic complex of Fort Edmonton Park, seen here, to the smaller (but still impressive) Alberta Aviation Museum, there is a variety and depth to the city's tourist attractions that make Edmonton the tourism capital of Western Canada.

(Photo courtesy Fort Edmonton Park)

Tourist Attractions

Edmonton is the tourism leader of Western Canada. While Toronto and Montreal dominate the eastern tourism market, Edmonton has the largest number of visits of any city west of Toronto. A total of 4,176,000 people visited the city in 1997, according to the most current statistics available.

The biggest single tourist draw in Edmonton is West Edmonton Mall, but there are many other attractions in the metropolitan area which have set records or are unique. As for hospitality, Edmonton boasts one of the highest number of restaurants in Canada. With more than 1,700 restaurants, you could eat dinner at a different establishment every night for four years and nine months.

Alberta Aviation Museum

The museum is located at the Edmonton City Centre Airport, in an historic aircraft hangar. The structure dating to the Second World War is the only double-wide, double-long original hangar left in Canada. The museum is dedicated to the love of aircraft and Edmonton's place in aviation history. That's shown by the fact that it's run by only two paid employees and 95 volunteers, including many people who restore the aircraft.

One of the most important displays is a World War Two-era Mosquito aircraft - one of only two of the record-setting fighter bomber aircraft left in Canada and the only one in Western Canada.

Another important aircraft is the 1929/30 Cranwell, the only one of its type left in the world. The historic aircraft also include the Fairchild 11C, used in 1935 to map out the north.

Part of the museum shows the history of the airport location, including the facility's day as the busiest in North America, on September 23, 1944, when 860 planes being used in the war effort were being refueled around the clock. The work was done largely by women.

The Aviation Heritage Museum is one of the fastest-growing attractions in Edmonton. There are many historic aircraft such as this Voodoo fighter jet (photo below), and volunteers are continually adding to the collection (photo opposite).
(Photo below by Allyson Quince. Photo opposite courtesy Ed Pywell)

Alberta Railway Museum

The Alberta Railway Museum on 34 St., 1.5 km south of Highway 37, is the only operating railway museum in Western Canada. The picturesque and peaceful complex displays the only surviving Northern Alberta Railways locomotive (No.73). It also has the only surviving Northern Alberta Railways passenger train, the only two pieces of equipment remaining from the Alberta Great Waterways Railway, the first freight diesel locomotive from Canadian National Railways (#9000) and the only operating Canadian Northern Railway steam locomotive left in Canada (#1392). The museum is open during summer months. Staff run a diesel locomotive every Sunday, and run the steam locomotive on each day of every long weekend.

Casino Edmonton

Established by the oldest casino company in Canada, this

complex on the city's south side is the largest facility of its kind in Western Canada, at more than 4,645 square metres (50,000 square feet).

Devonian Botanic Gardens

The University of Alberta's Devonian Botanic Gardens, just 25 km southwest of Edmonton, has nearly 10,000 plants including most native plants. Unique to the gardens is the Japanese Gardens, one of the only ornamental Japanese gardens in a boreal climate.

Edmonton Space and Science Centre

A stunning building designed by award-

Riding back into Edmonton's railway past is one of the treats at the Alberta Railway Museum.
(Photo courtesy Edmonton Railway Museum)

winning Edmonton architect Douglas Cardinal, the centre has almost 500,000 visitors a year and more than 1,858 square metres (20,000 square feet) of exhibit gallery space.

One of the centre's major attractions is its ultra-large screen IMAX theatre (the first in Western Canada), which has a seating capacity of 274. It is also home to the 250-seat Margaret Zeidler Star theatre, which has the largest planetarium dome in North America. The Zeidler theatre has a 23-metre- (75 feet) high projection screen, 17,000-watt audio system, 250 computer-controlled slide projectors and a laser display system.

The centre's Challenger Learning Centre was the first of its kind outside the United States. The Challenger centre is an experience-based learning area designed by families of the astronauts killed in the Challenger space shuttle explosion. Designed to promote team co-operation and problem solving, the centre has participants take part in a simulated space mission.

The Universe Gallery, opened in 1991, is dedicated to space and our solar system. It features the first moon rock on public display

outside of the U.S. Its Victor Echo 6 Sierra Charlie amateur radio station is a working interactive exhibit that is one of the best-equipped amateur radio stations in North America.

Edmonton Telephone Historical Information Centre

The centre in the historic Old Strathcona district is the only museum in Canada dedicated to the history of telecommunications. Considering the city's history in telephones (having the only city-owned phone company until Ed Tel was recently sold), the centre has a unique display of telecommunications history, making it the largest museum of its type in North America. There are numerous displays dating back to the 1870s, many of which are hands-on.

Fort Edmonton Park

In the North Saskatchewan River Valley (west of the university area) this is the largest living historical site in Canada. The park is a showcase of more than 70 restored buildings, organized along streets according to the era from which they came. The streets cover the eras of the 1846 fur trade fort, the 1885 settlement, the capital city of 1905, and the city during the 1920s.

Staff members dressed in period costumes show visitors the city's history through displays and hands-on demonstrations and interactive exhibits. Access to the site is by a short trip on an historic steam train, the Edmonton Yukon and Pacific, the only one of its kind in North America still running a regularly scheduled passenger route. There is also a loop of rail inside the park where visitors can ride a restored historic trolley.

Muttart Conservatory

Known by its distinctive four glass pyramids (the only such complex in Canada), the multi-million-dollar Muttart Conservatory sits in the North Saskatchewan River Valley just below the downtown skyline. The most northerly botanical conservatory in North America, it is home to the largest orchid species collection in Canada (including some flowers now extinct in the wild).

Each glass pyramid covers a separate pavilion, each of which is connected by tunnel to a central atrium. The pavilions are home to plants, flowers and birds from around the world, with each section set up according to a theme (tropical, temperate, arid and showcase). A 3,700-square-meter (39,828-square-foot) greenhouse sits next door.

Northlands Park

Northlands Park is Edmonton's oldest locally owned business and second-largest tourist attraction. Originating with the Edmonton Agricultural Society that was formed in 1879, Northlands Park now operates a 51-hectare (126-acre) site with an appraised value of $175 million in buildings including the Skyreach Centre, the Agricom and the Spectrum.

With more than 37,100 square metres (400,000 square feet) of indoor exhibition space, Northlands Park is the largest exhibition facility in Western Canada.

One of Fort Edmonton Park's best features is the staff, who wear period costumes to show just how life was during the city's early days.
(Photo courtesy Fort Edmonton Park)

The Muttart Conservatory has been a pioneer in the use of natural pest control. There are more than 140,000 ladybugs in the complex, which are let loose each spring to control bugs that would attack the plants.

Topped by four distinctive glass pyramids, Muttart Conservatory (a gift from the Muttart family) is one of Edmonton's best-loved and most beautiful attractions. (Photo courtesy City of Edmonton)

In 1986, the organization introduced to North America the concept of highlighting nations in international trade shows.

An estimated $150 million in annual economic spin-offs to Edmonton is recognized from events produced and supported by Northlands Park. And the Northlands' Agricom is Western Canada's largest and most modern exhibition facility. It offers more than 325,000 square feet of indoor event space.

Canada's most modern and luxurious horse racing and entertainment centre, the four-year-old, $21-million Spectrum at Northlands offers horse racing and gaming activities.

On-site thoroughbred racing takes place each summer and on-site harness racing runs throughout the spring and fall with global simulcast racing every day.

Highlights include the Canadian Derby and the Western Canadian Pacing Derby. With six ten-foot TV monitors, Uplinks is Alberta's largest state-of the art horse racing teletheatre.

Northlands Park has won awards, such as the 1998 Prize Fair Management of the Year Award for its planning. That was for excellence in the promotion and production of Klondike Days, Farmfair International and Canadian Finals Rodeo.

Attracting approximately 3.5 million guests a year to more than 2,600 events, Northlands Park is a not-for-profit community service organization with a business focus on event production.

The Provincial Museum of Alberta

The Provincial Museum of Alberta is the largest multi-disciplinary museum in Western Canada, and features unique

exhibits such as the Bug Room, which houses strange and rare live insects from around the world. The Bug Room was the first exhibit of its kind in Western Canada.

The new Natural History Gallery at the museum is home to Canada's only complete Columbian Mammoth skeleton. The mammoth was the largest land mammal to have ever lived in North America.

The Syncrude Gallery of Aboriginal Culture is a new permanent exhibition that occupies a quarter of the museum.

The gallery which focuses on Aboriginal life before and after European contact is the only one of its kind in Canada.

The gallery took five years to complete, and has artifacts dating back

9,000 years that are on display for the first time anywhere.

Rutherford House

The first provincial historic site in Alberta, this restored post-Edwardian house was the home of Alberta's first premier, Alexander Rutherford.

Ukrainian Cultural Heritage Village

The only village-style attraction in North America dedicated to early Ukrainian history, this was the site of the first mass settlement in Canada of Ukrainians.

The village is just outside the western boundary of the Metro Edmonton area.

It contains many restored buildings and costumed staff portray Ukrainian Canadians from 1892-1930 displaying what life was like for the early immigrants.

The entire historical complex, which is worth $20 million, is known also for its garden, which is recognized as one of the top displays in Canada for authenticity. Staff has recreated the proper size and dimensions of a period garden, and has used the same type of plants grown when the buildings were at their original site.

The Bug Room of The Provincial Museum of Alberta (photo opposite) is one of Edmonton's unique attractions, and is especially popular with kids. Northlands Park has been one of Western Canada's top tourist destinations for decades. Northlands' horseracing (photo right) has set records for betting, and has produced champion horses such as Native Brass, seen here winning the 1999 Canadian Derby at Northlands Park. The horse is owned by Bob and Roberta Giffin, and was bred by Denny Andrews. It was the fourth race in a row the filly won.

(Photo opposite courtesy The Provincial Museum of Alberta, photo right courtesy Bob and Roberta Giffin)

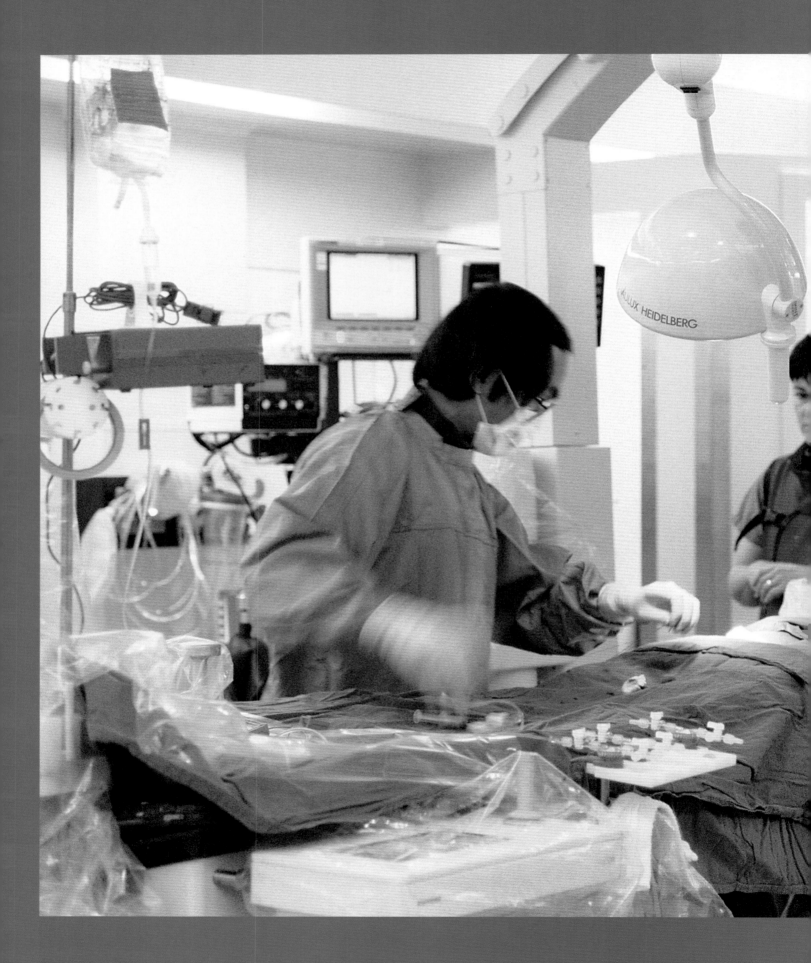

Medicine

Edmonton is one of Canada's leading centres for medical treatment and research. In everything from the sheer size of the area it covers, to the leading-edge services it provides, the Edmonton medical community has an impressive list of achievements.

Despite radical changes during the past decade in how medical services are provided, the professionals here have managed to continue offering the best service available.

(Photo courtesy Capital Health)

Medicine

Edmonton's medical community has been lauded for providing the best quality health care in 1999, out of 16 major Canadian cities. A survey in *Maclean's* magazine puts Edmonton first in Canada in the provision of health care. The magazine's *National Health Report* considered 13 areas of care, including the number of general practitioners and specialists per capita.

Edmonton is one of Canada's leading cities in medical research and treatment. Capital Health, which administers medical care in the metropolitan area, is the largest academic integrated health region in Canada. The system oversees all areas of health care, from community-level treatment to the most advanced surgeries.

One of the reasons Edmonton's health-care system is so large and all-encompassing is that it serves not just the city, but all of Northern Alberta and much of Northern Canada. The region has more than 1,800 physicians, the most of any health authority in Canada.

The system handles 304,000 emergency-room visits a year, with more than 90,000 patients being admitted to a hospital bed.

Efficiency is one of Capital Health Region's accomplishments. It has managed to have the lowest administrative costs in Canada.

Edmonton hospitals offer the only top-level specialty treatments in Alberta for conditions such as burns. Many of the programs or treatments were the first of their kind.

One area where treatments were pioneered here was in operating on infants still in the womb.

One of the system's firsts is having Canada's largest comprehensive tissue centre, which acts as a bank for human organs and tissue needed for transplantation.

The centre, in the Red Cross Building, has the first heart-valve bank in Western Canada. The centre freezes and saves bone, heart valves, corneas, ligaments, tendons and skin for medical use.

Transplantation is one of the system's areas of excellence. Edmonton doctors performed 63 heart, lung and liver transplants in 1997 and 1998, as well as 92 kidney transplants.

One of the most recent awards to an Edmonton doctor went to neuroscientist Dr. Richard Stein. He received the 1999 Canadian Medical Association's Medal of Honour. The award was for "outstanding contributions to the advancement of medical research in the areas of spinal cord injuiries, locomotion and functional electrical stimulation."

Stein's work focuses on using electrical stimulation to prompt body movement in people who have suffered from strokes or injuries. The Medal of Honour is the highest award given by the CMA to someone not of the medical profession (Stein has his PhD in Physiology from Oxford).

The University of Alberta Hospital complex is also a world-renown centre of medical excellence. Professionals there are at the leading edge of Canadian medical research and treatment in transplantation, with the hospital's official designation as Transplant Centre for Western Canada.

Three standout transplant programs which are the first of their kind in

Western Canada are the heart (1985), heart-lung (1986) and liver transplant programs (1989).

The first pancreatic islet transplant in Canada was performed at the hospital, in 1989, as were the first transplant of a kidney from a relative who had recently died, and the first liver transplant from one living relative to another (1998).

The first heart transplant in Western Canada came at the U of A Hospital, in 1985, and was followed within two years by the region's first heart-lung transplant.

The first pediatric liver transplant in Western Canada was performed at the

Leading-edge surgical techniques and treatments have been developed in Edmonton.
(Photo courtesy Capital Health)

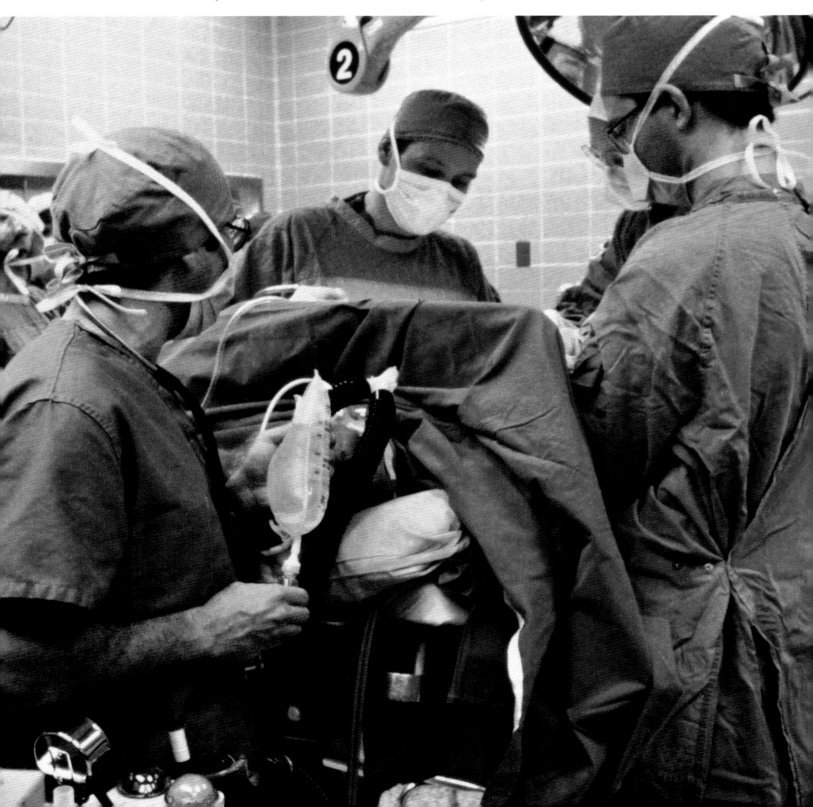

A patient is wheeled through the spectacular atrium at the renovated and expanded Royal Alexandra Hospital. (Photo by Emir Poelzer, courtesy Royal Alexandra Hospital)

hospital in 1990.

University of Alberta Hospital's Dr. Lorne Tyrrell developed the anti-hepatitis B drug lamivudine, which was used for the first time in the liver transplant of a hepatitis B patient (in 1994). It has since become the world standard treatment.

Research and treatment of children's illnesses is also one of the specialty areas at University hospital. Pediatric cardiovascular (heart and blood vessels) research and treatment at the hospital is a Canadian and world leader.

Pediatric oncology (cancer) is one of the areas where research and treatment have been among the world's best. In the 1950s, most children with cancer did not survive. But as part of a push to have cancer specialists and pediatricians focus on the area, the first program in the Prairies to focus on children's cancer began at Cross Cancer Institute in the 1970s.

Research in Edmonton has led the world in advances such as classifying types of pediatric cancer, diagnosing, and determining what type of treatment is best for each. This has led to treatment protocols (or plans) which are used around the world, and have boosted the survival rate to almost 80 per cent. In some cases, such as kidney tumors, the survival rate is almost 100 per cent.

Research and treatment in pediatric cancer is being boosted again with the move to combine Cross Cancer's work more closely with The University of Alberta Hospital's pediatric unit.

One of the more spectacular areas where Edmonton medical research and treatment has been at the forefront is the referral centre for bone-anchored prosthetics to replace parts of the head and face missing due to cancer, birth defects, injuries or burns.

Some of the doctors at the hospital have invented procedures and devices that are the first of their kind in the world. Dr. Yashu Coe has invented several instruments for heart surgery, which allow safer, less expensive and less stressful operations. The devices often use balloon-like instruments that open or support damaged valves or vessels.

Another world-reknown U of A surgeon was Dr. Bruce Weir. Named to the Order of Canada in 1996, he was chair of the department of surgery, and surgeon-in-chief of the U of A Hospital. He led the first international symposium on his research specialty, cerebral vasospasm, a condition that affects blood vessels of the brain after a stroke.

The Royal Alexandra Hospital is the city's other major health centre, and is the designated centre for health care for all of Northern Alberta, including having the leading perinatal (shortly before and after birth) clinic for high-risk pregnancies.

Some of the doctors at the Royal Alexandra are leaders in their field, including Dr. Kathy Flood, who is the only urogynecologist in Alberta.

One of the technologies pioneered at the Royal Alexandra is the performing of internal heart x-rays by inserting a device through the wrist artery instead of the leg. The Alex, as the hospital is known locally, has Alberta's only Obstetrical Intensive Care Unit, the province's largest gynecological service, and is the birthplace of more Alberta babies than any other hospital.

Education

When politicians speak of "The Alberta Advantage," one of its cornerstones is education. Edmonton has always been at the leading edge of education, from having the province's first university, seen here, to attracting the best instructors at every level.

Today, with a network of education institutions to serve people of all ages, Edmonton has firmly established itself as a leader in the field.

(Photo by Allyson Quince)

Education

Edmonton has a long history of excellence in education, from its public schools to being home to one of Canada's top universities.

Whether won by students or teachers, awards and achievements have been common for many years.

University of Alberta

Established in 1906, University of Alberta was the first in the province. It has grown to become the largest post-secondary institution between Toronto and Vancouver. The 1998/99 school year saw the university with an undergraduate student population of 25,667, and a graduate student population of 2,766. The university hands out more than 5,300 bachelor's degrees and close to 800 master's degrees each year.

The university is also one of the oldest collecting institutions in Western Canada. The university has more than 30 different museums, collections and exhibits on campus, with more than 17 million artifacts and exhibits.

University of Alberta's library has more than nine million holdings, giving it the largest number of items per full-time student of any Canadian university.

But the university is about more than just record-breaking numbers; it's also a leader in quality.

According to the 1999 Maclean's poll of post-secondary institutions, University of Alberta ranks as the best overall university outside Ontario, and the best non-Ontario university for innovation and training the leaders of tomorrow. It also ranked fourth in Canada for student grade improvement between high school and graduation.

Instructors at the University of Alberta have won many awards for their work both inside and outside the institution.

Richard Taylor won the 1990 Nobel Prize for physics (the first by a Canadian) for work in proving the existence of the sub-atomic particles known as quarks.

Environmental scientist Dr. David Schindler has won many awards, including the 1991 Stockholm Water Prize for his work on North American pollution policies, and the 1998 Volvo Environmental Prize for his work on chemical pollution in fresh water.

Three U of A professors have each won a Governor General's Literary Award, which is the country's top writer's prize. Rudy Wiebe won twice: in 1973 for *The Temptations of Big Bear*, and in 1994 for *A Discovery of Strangers*; Greg Hollingshead won in 1995 for *Roaring Girl*; and Ted Blodgett won in 1996 for *Apostrophes*.

History professor Olive Dickason, a writer and historian, is best known for her work in native studies. She was named to the Order of Canada in 1996, and in 1992 won the MacDonald Prize for her book *Canada's First Nations; A History of Founding Peoples from Earliest Times*.

University of Alberta's Juliet McMaster has also won several awards for her literary works, including the Canada Council Molson Prize in the Humanities and Social Sciences.

Anne Naeth won the Canadian Land Reclamation Association's national award for her research focusing on reclaiming land once used for mining, pipelines or well sites. Dr. Lorne Tyrrell, the Dean of Medicine and Oral Health

The three major literary award-winners at University of Alberta: Greg Hollingshead, Ted Blodgett and Rudy Wiebe.
(Photo courtesy University of Alberta)

Sciences and Director of the Glaxo Heritage Research Institute, developed the world's first antiviral treatment for hepatitis B.

Chemistry professor Jed Harrison won the prestigious E.W.R. Steacie Memorial Fellowship for developing miniature chemical analysis systems on silicon chips. Math professor Andy Liu has been named Canadian University Professor of the Year by both the Toronto-based Canadian Council for the Advancement of Education, and the New York-based Council for the Advancement and Support of Education.

Professor emeritus Dr. Chuji Hiruki has won close to 30 prestigious awards from around the world for his work in plant pathology - the study of organisms which attack plants. Dr. Hiruki was among the first recipients of the Mycoplasma Recognition Award, in 1999. He has also won the 1996 Outstanding Research Award Gold Medal from the Canadian Phytopathological Society, and in 1993 was given the Award for Lifetime Achievement from the American Phytopathological Society.

And University of Alberta leads the nation in the number of professors who have been awarded 3M Teaching Fellowships (to 1997), Canada's top award for university undergraduate teaching. University staff members have taken 17 of the fellowships, compared to 15 for University of Western Ontario, seven for University of Guelph.

The University of Alberta has been named as the editorial headquarters for one of the world's most prestigious academic journals in the social sciences, arts and humanities. Starting in 2000,

political science professor Andy Knight will become lead editor of *Global Governance: A Review of Multilateralism and International Organizations*.

The university also has had 62 scholars elected as Fellows of the prestigious Royal Society of Canada.

Not all of the achievements have been purely academic. University of Alberta's Dr. Larry Wong invented and developed the unique Canadian Cold Buster food bar in 1991. The high-energy bar is also known as Access Bar, and is sold worldwide.

University of Alberta also attracts people with a history of awards as professors. In 1993, Edmonton-raised international pianist Marek Jablonski returned to the music faculty after years of international acclaim. His awards include being unanimously chosen in 1961 as the grand prize winner in the first Jeunesses Musicales of Canada National Music Competition. The same year, he won the national competition at the Julliard School in New York.

Students at University of Alberta have also won awards. Engineering student Michelle St. Cyr became, in 1999, the first University of Alberta undergraduate to win a Canadian Engineering Memorial Foundation scholarship, and won the overall national award for her leadership, community involvement and academic achievement.

Grant MacEwan Community College

Built on three campus locations in the city, Grant MacEwan Community College (GMCC) is the largest college in

Grant MacEwan Community College's downtown campus has become a city landmark, thanks in part to its distinctive architecture.
(Photo by Allyson Quince)

Alberta, with more than 57,000 students, and some of the best facilities available in community colleges anywhere.

More than 86 per cent of students successfully transferred their GMCC qualifications to post-secondary institutions, the highest rate of any similar institution in Alberta.

GMCC's music program is the only one in Western Canada to focus on contemporary music, such as folk, jazz and pop. It's theatre arts program is the only one in Western Canada to focus equally on acting, dancing and singing.

The college's Arts Outreach program won an award of excellence from the California-based Learning Resources Network, for outstanding design of the program's brochure.

Brian Webb, chair of GMCC's dance program, won the Telus Award for Arts of the Future in 1998. The college's dance program was highlighted in the prestigious U.S. magazine *Dance Teacher Now*, the first Canadian modern dance program to be so recognized.

Northern Alberta Institute of Technology

While not the first or largest school of its kind in Alberta, the Northern Alberta Institute of Technology (NAIT) is the single-largest provider of Business Administration diploma programming in Alberta. NAIT also offers the only non-university finance program in Western Canada. NAIT offers many programs aimed at applied education and training. There are 92 full-time programs, more than 1,200 continuing-education courses and 32 apprenticeship programs, in one- two- and four-year programs.

Alberta College

The college is Alberta's oldest post-secondary institution, having been established in 1903. A leader in adult education, it also has Western Canada's largest Conservatory of Music.

The College's excellence in music education was enhanced in 1998 with the establishment of Canada's first International Music Academy. That program combines education in music, regular high school academics and English as a Second Language.

The King's University College

The King's University College was the first private institution in Canada approved to offer a certified and accredited education degree program.

Geoff Abma, a King's graduate in environmental studies, won the Association of Universities and Colleges in Canada Governor General's Environmental Award in 1999.

Public and Separate Schools

Edmonton's school system has a mixture of schools, offering unique options for parents and students. The largest system is Edmonton Public Schools, which has more than 79,000 students in 206 schools.

Right from the start, the public system has established a record of pioneering. In 1881, the system put up the first free-education schoolhouse in the Alberta district of the Northwest Territories. It was also the first frame-lumber building in Edmonton, and served as Edmonton's first courthouse. The building still stands as a museum, next to the public school archives in the former McKay Avenue School.

Edmonton Protestant Public School District #7 was the first public school system in Alberta and the Northwest Territories, in 1885. The number seven referred to the region of the territories where it was located.

Women in education have marked firsts in Edmonton. The city hired its first female teacher, Lillian Osborne, in 1899. And the public system had the first female trustee in Alberta, when Bessie Nicols was elected in 1912. Florence Phillips became the first female high school principal in Alberta, in 1975.

When it comes to administration, the system was the first in Canada to switch to school-controlled spending. Starting in the 1970s, superintendent Michael Strembitsky led the move away from having all spending controlled by the central

The Victoria Composite High School cheerleading squad won the 1994 gold medal at the international championships. Back row, left to right: Doug Adair, Amber Dryhorub, Wade Daniels, Dianne Greenough, Tom Toma, Pamela Jones and Dean Cooper. Middle row, left to right: Cathy Bowen, Melisa Harper, Lindsay Thomas, Jenny Berg, Tara Wood and Maria Lee. Front row, left to right: Caroline Spencer, Julie Stoehr, Tanya Elund, Jen Pope, Kim Cutmore and Anne Heaney.

(Photo courtesy of Jostens Canada and Dianne Greenough)

government education office. The move would be widely copied by the provincial government in the following two decades.

Strembitsky was so successful, that he has become a leading consultant to education systems in the United States.

Several public school teachers have won national Prime Minister's Awards for Teaching Excellence.

Tami Dowler-Coltman, Robyn Shewchuk and William Kao won in 1988. Frank Jenkins and Laurie Jewell won in 1997. Michael Dzwiniel and Jane Skinner won in 1996. Karen Slevinsky won in 1994, and Jean Hetherington won in 1993.

Teacher Barry Edgar was named to the 1999 Honour Roll of the Association of Science Technology Centres in Washington, D.C., for going beyond ordinary duties in teaching science.

The system also leads the nation in specialized education, with such national firsts as Victoria Composite High School's performing arts program and Vimy Ridge Academy's structured, military-style education, taking place in public schools.

Another first-of-its-kind program has students do home schooling via a computer link with their local school. This lets parents take a more active role in education, but still has the student free to take part in field trips, extra-curricular activities and social events at

the school.

Many public school students have won awards and established a precedent of high achievement.

Students from Old Scona High School won the 1999 University of Toronto national biology competition. The team beat out 344 other teams from across Canada in its first time at the competition.

Student Salim Rajwani won the World Speech and Debate Championship in 1997. Ranjan Agarwal won the 1995 Canadian Student Debating Federation's Cup, the Founder's Cup and other awards for his debating skills.

One of the highest levels of academic achievement in the world is the International Baccalaureate program, which has high school students earn university credits through advanced study and community service, and has extra essay and examination requirements. The program operates around the world, and Edmonton students regularly score highly.

In 1998, the most recent results available, Edmonton students scored significantly above-average in all but one of the 11 study sections - German studies. In the Mandarin studies section, they came close to a perfect score, with the group receiving 6.37 out of a possible seven points.

Five Edmonton Public Schools students have scored perfect marks on the International Baccalaureate program's overall exam (45 points out of 45) in the past few years. Jean Christophe Rochet achieved the feat in 1986/87. Two students scored perfect marks in 1993/94: Robert Radovanovic and Lance Robert Doherty. Another double came in 1995/96, when Tim Poon and Wynne Leung also earned perfect scores on the exam. Annually, only about a dozen students around the world receive perfect scores.

School groups have also had outstanding achievements. The Strathcona High School yearbook committee won the Canadian Scholastic Review Award for yearbooks two years in a row: 1995/96 and 1996/97.

The Queen Elizabeth Knights' Cheerleading Squad has taken Edmonton's championship attitude around the world, winning the 1995 gold medal in the Miss Drill Team International Cheerleading Championships. That title followed the 1994 gold medal performance by Victoria Composite High School's squad.

Three Edmonton students won awards at the 1999 Canada-Wide Science Fair, which was held in Edmonton. Leyla Asadi won a gold medal in the intermediate earth and environmental science division for a project called *With The Canola Cure?* Tanya White received a junior gold in life science for a project on the health risks of magnetic fields.

Ivan Sly also won a gold medal, in the engineering junior division, for his project called *The Glasslamp*.

Many famous achievers have come through the Edmonton Public Schools system, including the following:

Capt. Roy Brown, D.S.C., shot down the Red Baron on April 18, 1918. The Edmonton flyer was in a dogfight alongside fellow Edmontonian (and Victoria Composite schoolmate) Wop May, who dropped out of battle when his plane's motor failed. Baron Manfred Von Richtofen went to attack May, and Brown sprayed the German aircraft with bullets, killing the feared Red Baron and saving May.

Mary Lobay, the sister of long-time Edmonton Mayor William Hawrelak, was chairman of the Edmonton Police Commission, the first woman in Canada to hold such a position.

Martin Yan is the host of the long-running Yan Can television cooking show, and author of many best-selling books on oriental cooking.

Edmonton Catholic Schools is the city's leading separate school system (there are also charter schools), with 84 schools and more than 32,000 students.

The system, its teachers and students have won awards over the years, including the Microsoft Award for excellence in integrating technology - the only Canadian school division to receive the award.

Teacher Lynne Holzmann was named to the 1999 Honour Roll of the Association of Science Technology Centres in Washington, D.C., for going beyond ordinary duties in teaching science.

Some of the award-winning and notable students to have graduated from Edmonton Catholic Schools are Broadway singer Robert Goulet, musicians Marek Jablonski and Juliette Kang, record-setting CFL athlete Hank Ilesic, and actor Nathan Fillion.

One of the more recent grads is actor Nathan Fillion. After winning acting awards in Edmonton, he began acting in the U.S., and won a speaking role in the Academy Award-winning movie *Saving Private Ryan*.

Business

Edmonton means business. From its very start as a trading fort, the settlement was intended as a business venture. That spirit still exists in Edmonton, with many leading-edge firms doing research and manufacturing in everything from retail to biotechnology. And of course, the petroleum industry has been the major driving force in the city's economy for decades. While firms are often reluctant to discuss their achievements, there are enough firsts and bests in Edmonton's business community to make any city proud.

(Photo courtesy City of Edmonton Archives)

Business

It's been said that Edmontonians work for either the government or the oil industry, and love to spend their money in shopping malls.

While it is true that Edmonton has traditionally relied on government (and government-supported organizations) along with resource industries for employment and business income, that tells only part of the story.

Edmonton was established as an entrepreneurial centre at its inception as a trading hub for the region. That early business focus resulted in Edmonton establishing the first Board of Trade west of Winnipeg, in 1889.

Since the late 1980s, Edmonton has seen a diversification of its industries. Tourism, high-tech firms and a broader resource-industry base are some of the areas that have driven recent business growth in Edmonton.

In fact, Edmonton is the industrial heart of Alberta. Nearly 45 per cent of Alberta's value-added manufacturing occurs in the Edmonton area, creating approximately $15 billion in goods in 1997.

That means Edmonton also leads the province in industrial employment. In the manufacturing sector, Edmonton's workforce increased by 8,000 in 1997, to 50,600.

Edmonton has been cited several times for its excellent business climate.

Edmonton is the best city for business in North America, according to a spring 1999 study by KPMG. The ranking was based on the typical operating costs for a medium-sized business.

Edmonton was ranked as having the most diverse economy in Canada, according to the Conference Board of Canada. The organization's summer 1999 report on top-ranking economies put Edmonton at number one. The board estimated the metro region's gross domestic economy will grow by 3.8 per cent in 2000.

The board also said that Edmonton has the lowest commercial lease rates of any Canadian city, at $3.90 per square foot. Retail sales are expected to be the highest of any city except Toronto in 1999, topping $11 billion.

A survey by *Industry Week* magazine in April 1999 concluded that Edmonton has the best worker productivity of any city in Canada.

One of the areas where Edmonton is seeing continuing success is in leading-edge technology business.

The International Development Research Committee named Edmonton as the only Canadian city on its list of Smart Cities; and only six cities in the world were chosen in total.

Edmonton was cited for creating an environment that fosters creativity and knowledge-based business and research. The city does this by bringing together the various post-secondary institutions, research organizations, business, government and the Edmonton Arts Council.

But it isn't the first time such a distinction has come to Edmonton.

The *Globe and Mail Report on Business* named Edmonton as one of its five Smart Cities in 1995. The city was also rated one of the top five cities for business in 1993, and received honorable mentions in 1992 (for business climate) and in 1997 (for export business).

Economic Development Edmonton, the city's business-development arm, has earned the city attention from outside Canada. It's Model 7/25 strategy, designed to diversify the city's economic base, earned Edmonton the honour of being the only Canadian city chosen for a $1-million study of six major 'smart cities' by the International Development Research Council.

Edmontonians are among the most educated people in North America. More than 40 per cent of the workforce has a post-secondary diploma or degree. Edmonton has a workforce in excess of 500,000 people with a participation level of approximately 72 per cent, and a low unemployment rate of six per cent in 1998.

The intellectual advantage, along with low start-up and operating costs, is one of the reasons why Edmonton has emerged as a leader in high-tech industries. There are more than 900 high-tech companies in Edmonton.

A continent-wide study by KPMG chartered accountants in 1996 found that Edmonton was the most cost-effective place in North America to construct a semi-conductor fabrication plant.

The Edmonton Research Park is a

Refineries in the metropolitan Edmonton area process a massive amount of the nation's petroleum supplies. The massive complexes look like miniature cities in the night. The huge amount processed and sent through Edmonton is a major reason for the city's claim to being the oil capital of Canada.

(Photo courtesy City of Edmonton Archives)

development area in the city's south, aimed at scientific and emerging technology companies. It is the second-largest research park in the country. The 130-hectare (320-acre) park is home to more than 1,200 employees in areas such as medical diagnosis, software development, biotechnology, electronics, telecommunications, petroleum research and environmental testing. It also includes the Advanced Technology Centre, an incubator for emerging-technology businesses. The centre is completely occupied, as is Research Centre One, a second-stage incubator facility.

There is constant growth at the research park, with Miza Pharmaceuticals Inc., Bently Nevada Canada Corp., Intelligene Expression Inc. and other cutting-edge companies recently purchasing lots and developing their own facilities.

The new Biotechnology Lease Initiative is a leader in the emerging industry, allowing biotechnology companies to lease property in the park for $1 a year, for up to 10 years. These companies have the option to buy the property at market value any time during the agreement, but must develop the land within six months of the purchase.

Economic Development Edmonton

High-tech research and development is a big part of Edmonton's business edge. The Alberta Research Park provides cutting-edge programs and facilities which have helped to lead the city's economy into the 21st century.
(Photo courtesy Alberta Research Council)

(EDE) operates the park. EDE is also the setting for the Edmonton Capital Region Innovation Centre. The EDE offices at the Shaw Conference Centre house the centre itself, which supports and promotes the commercialization of new products, services and ideas. The conference centre is also a record-setter. Chefs at the centre make up Culinary Team Canada, which won world championship gold medals in both 1998 and 1997. Executive Chef Simon Smotkowicz was named Canadian Federation of Chefs and Cooks' 1998 Chef of the Year.

The Alberta Research Council (ARC), which partners the private and government sectors to develop new technologies, has won many awards over the years. One of the most recent is the 1996 award from the Canadian Land Reclamation Association for the development of special plants used to reclaim land from industrial or other large-scale use.

The ARC's complex in the research park has been at the forefront of many technological innovations, from using straw to make panel board, to reducing air pollution by pumping it into the ground to release methane deposits.

Albertans have the lowest overall personal and business taxes in Canada, with no general capital, payroll or provincial sales taxes.

Municipal tax rates and utility costs in metro Edmonton are among the lowest in Canada, and the city has an abundance of clean water, natural gas and electricity.

Residential taxes are the fifth lowest of major Canadian cities.

Edmonton is in the final stages of an award-winning debt-retirement program that will free the city from tax-supported debt by 2004. The province of Alberta has posted consecutive surplus budgets and must, by law, balance its budget each year.

Edmonton is the major business centre for all of Northern Alberta. There are virtually no major projects completed in Northern Alberta without Edmonton businesses benefiting economically. Many of these projects are traditionally in the resource area, such as oil & gas, mining, and more recently, forestry.

Since the Leduc #1 discovery, Edmonton has billed itself as the oil capital of Canada. While Calgary may try to claim that title for its spate of head offices, or Fort McMurray may claim it for its heavy reliance on the industry, nowhere compares to Edmonton for being the overall centre of the nuts and bolts of Canada's petroleum operations. In fact, the amount of crude oil processed in Metro Edmonton in one day would be enough to change the oil of every car in Canada.

More than 80 per cent of Canada's oil reserves are in Alberta and more than 80 per cent of the province's producing oil wells are in the Edmonton service area. That means Edmonton has scores of businesses dedicated to exploration and extraction, as well as the refining and distributing of oil and petroleum products.

Edmonton is home to some of the largest petroleum refineries in Canada, and there are more than 20 major chemical producers in the area. Metro Edmonton is the hub of Western Canada's oil and gas pipeline network,

Dr. Karl Clark played a huge role in the development of northern Alberta's oil industry, by unlocking the secret of extracting petroleum from the tar sands.
(Photo courtesy Alberta Research Council)

and the supply and service centre for Canada's petroleum industry, as well as the rapidly expanding mining and forestry industries in Alberta and Northern Canada.

An illustration of Edmonton's strengths in oilfield supply is Score Energy Products, which created the largest triple offset design butterfly valve ever built in Canada. The 152-cm valve was built for Nova Chemical, and cost $120,000.

As well as the city being the centre of the province's oil production business, Edmonton is a home to many scientists who have been at the forefront of petroleum-related innovations. One of the most influential was Dr. Karl Clark, who discovered the secret to tar sands processing. Clark uncovered the chemical secrets of the sands that would make it easy to remove the oil by using hot-water

extraction.

Similarly, retired University of Alberta professor Raymond Lemieux turned his ground-breaking chemistry research into big business. His work on synthetic chemical structures led to co-founding with the university of ChemBioMed Ltd. in 1977. The company has become a world leader in creating biomedical compounds used in organ transplant and blood transfusions.

Northern Alberta has one of the world's largest remaining untapped forest resources, and the past 10 years has seen the forestry industry grow tremendously, with new plants being built throughout the area. While there are larger forestry-related plants in rural centres, Edmonton leads the province in numbers, with 13 forestry-related businesses. Most of these are secondary manufacturing and panelboard manufacturing.

The Edmonton market area contains more than two-thirds of the province's farms, totaling more than 30 million hectares (74 million acres).

Edmonton can lay claim to being the banking centre of Western Canada, being the location of the only major-chartered bank outside Toronto and Montreal, and the home of Canada's only 100-per-cent native-owned financial institution.

Canadian Western Bank is a niche-market institution, which meets the same regulatory requirements as its better-known eastern rivals. But the 16-year-old bank focuses on western-Canadian businesses; specifically small-to medium-sized companies and especially those in the petroleum industry. About 75 per cent of the bank's lending is to such companies, with the rest going to individuals' loans. Total assets of the bank in 1998 were about $2.2 billion, on a net income of more than $19 million.

Peace Hills Trust is a unique institution, having been started by the Samson Cree Nation of Hobbema in central Alberta. Headquartered in Edmonton, the company was begun in 1981, and now has branches in seven cities across Western Canada. While the company's main focus is on First Nations business and customers, the institution is open to anyone. Peace Hills Trust has assets of more than $692 million, with equity of more than $41 million.

Capital City Savings is the biggest credit union east of B.C. and the fifth-largest in Canada. The credit union has 14 branches in Edmonton and 10 others in the surrounding area. In 1998, Capital City Savings had total assets of slightly more than $1 billion dollars, an increase from $893 million the previous year. That raised the members' equity to $44 million in 1998, from $39 million the year before.

Edmonton can also boast records in making itself ready for business travelers.

Edmonton has the lowest meal costs for travelers of any major Canadian city, and the lowest overall business-travel costs of world cities surveyed by the Runzheimer Guide to Daily Travel Prices' 1998 edition.

And there are many aspects of the city which make it attractive to business. With 4.2 million visits a year, Edmonton is the biggest tourist centre in Western Canada, with only Toronto and Montreal drawing more visitors. Edmonton's

tourism industry contributes $1 billion a year to the local economy.

One reason tourists enjoy Edmonton is the high level of excellence in the local hospitality industry. As well as the award-winning chefs at the Shaw Conference Centre, Michelle Blanchett of the Sheraton Grande Edmonton is representing Canada at the 1999 World Culinary Skills Competition in November.

There is an abundance of land available for growth in metro Edmonton, with purchase costs as low as $6,071 per hectare ($15,000 per acre) for unserviced parcels.

Edmonton's communications systems are fully digital and include hundreds of kilometres of fibre-optic line.

As a regional distribution centre for Northern Alberta, Edmonton has 510,000 square metres (5.5 million square feet) of warehouse space, including 232,000 square metres (2.5

One Edmonton business came up with a big (literally) promotional idea for its retail outlet. Western Boot Factory built the world's tallest boot (standing about four stories high), which sits outside the company outlet at 10007 167 St.

million square feet) of public warehouse space.

Edmonton is Canada's Gateway to the North, serving as the supply and service hub for northern activity. This began with the 1887 Klondike Gold Rush, and continues today with approximately $42 billion in investment for major projects in the North.

And yes, retail sales are big business in Edmonton, supplying the city with some of its most important business records. Edmonton has the most retail stores per capita of any major Canadian city. Edmonton has close to 77 shopping centres and several designated retail districts. As well as being home to the world's largest shopping mall (West Edmonton Mall), the city is the home of Canada's first shopping centre - Westmount Mall - only the second modern shopping centre in North America.

The oil boom of the 1970s brought many success stories to the Edmonton business scene. One of the most famous is The Brick. Canada's largest dollar-volume furniture retailer, the nation-wide chain of stores began in a red-brick warehouse (the origin of the name). The business founded by Bill Comrie was built on the innovative concepts of mass purchasing to lower prices, and offering services such as in-house repair technicians and delivery across the province.

In 1996, the latest figures available, The Brick had about 50 stores in Canada, more than 3,000 employees, and a fleet of about 400 tractor-trailer and delivery trucks.

Another local success story is RTO Enterprises, a retail furniture outlet

begun in Edmonton. It was the second-fastest-growing company in Canada in 1998 according to *Profit* magazine. It was still on the list in 1999, at number 26. The only other Edmonton company to make the list in 1999 was the engineering firm Matrikon Consulting Group, which hit number 98.

Edmonton is home to the largest privately owned drug-store chain in Canada. The Katz Group is owned by Donald Beeler, who in 1999 signed an agreement to buy the American 141-store chain Snyder Drug Stores Inc. The Katz Group began with one Edmonton drug store in 1991, and grew to more than 300 stores across Canada. The U.S. deal will boost its annual revenue to about $1.1 billion.

One of the big success stories in the food industry is Three Blondes & a Brownie. Started in 1986, the company which specializes in low-fat baked goods, was the first all-female company to supply food products to McDonald's nation-wide. The company is owned by Terry Lynne Meyer (who was also the

first Edmontonian to become Miss Canada, in 1975), Candace Brinsmead and Nadja Piatka.

Founded in 1988, employee-owned Quality Group of Companies is one of Canada's leading printing companies, and was among the first in the world to introduce advanced equipment such as computer-to-plate technology that is faster, more efficient and of higher quality than traditional printing methods.

Quality companies also include one of the largest pre-press facilities in Western Canada - Screaming Colour. One of the areas where Quality leads the industry is in using environmentally friendly technology, including having the first chemical recycling unit of its type in Western Canada.

One of the unique retail districts in Edmonton is Old Strathcona. Once a run-down section on what was considered by some as the wrong side of the tracks, the area is one of the oldest in Edmonton.

City planners had decided to run a freeway through the district to downtown, but the amount of older, significant buildings in the area attracted the attention of several local business people and activists. By using city grants, historical designations and special zoning, the district is now home to some of the best shopping and entertainment in the city, and has been a showcase for similar heritage developments across Canada.

The restoration of Old Strathcona (centered on Whyte Avenue) has won several awards for historical preservation, and businesses have won awards. One of those is Alikatu, a gift shop, which won the 1999 National Award of Merit from the Canadian Gift and Tablewares Association as the best non-chain store in Western Canada.

With mining in the North, Edmonton has long been connected to the minerals and metals business. It is also recently building links with the diamond exploration going on in the North.

An example of how this has led to awards came in 1996, when Edmonton jeweller Mark Katzeff won first place in the Canadian Jeweller Buyer's Choice design competition, for his design of a gold, diamond, ruby and sapphire brooch.

Edmonton businesses are known for their commitment to the environment, many working directly in the field of energy conservation and pollution prevention and clean-up. A first in this area came in 1994, when Challenger Homes won the provincial small business Emerald Award for building the first EnviroHome in Canada. The home uses environmentally friendly materials and techniques in everything from creating materials to finished product.

Media

Edmonton has been home to some of North America's earliest news institutions. The media in Edmonton has established a tradition of winning accolades. Continuing through to modern times, the city's media has regularly won honours. This 1987 *Edmonton Journal* photograph of a firefighter rescuing a child won photographer Rick MacWilliam a National Newspaper Award.

Media

As the province's centre for media production, Edmonton is home to newspapers, television and radio stations that have garnered many awards.

As the oldest existing media outlet in town, *The Edmonton Journal* has won awards for many years, including a Pulitzer Prize in 1938 for fighting against government control of the media.

The Journal is a two-time winner of the national Michener Awards, established in 1970 for meritorious public service in journalism. In 1980, writer Wendy Koenig won for a series of stories on abuses in the Alberta child welfare system. In 1992, writer Tom Barrett won for a story about the use of psychiatric testimony in Alberta courts.

Journal staff members have won many National Newspaper Awards, given by the Canadian Newspaper Association. In l963, reporter Bob Hill won for his coverage of the rescue of Helen Klaben and Ralph Flores from a plane crash in the wilderness of Northern British Columbia. In 1969 and 1979, Edd Uluschak won cartooning awards. In 1988, Rick MacWilliam won for spot news photography. In 1991, John Lucas won for feature photography. In 1992, reporters Greg Owens and David Staples won for their coverage of the Yellowknife mine explosion. In 1993, a team of writers won for a series of articles on men's and women's health. In 1991 and 1994, columnist Linda Goyette won for column writing. In 1995 and 1996, Shawn Ohler was the recipient of the Hon. Edward Goff Penny Memorial Prizes for Young Canadian Journalists. In 1998, editor Murdoch Davis won for three editorials.

In 1993, writer Ed Struzik won a Canadian Science Writers Association award for an article exploring the impact that advances in genetic engineering would have on the future of food technology.

The Edmonton Journal is a four-time winner of the Annual Media Human Rights Awards, sponsored by the League for Human Rights of B'nai Brith Canada and awarded since 1974. Koenig's 1980 story on child welfare abuse (the Michener winner) was a B'nai Brith award winner. In l983, the paper won for its coverage of the controversy surrounding Jim Keegstra's anti-Semitic teachings in an Eckville school. In l998, reporter Graham Thomson and photographer Shaughn Butts won for their investigative report on the lives of people forcibly sterilized under government decree.

Journal photographers have also won many awards. The Canadian Press

Al McCann of CFRN-TV has been a much-respected figure on the city's broadcasting scene for many years. In 1993, he won the The Bell Memorial Award from the Alberta Sports Hall of Fame.

(Photo courtesy Al McCann)

(CP) News Picture of the Year was awarded to Steve Simon (1987), Rick MacWilliam (1988) and Jim Cochrane (1993). The CP Feature Picture of the Year went to Michael Dean in 1976.

MacWilliam also won the National Newspaper Awards (NNA) News Picture of the Year in 1988. The NNA Feature Picture of the Year went to John Lucas in 1991.

Dean Bicknell (1982) and Simon (1993) were named Canadian News Photographers of the Year. Western News Photographers of the Year went to Bicknell (1982 and 1980) and Brian Gavriloff (1981).

The Western Canadian News Photographers Association (WCNPA) has given Picture of the Year awards to many *Journal* photographers. Jackie Northam won in the sports category in 1981. In 1984, Karen Sorenburger won for news and Chris Schwarz won for sports. In 1985, Schwartz won for both

news and portrait, Sorenburger won for feature photograph, and Cochrane won for sports.

The WCNPA Picture of the Year was awarded to Schwartz (sports) and Mike Pinder (feature) in 1986. The next year, the Journal winners were Simon (news), Cheryl Choji (portrait) and Cochrane (photographers choice). Larry Wong won in 1988, while Simon (picture story) and Ian Scott (photographers choice) won in 1989.

The WCNPA awards for Picture of the Year kept coming in the 1990s. Simon won the Ted Grant Annual Human Interest Award in 1992. The following year, the winners were Ed Kaiser (sports), Wong (portrait), Cochrane (photographers choice), and Simon (one for pictorial and that year's Ted Grant award).

Brian Gavriloff won three WCNPA awards in 1998, for Feature, General News and picture story. Bruce Edwards

News photography is one area in which Edmonton has produced many award-winners. This picture won a Western Canadian News Photographers Award in 1991 for Edmonton Sun photographer Walter Tychnowicz.
(Photo courtesy The Edmonton Sun)

photography.

Simon won the multi-picture category in 1994, when Gavriloff won for sports. Gavriloff also won in 1995, for news, and Simon took that year's Ted Grant Award. 1996 saw Kaiser win for sports. Gavriloff won for feature photograph in 1997.

The most recent award to *The Edmonton Journal* was the 1999 B'nai Brith award, given to writer Satya Das for his series on human rights issues on the fiftieth anniversary of the United Nations Declaration of Human Rights.

The Edmonton Sun is the city's younger daily newspaper, but it has also won several awards.

Columnist Doug Gilbert received the 1978 National Newspaper Award as top sportswriter in Canada, for his coverage of the Commonwealth Games. Gilbert died after being hit by a car while covering the 1979 Pan Am Games in Puerto Rico. The Sports Federation of Canada immediately renamed its sportswriter and sportscaster of the year awards in his honour. Canada and East Germany also named awards in his honour, for sports writers contributing to international understanding.

Sun photographers have won many awards over the years. Robert Taylor won the National Newspaper Award for spot news photography in 1982, for a shot of Peter Pocklington's wife running for safety when the businessman was taken hostage.

Gorm Larsen won a National Newspaper Award in 1989 for a shot of Wayne Gretzky breaking Gordie Howe's point-scoring record.

Walter Tychnowicz won Western Canadian News Photographers

Edmonton Sun photographer Walter Tychnowicz won a Western Canadian News Photographers Award in 1996 for this shot of a man being arrested.
(Photo courtesy The Edmonton Sun)

Canadian News Photographers Association awards in 1991 (an environmental protestor giving members of a forestry hearing a one-finger salute), 1994 (three prizes, including a first for coverage of a violent strike) and in 1996 (for a photograph of a man being arrested).

Dan Riedlhuber won the 1993 Western Canadian News Photographers Association award for his picture of a couple who had just escaped from a car crash. The same photo also won an award from Photo Digest.

The Canadian Association for Distance Education gave radio station CKUA (along with Athabasca University) the Award for Excellence in Partnership in 1998.

CFRN and its staff members have won many awards over the years. Some of the more recent include the following CANPRO Awards: 1990 for *New Performers* and for *Down Came The Rain*; 1995 for the *Melrose Place* promotional campaign; and 1996 for both *Acorn The Nature Nut* and the Edmonton Oilers promotional campaign.

CFRN news coverage has won several Radio Television News Directors' Association (RTNDA) awards: 1987 for coverage of the Edmonton tornado disaster, and for *The Battle of the Bulge*; 1988 for coverage of a bone marrow transplant, and for the Code Inquiry; 1992 for coverage of an airplane crash; and 1997 for it's *Vegas Series*.

A long-serving and locally notable member of CFRN was Bruce Hogle, who won many prestigious awards in his career in Western Canada, including his more than 20 years with the station.

In 1960, Hogle was made an

CFRN's Bruce Hogle is a legend in the city's media history, with many awards and firsts to his credit.
(Photo courtesy CFRN)

honorary life member of the Trail, B.C. Safety Council for work as an editor of the *Trail Times*, helping to create safety awareness. In 1962, The Keep our Doctors Association of Saskatchewan honoured Hogle for his editorials on CFRN radio.

Hogle received a medal from The Vatican in 1975, for his work as a director of the Salesian Fathers St. Mary's High School in Edmonton. Other community service honours were given to Hogle, for services in the fields of education and crippled children.

In 1988, Hogle was given a Certificate of Appreciation from Alberta Social Services for the CFRN feature *Wednesday's Child*, which helped find homes for unadoptable foster children. Other awards included the 1992 Melvin Jones Fellowship (the highest honour of Lions International) for community service, the 1993 Queen's Commemorative Medal for public service, and being named a Member of the Order of Canada in 1998.

Later to become one of Edmonton's most popular television personalities, Terry Lynne Meyer (photo right) was the first Edmontonian to win the Miss Canada title, in 1975. Cynthia Kereluk won the title in 1984, and Leslie McLaren was the last woman from the city to be named Miss Canada, winning the title in 1991. Miss Teen Canadas from Edmonton have been: Emily Sertic (1982) and Lori Assheton-Smith (1983).

(Photo courtesy Terry Lynne Meyer)

Hogle's professional awards are also many and varied. In 1966, he won one of the first RTNDA awards, for the documentary *What About the Victim?* The National Headliners Club of the U.S. gave its first award outside America to Hogle, for a series of editorials in 1967 against a move by police to withhold some crime news from the public. Hogle won the first RTNDA Community Leadership award in 1976, for editorials on unscrupulous landlords. The *Wednesday's Child* feature won Hogle his own CANPRO award in 1982, for which he also won the Canadian Broadcasters' Association Gold Medal. In 1985, Hogle won another RTNDA, for a series of editorials. Hogle was made a life member of the Western Association of Broadcasters in 1993.

Videon (which was until recently known as Videotron) has won national awards for programming, most of them

for the local-affairs program *The Edge*. The Canadian Cable Television Award for programming went to Videon in 1992, 1996, 1997, 1998 and 1999.

The Canadian Broadcasting Corporation's Edmonton television operation has won a number of awards. In 1996, the news story *No Way Out: The Cinnamon Bear*, won the best of category award at the International Wildlife Film Festival. That same year, the Columbus International Film and Video Festival gave a bronze plaque to the documentary *Diary of Hope*.

CBC reporter Matt McClure and producer Brian Murphy won the 1993 Canadian Association of Journalists award for investigative journalism, for their report *Autistic Abuse*.

ACCESS, the Edmonton-based provincial education-oriented TV and radio broadcaster, has won many awards for its productions. The highlights come from around the world.

One of the station's most popular programs, *L&J News*, won the World Medal in 1997 from The New York Festival. The Festival gave the 1996 Gold Award to the young adult special *Opportunities For You*.

The Living Flow: Hour Two - Flow, Tides, Symphony, won the Gold Apple Award at the 1994 National Educational Film & Video Festival. At the 1993 Columbus International Film & Video Festival, the show *The Living Flow* won the Edgar Dale Screenwriting Award. The 1992 BMPE International Gold Medallion Award went to the 30-second promotional video *Thighs, Lies and Beauty*.

In 1988, two BPME International Gold Medallion awards went to *We Are*

The Difference.

Lynda Hodges won the 1983 ACTRA award for Best Writer Radio Documentary/Public Affairs, for *The Falklands Islands Crisis.*

1983 ACTRA awards were also handed out to Peter Adamski and Michael Sturko for Best Writer Television Drama, for *Game Plan*. Joe Galland won the Earl Grey Award for Best Acting Performance in that show.

ACTRA also handed out Best Radio Program and Best Writer, Radio Drama (Bill Williams) for the 1983 broadcast *Listening to Literature: The Great Gilly Hopkins.*

The Children's Broadcast Institute gave an Award of Excellence to *The Garage Gazette: Our Own Newspaper*, in 1983/84.

Basic Life Science - Listen To The Prairie: Prairie Rattlesnake, won the Minister of Educational Prize at the 1981 Japan Prize Educational Program Content.

The adult literacy program *Safer Than a Sock* won awards for best dramatic script, best entertainment short feature, and best actor at the 1980 Chicago International Film Festival.

Also in 1980, the Houston International Film Festival gave the Gold Award to *Native Religious Traditions: The Sacred Circle*. That same year, the program *Festival '78: I Can Still Hear the Drums*, won the Maeda Prize at the Japan Prize Competition.

The Ohio State Awards gave first place in 1979 to the show *The Way I See: Reptiles*.

ITV and its staff have won many provincial and national awards.

Probably the most prestigious award came to ITV in 1982, when the station received an Emmy Award for graphic title design. The station has also been home to award-winning productions such as *SCTV*, which featured such famous and award-winning performers as John Candy, Martin Short and Dave Thomas.

Edmonton may not have the best weather in the world, but we do have the best weatherman. ITV's Bill Matheson won the 1995 award as the world's best television weather forecaster from the Festival Internationale de Meteo.

The Radio/Television News Directors Association gave commentator Bob Layton the 1999 Sam Ross Award for best editorial, and named ITV as having the best television newscast in large markets in 1995.

The Canadian Association of Broadcasters has handed out many awards to ITV, such as the 1994 and 1995 Gold Ribbon Awards for the station's *It's Ours* promotion. ITV has won CAN PRO Gold Awards in 1992 (for station promotion), 1994 (one for news promotion, and one for the special *Just A Little Closer to Heaven*), 1995 (one for the *Trouble Shooters* news segment, and one for the *News Makers* newsmagazine).

ITV has also won the 1991 CNN International award for its feature report on the Glendon perogy monument. The station was named Television Station of the Year by the Western Canadian News Photographers Association in 1991, 1992, 1993, and 1994.

In 1999, radio station Power 92 (CKNG-FM) gave away $110,000 Cdn. to a listener - the biggest single cash give-away prize by any radio station in the world.

Historic Events

All great cities are a culmination of circumstances. Edmonton is no different, with its pioneering spirit, determination and compassion honed through decades of first, biggest and best events. For modern-day Edmontonians, nothing has had as great an effect as the 1987 tornado which left a swath of death and destruction. This award-winning photograph by *Edmonton Journal* staffer Steve Simon shows the magnitude of the tornado.

Historic Events

Edmonton has been shaped by its eventful history. A city proud of its heritage, many of these events were record-setting or the first of their kind. Some were happy, others tragic. But no history is complete without both the good and the bad, and Edmonton has grown into the cosmopolitan centre it is today because of the effect of each of these events.

1795

-With the Northwest Company already operating in the area, a Hudson's Bay Company party stopped along the North Saskatchewan River near what is now Fort Saskatchewan, looking for a place to build a trading post. Within eight days Edmonton House was being built.

1802

-Edmonton House was moved upstream to near today's Rossdale Power Plant. It would be relocated three more times over the next 30 years. Its last site was near the current Alberta Legislature.

1823

-Edmonton House became the west's most important depot, handling the largest amount of goods and business in the west.

1861

-The first Roman Catholic mission (in St. Albert) was started by Father Lacombe.

1871

-Methodist Rev. George McDougall moved to Edmonton

Pioneering priest Father Lacombe played a major role in the area's early history.
(Photo courtesy City of Edmonton Archives)

House, bringing a small organ with him. It was the first such musical instrument west of Winnipeg.

1875

-The Northcote became the first steamboat to reach Edmonton. The flat-bottomed boat ushered in a more convenient way for settlers to come to Edmonton from the east, helping to fuel the city's early growth. Steamboats continued regular service until World War One.

1879

-Edmonton's first agricultural fair was held at Fort Edmonton.
-A telegraph line was extended from Hay Lakes to Edmonton.

1880

-The first telegraph message was sent to Edmonton on January 1.
-*The Bulletin*, Edmonton's first newspaper (and the second newspaper to be established in the North West Territories of Canada), was started by Alex Taylor and Frank Oliver with $20 of capital. It was physically the world's smallest newspaper, measuring five inches by five inches, and the first issue had four pages.

1882

-The Belle of Edmonton, the first cable ferry west of Winnipeg, made a trial run on April 26 across the North Saskatchewan River. Constructed and operated by Edmonton pioneer John Walter,

Quick Facts

the ferry ran in the area where today's downtown bridges are, and was in operation for more than 30 years.
-Edmonton's first public school opened (with 25 students) on the brow of the hill at 99 Ave. and 105 St. It also served as the city's first courthouse. One hundred years later, the building was restored as a museum on the original site.

1883

- The McPherson and Coleman stagecoach made its first run from Edmonton to Calgary.

1888

-The first Edmonton Roman Catholic Separate School opened on 110 Street, on November 2. The move came after a vote by the city's Catholic ratepayers who were dissatisfied with the existing public system.

1891

-The first train arrived from Calgary, signaling the start of the regular service between the two cities for decades.
-On December 22, Edmonton's first electric light was turned on.

1892

-Matt McCauley became the first mayor of the newly incorporated town of Edmonton. The first meeting of Edmonton's town council was held February 15.

1899

-South Edmonton was incorporated as a town and renamed Strathcona.
-In August, the North Saskatchewan River flooded the valley and rose about 41 feet above its winter level.

1900

-The Low Level Bridge was opened on April 4. It was the first bridge to span the North Saskatchewan River in Edmonton. It played a major role in Edmonton's early growth by giving easy access to the city.

1902

-The Edmonton, Yukon and Pacific Railway crossed the Low Level Bridge and established Edmonton's first connection to a railway system.

1903

-The first edition of the *The Edmonton Journal* appeared on November 11. Although not the city's first newspaper, it has often been the only daily newspaper in Edmonton and today is the city's oldest daily.

1904

-Edmonton was incorporated as a city.
-The city purchased the Edmonton District Telephone Company. It was known as Edmonton Telephones and was the only city-owned phone system in Canada. The company was sold in 1995 for $720 million to AGT, which was the then-privatized provincial government telephone system. The sale was highly controversial and came only after early attempts had been blocked

John Rowand, Chief Factor of Edmonton House in the mid-1800s, was the first Edmontonian to take a Hawaiian winter vacation. When the Hudson's Bay Company sent Rowand and Sir George Simpson to tour their worldwide interests in 1841, the pair reached Honolulu in January. The pair settled in at the beach for two months before continuing their journey.

by public pressure.

-Successful Edmonton businessman Joseph Morris brought the first car to Edmonton.

1905

-Alberta was incorporated as a province on September 1.

-The Canadian Northern Railway reached Edmonton.

1906

-Edmonton became the provincial capital on April 25.

-The University of Alberta was founded - Alberta's first university. Calgary had lobbied heavily to be the home of the University, saying Edmonton had already received its share by being made capital. Premier Alexander Rutherford agreed, but said that since Calgary had been given the Normal School, he would give the university to a third community. He placed it in the then-separate community of Strathcona, directly across the river from Edmonton.

1907

-Construction began on the Alberta Legislature.

Joseph Morris shows off his new car - which was the first one in Edmonton.
(Photo courtesy City of Edmonton Archives)

- The city suffered its first major disaster when six workers died in a mine fire at the Strathcona Coal Company. The accident occurred at Walter's mine, just east of today's High Level Bridge on the south side of the North Saskatchewan River. The funeral services attracted hundreds of mourners and left the community stunned. But as coal mining was an important industry in Edmonton, the mine was reopened and operated for four more years.
- The City of Strathcona was incorporated on March 15.

1908

-Registration of the first students at the University of Alberta began on September 23. The first classes were held at Duggan Street School, which is now known as Queen Alexandra School. The university had 40 students and a staff of five. The university has since become the largest in Western Canada, and a regular winner of awards.
-The first streetcar service began. Edmonton's streetcar service would become the backbone of civic transportation for decades. Today a volunteer group restores and operates old streetcars but public transportation no longer uses the vehicles for regular service.
-Edmonton became the first city in Alberta with an automatic dial system for its telephones.

1909

- On Labour Day, Edmonton carpenter Reg Hunt made the first aerial flight over Edmonton and became the first person

in Western Canada to fly a man-made, heavier-than-air, machine. The flight lasted 35 minutes, and Hunt soared 10 to 15 metres (30 to 50 feet) above the ground.
-The Grand Trunk Pacific Railway reached Edmonton for the first time.
- John Walter launched the City of Edmonton steamer.

1912

-On February 1, the City of Strathcona was voted out of existence by a 2-1 margin. It was merged with the City of Edmonton.
-During the city's biggest real estate boom, the Hudson's Bay Company decided to sell its land holdings. In selling its huge tract of land by lottery, the company had so many would-be customers that hundreds of people lined up for a chance to draw ticket number one and have first pick of the 1,500 lots for sale. A few months later, the real estate market collapsed and many of the lots reverted to the city for non-payment of taxes.

1913

-The Alberta Legislature building opened.
-The High Level Bridge was completed, with the first train crossing on June 2. The bridge, built by Canadian Pacific Railway Co., cost $2 million and was the fourth largest in Canada. As it was built at grade with the top of the North Saskatchewan River Valley, it made bringing trains to the city much easier and helped to fuel growth for decades to come.

1914

-The Edmonton Newsboys' Band was established. The band, started by colourful local businessman John Michaels as a way to reduce juvenile delinquency, became recognized as the best boys band in Canada. The band was made up of newspaper delivery boys and had close to 1,200 members over the years. It was the only band in Canada chosen to play at the British Imperial Exposition in 1924.

1915

-On January 4, the 49th Battalion was formed. It would distinguish itself in several of the century's biggest battles.
-The North Saskatchewan River flooded due to heavy July rains. The flood was the worst in the city's history with the river rising three metres (10 feet) in 10 hours. The river crested at 15 metres (50 feet) above its normal level, leaving 2,000 people homeless and causing $750,000 in damage. The damage was so extensive that it spelled the end of the river valley as an industrial area.
-The Hotel Macdonald - the city's most recognized landmark for decades - opened on July 5.
-Fort Edmonton was dismantled from its site on the south grounds of the Alberta Legislature, despite opposition from many Edmontonians about the loss of an historic landmark. People were assured that the wooden structure was being catalogued for an eventual rebuilding elsewhere. The fort was never re-built, and the numbered pieces have since disappeared.
-The Princess Theatre opened at a cost of $75,000. It was the first marble-faced building west of Winnipeg.

1918

-Aviatrix Katherine Stinson flew from Calgary to make the first air mail delivery to Edmonton on July 10.

1919

-The men of the 49th Battalion returned home. Of the 4,050 men who were members during the war, 977 never returned and another 2,282 were wounded. The whole city turned out to welcome the men home.
-Edward, Prince of Wales, visited Edmonton in September as part of a Canadian tour. In what was then unheard-of behavior, the Prince attended a baseball game where he donned a team cap and threw two pitches to the Lieutenant Governor. He then ignored the royal seats and sat on the grass near the first base line where he cheered for the home team.

1921

-The Edmonton Federation of Community Leagues was founded January 24 to address the concerns of the 10 community leagues in Edmonton. The federation became the largest volunteer organization in North America and had a tremendous effect on the city. As well as organizing volunteers, the federation has had a powerful political influence at times. Today, about half of Edmonton households are signed up with the 138 community leagues.

1922

-Alberta's first radio station, CJCA, began operating in Edmonton.

1926

-Blatchford Field (now City Centre

Airport) north of downtown Edmonton became the first licensed municipal airport in Canada.

-During the Christmas/New Year season, Wilfrid 'Wop' May and Vic Horner flew 1,125 km (700 miles) through sub-zero weather in an open-cockpit airplane to deliver an anti-diphtheria serum to Fort Vermillion. News of the flight moved the people of Edmonton, and thousands of cheering Edmontonians greeted them on their return to Blatchford Field on January 6. Conditions were so bad that May's scarf froze to the lower part of his face, stripping off layers of skin when he removed it after landing.

1932

-The city's worst public uprising, the Market Square riot, broke out on December 20. In the midst of the Great Depression, a hunger march from rural Alberta converged on Edmonton. The object of the march was to draw attention to the plight of the farmers. Nearly 2,000 marchers attempted to move from the Market Square (on the south side of what is now Sir Winston Churchill Square) to the Legislature. The marchers had been refused a permit to parade and were confronted by the RCMP and city police. A riot broke out, lasting more than two hours, and leaving many marchers and police officers injured.

Vic Horner (centre) and Wop May (right) return to Edmonton after their mercy flight. May, usually known for his beaming smile, is shown just after pulling off the scarf that had frozen to his face.
(Photo courtesy City of Edmonton Archives)

1938

-*The Edmonton Journal* was awarded the Pulitzer Prize; the first ever awarded to a non-U.S. newspaper. The prize, a bronze medal mounted on a plaque, was for leading the fight against Alberta's 1937 Press Act, which called for papers to reveal all their sources, and print anything provided by the provincial government (the move was designed to attack political opponents). The Supreme Court of Canada eventually struck down the law as unconstitutional.
-Clarke Stadium was opened. The complex was named after Mayor Joseph A. Clarke for his efforts to acquire the site from the Dominion government. It has been the site of many landmark events and continues to play a role today. A planned renovation project helped to secure the 2001 World Track and Field championships for Edmonton; the first time the event will be held in North America.

1942

-The Alaska Highway was officially opened on November 2. The road from Edmonton to Fairbanks, Alaska, was built as a military supply route because of fears of a Japanese invasion of Alaska. The massive project was the largest of its kind, and had a tremendous impact on the growth of Edmonton and its role as 'Gateway to the North.'

1944

-The highest scoring squadron in the Royal Canadian Air Force during the Second World War, the 418 Squadron was adopted by the city and the name was changed to the City of Edmonton Squadron. In exchange for the name

Leduc #1 (opposite page photo) was a milestone in Edmonton's history. After the discovery, Edmonton became known as the Oil Capital of Canada.
(Photo courtesy City of Edmonton Archives)

change, enthusiastic and appreciative Edmonton citizens provided luxuries such as chocolates and cigarettes to the unit.

1947

-Likely the most influential event in Edmonton's history came on February 13, when Imperial Oil's Leduc #1 drilling site blew in. The city almost immediately became a boomtown, with a new oil-based economy that fuelled a period of massive growth and continues to help drive the city today.

1948

-The first oil refinery in the Clover Bar area was opened. The district now holds the record for total refinery activity in Canada.

1950

-The first inter-provincial pipeline was completed, from Edmonton to Ontario.

1952

-Canada's first underground parking garage opened, adjacent to the extension to the Hotel Macdonald.

1954

-CFRN television, Alberta's first TV station, was started. It was part of the CBC network, and the first privately owned television station in Alberta. Later, when CBC started its own station in Edmonton, CFRN joined CTV.
-The Edmonton Eskimo Football Club won its first Grey Cup by beating the heavily favored Montreal Alouettes. The city went wild and the event became the first in a long string of championships in several sports by

Edmonton teams. The era was the beginning of the city gaining a self-confidence and pride that would lead to its eventually adopting the motto 'City of Champions.'

1960

-Edmonton International Airport opened.
-The Queen Elizabeth Planetarium, the first civic planetarium in Canada, was opened. No longer a planetarium, the building is now being used as office space. But since it is still intact, an effort is underway to have it declared an historic site.

1961

-The town of Beverly became part of Edmonton on December 31. A town on the city's northeast since 1913, Beverly was incorporated into the city after decades of failed attempts at growing its own economic base.

1962

-The first exhibition to be known as Klondike Days was held. Although the Edmonton Exhibition Association had already been running a summer fair, the new Klondike theme would prove to be sometimes controversial. It has become the city's single-largest tourist event, attracting hundreds of thousands of people each year and growing to include many off-site activities geared to the Klondike theme, such as the popular Sourdough Raft Race.

1963

-The town of Jasper Place was annexed by the city. Growth had led the town west of Edmonton to become simply another section of the city.

1964

-The Citadel Theatre was founded. The Citadel is Canada's largest theatre complex and has provided early career boosts to many world-famous actors.

1967

-The Provincial Museum of Alberta opened; now the largest multi-disciplinary museum in Western Canada.

1974

-Northlands Coliseum opened on November 10. Now named Skyreach Centre, it holds about 17,500 people in stadium seats and private boxes. Skyreach has a reputation as having the best ice surface of any National Hockey League arena, and staff are routinely consulted to solve other arenas' deficiencies.

1978

-The XI Commonwealth Games were held in Edmonton from August 3 to 12. The event, which was the biggest of its kind ever staged in Edmonton, featured competitors from 46 countries and relied on thousands of local volunteers for its success. As well as bringing Edmonton international television exposure, the games spurred the upgrade of some facilities and the construction of many others. Many athletic records and firsts were established at the games.
-The Light Rail Transit (LRT) system was opened on April 22. The line was the first of its kind in Canada. Originally 7.25 km (4.5 miles) with five stations, the LRT cost $65 million and took four years to build. The LRT has since expanded and has helped Edmonton successfully

bid for major events such as the 2001 World Track and Field Championship.

1980

-Artist Peter Lewis' *The Great Divide* waterfall was constructed on the High Level Bridge for Alberta's 75th anniversary. The waterfall is 7.3 metres (24 feet) higher than Niagara Falls and is the largest man-made waterfall in the world. It is operated on holidays and during some civic celebrations.

1981

-Phase One of West Edmonton Mall opened on September 16. The mall would become the city's top tourist attraction and, along with Wayne Gretzky, one of the two record-setters with which Edmonton would become identified. The mall has set many records, including being the largest shopping and entertainment complex in the world, and it is continuing to expand.

1982

-The first Edmonton Fringe Theatre Festival was founded. Designed to showcase offbeat or new talent in the city's live theatre scene, the festival stages plays in many venues in the Old Strathcona district. The event has become the biggest of its kind in North America, and only slightly smaller than the original fringe festival, held in Scotland.

1983

-Edmonton hosted the World University Games. It was the first of the amateur games events ever held in Canada.
-The Edmonton Convention Centre, a

unique building slotted into the bank of the North Saskatchewan River, opened on June 22. Despite massive cost overruns, much public controversy and a final price tag of $82 million, the centre has become a major tourist attraction and has brought millions of dollars in convention and tourism business to the city. Now known as the Shaw Conference Centre, the complex is the largest convention centre in Western Canada.

-Phase Two of West Edmonton Mall opened.

1986

-The Mindbender roller coaster at West Edmonton Mall crashed, killing three people. The ride was given extensive safety upgrades and has run trouble-free ever since.

-A violent labor dispute at Gainer's Meat Processing Company took place. With daily attacks on replacement workers and clashes between police and strikers, it was the most violent labour dispute in Western Canada since The Great Depression.

-The North Saskatchewan River flooded much of the river valley floor.

1987

-A massive tornado struck Edmonton on July 31, killing 27 people, injuring more than 300 others, and causing more than $300 million in damage. The event, which became known as Black Friday, remains the worst disaster in the city's history. The tornado left a trail of damage 40 km (25 miles) long, ripping through industrial and residential areas. The worst of the death and destruction came in the city's northeast, at the

Evergreen Trailer Park. Community efforts to help those still alive led to the founding of the Edmonton Emergency Relief Agency, which still coordinates aid for disaster victims.

1991

-After years of neglect, the historic Hotel Macdonald re-opened with a multi-million-dollar renovation. The interior

The Fringe Theatre Festival has become one of the leaders of Canada's cultural scene.
(Photo courtesy City of Edmonton Archives)

work won a national interior design award from the Ontario Interior Design Association. The hotel would also win the 1997 Hotel of the Year award from the Canadian Professional Sales Association, the 1995 Emerald Award for environmental awareness, and be given Mobil Travel Guide's four-star rating for quality seven years in a row. The hotel is the only one in Alberta, and one of only 13 in Canada, to get the rating, the highest which is ever given to Canadian hotels.

1993

-Edmonton's new city hall was opened. The building which combined new materials with salvaged materials from the old city hall won three awards: The Canadian Institute of Steel Construction's 1992 award for the most effective use of structural steel; the American Concrete Institute (Alberta Chapter) 1993 award for excellence in concrete design and construction; and the Urban Design Review Panel (Downtown Business Association) 1994

Some people scoffed at the idea of a waterfall in the prairies, but the spectacular sight has become a regular tourist draw. (Photo courtesy City of Edmonton Archives)

certificate of recognition for Outstanding Contribution to Urban Design.

1995

-Northlands Spectrum, a sports and entertainment facility, opened as an expansion of the existing horseracing complex.

1996

-Edmonton annexed the Namao armed forces base, making it one of the city's major employers.

-The 1996 World Figure Skating Championships were held in Edmonton, breaking attendance records.

1997

-The Winspear Centre for Music opened after years of planning. The major concert hall was made possible in part by a $6-million donation from namesake Francis Winspear. It remains the largest private arts donation ever in Canada.
-The Syncrude Gallery of Aboriginal Culture opened at the Provincial Museum of Alberta. It was the first gallery of its kind in Canada.

1998

-A group of businessmen from Edmonton and other Alberta communities purchased the Edmonton Oilers, which had been taken over by Alberta Treasury Branches from financially troubled owner Peter Pocklington. It was the first time the National Hockey League allowed a team to be owned by a group of community-based investors.
-The federal government realigned its armed forces bases, making Edmonton the main and largest land forces base in Western Canada. More than 1,200 soldiers were transferred to the city from Calgary and British Columbia.

1999

-Edmonton war veteran Cyril Martin was presented with the Legion of Honour, France's highest medal, for fighting in World War One. He is one of fewer than 100 Canadians to receive the honour. Martin was also presented with a certificate from Queen Elizabeth II and Canada's John McCrae Medallion.

Citation Winners

t accomplishments don't always bring great rewards. And despite the fact that great Edmontonian
uch as Francis Winspear (left) don't seek out fame and awards, they have been recognized regularly for
mplishments. Whether it be in sport, politics or community service, national and provincial bodies have
wn - and given recognition for - just how much the people of this city have sacrificed and
ed.

(Photo courtesy City of Edmonton Archives)

Citation Winners

Order of Canada
C.M. = Member
O.M. = Officer
C.C. = Companion
Date is for year named to Order.

Anne Anderson, C.M. 1991. Author of Cree language books and promoter of native culture.

Charles Anderson, C.M. 1996. Expert and preservationist of railways and music.

Margaret Andrekson, C.M. 1996. Community volunteer.

Violet Archer, C.M. 1983. Composer.

Tommy Banks, O.C. 1991. Composer, musician, actor.

Fred Bentley, O.C. 1994. Agricultural scientist.

James Bentley, O.C. 1967. President of the Canadian Federation of Agriculture.

Norbert Berkowitz, C.M. 1984. Energy sector scientist.

Gurcharan Singh Bhatia, C.M. 1997. Journalist and multicultural booster.

Marjorie Bowker, C.M. 1990. Law and social activism.

Wilbur Bowker, O.C. 1990. Law.

Anne Burrows, C.M. 1992. Music teacher, writer and advocate for the blind.

John Callaghan, O.C. 1985. Pioneering heart surgeon.

Ruth Carse, C.M. 1991. Founder of Alberta Ballet School.

Allan Collins, O.C. 1991. Public service.

Ron Collister, C.M. 1994. Journalist.

Herbert Coutts, C.M. 1974. Education.

Mary Davis, C.M. 1995. Seniors activist.

Louis Day, C.M. 1981. Fire chief, community service.

Laurence Decore, C.M. 1983. Former mayor, lawyer and multicultural booster.

Ivor Dent, C.M. 1983. Former mayor, professor.

Louis Desrochers, C.M. 1993. French culture and language activist.

Samuel Donaghey, C.M. 1981. Police officer, community sports activist.

Fred Dumont, C.M. 1985. Education and aboriginal activist.

James Edwards, C.M. 1982. Addictions activist.

Zane Feldman, C.M. 1992. Philanthropist, former president of Edmonton Oilers.

Robert Folinsbee, O.C. 1973. Geological scientist.

The Hon. Jean Beatrice Forest, O.C. 1987. Community service.

Zoie Gardner, C.M. 1997. Cared for physically and mentally disabled youth.

Pierre Gariepy, C.M. 1978. Handicapped activist.

Eric Geddes, C.M. 1989. Entrepreneur, philanthropist and community service.

Donald Getty, O.C. 1998. Former premier, Edmonton Eskimo player.

Helen Gibson, C.M. 1973. Community service.

James Gilbert, C.M. 1997. Medical education.

Cecil Goldstick, C.M. 1990. Athlete and children's charity activist.

Leslie Green, C.M. 1993. Legal scholar.

Harry Gunning, O.C. 1979. Scientist and educator.

Robert Hardy, O.C. 1974. Educator.

W.G. Hardy, C.M. 1973. Educator and writer.

Walter Harris, C.M. 1998. Chemistry researcher and teacher.

Helen Hays, C.M. 1986. Palliative care activist.

Bruce Hogle, C.M. 1998. Broadcaster and community service.

Peggy Holmes, C.M. 1989. Seniors activist and community service.

Mel Hurtig, O.C. 1980. Publisher.

Helen Huston, O.C. 1994. Medical missionary in Nepal.

Louis Hyndman, O.C. 1992. Public service.

The Right Rev. William Irwin, O.C. 1998. C.M. 1988. Social services activist.

Werner Israel, O.C. 1993. Theoretical physicist.

LCdr. The Rev. Canon Randall Ivany, C.M. 1985. Former Alberta and University of Alberta ombudsman.

Walter Johns, O.C. 1978. Former University of Alberta President.

R. Norman Jones, O.C. 1998. Molecular scientist.

Krishan Joshee, C.M. 1987. Community service.

Walter Kaasa, C.M. 1996. Public service and cultural booster.

Cyril Kay, C.M. 1995. Biochemist.

Robinson Koilpillai, C.M. 1996. Multicultural activist.

Henry Kreisel, O.C. 1987. Author and educator.

Ernie Kuyt, C.M. 1992. Wildlife biologist.

Raymond Lemieux, C.C. 1994. O.C. Chemistry scientist and professor.

Le reverende pere Joseph Levaque, C.M. 1987. Missionary and native services activist.

Mary Lobay, C.M. 1987. Community service.

Dr. Neil MacDonald FRCP (C), C.M. Cancer research and treatment.

Peter Macdonnell, C.M. 1979. Lawyer and businessman.

James MacGregor, C.M. 1973. Historian and author.

Walter MacKenzie, O.C. 1970. Dean of University of Alberta Faculty of Medicine.

Sandy Mactaggart, O.C. 1997. Businessman and philanthropist.

James Marsh, C.M. 1988. Editor-in-Chief of *The Canadian Encyclopedia*.

Sister Mary of the Annunciation, O.C. 1969. Community service.

Robert Matheson, C.M. 1989. Lawyer and community service.

Stanley McCuaig, C.M. 1972. Lawyer.

Arliss Miller, C.M. 1999. Community service.

The Hon. H.R. Milner, C.C. 1969. Lawyer, businessman, community service.

Roman Ostashewsky, C.M. 1979. Ukranian cutlural activist.

Charles Peacocke, C.M. 1995. Actor and professor.

H.J. Pearson, C.M. 1993. Community service.

Hugh Pearson, C.M. 1976. Broadcaster.

John Poole, O.C. 1996. Businessman, philanthropist.

John Primrose, C.M. 1985. World champion trap shooter.

Steven Ramsankar, C.M. 1983. Inner-city teacher and principal.

Bruce Rawson, O.C. 1990. Public service.

C. Neil Reimer, O.C. 1988. Labour organizer and politician.

G.R.A. Rice, C.M. 1984. Pioneering broadcaster.

Alan Ridge, C.M. 1985. Historical preservation.

The Hon. Douglas Roche, O.C. 1992. Public service.

Peter Savaryn, C.M. 1987. Ukrainian cultural activist.

Thelma Scambler, C.M. 1988. Public service and seniors activist.

Otto Schaefer, C.M. 1976. Medical research.

John Schlosser, C.M. 1983. Businessman and community service.

Joseph Shoctor, O.C. 1985. Founder of Citadel Theatre.

Frederick Sloane, C.M. 1982. Former Chief of Police, and community service.

Chief Robert Smallboy, C.M. 1979. Native community service.

Hank Smith, C.M. 1994. Country music entertainer.

Bernard Snell, C.M. 1996. Health care services, and community service.

Robert Steadward, O.C. 1999. Disabled sports administrator.

George Steer, O.C. 1971. Legal work.

Charles Stelck, O.C. 1996. Geology professor.

The Hon. William Stevenson, O.C. 1996. Lawyer.

Jake Superstein, C.M. 1986.

Business and community service.

The Rev. Father Anthony Sylla, O.C. 1971. Oblate missionary.

F. Elva Taylor, C.M. 1991. Nursing.

Nena Timperley, C.M. 1982. Community service.

Maxwell Ward, O.C. 1975. Aviator and businessman.

Donald Wilson, O.C. 1980. Medical research and treatment administrator.

Francis Winspear, O.C. 1967. Businessman, philanthropist.

Henry Wojcicki, C.M. 1989. Psychiatric care specialist and activist.

Margaret Zeidler, C.M. 1994. Businesswoman and community service.

Canadian Sports Hall of Fame

Kurt Browning - 1994. Figure skating.

Matt Baldwin - 1973. Curling.

Norm Kwong - 1975. Football.

Susan Nattrass - 1977. Shooting.

J. Percy Page - 1955. Basketball.

Jackie Parker - 1987. Football.

Karen Percy - 1994. Skiing.

John Primrose - 1977. Shooting.

Graham Smith - 1986. Swimming.

Alberta Sports Hall of Fame

Individuals

Kurt Browning - 1992. Figure skating.

Alexander Keith - 1986. Golf.

Matt Baldwin - 1980. Curling.

Elsie Barlow - 1966. Softball, Speed Skating.

Pamela Barnard - 1978. Table tennis (disabled).

Gordon Bertie - 1987. Wrestling.

Doug Bovee - 1976. Wheelchair sports.

Nancy Brawley - 1985. Diving.

Johnny Bright - 1980. Football.

Max Ward was one of the city's aviation pioneers.
(Photo courtesy City of Edmonton Archives)

Edward Brooke - 1986. Fencing.
James "Buster" Brown - 1980. Track and field.
Johnny Bucyk - 1996. Hockey.
Hugh Campbell - 1997. Football.
Elizabeth Carruthers - 1974. Diving.
Betty Stanhope Cole - 1980. Golf, curling.
Neil Colville - 1980. Hockey.
H. "Boots" Cooper - 1987. Wheelchair sports.
June Causgrove Cox - 1984. Multisport.
C.M. Sam Donaghey - 1999. Soccer.
Clare Drake - 1980. Hockey.
John Eugene Ducey - 1980. Baseball.
Dianne Crowe Earl - 1976. Track & Field.
Elaine Ell - 1976. Wheelchair sports.
M.E. Eurchuk - 1985. Wrestling.
Jim Flemming - 1987. Soccer.
John Gattens - 1980. Multisport.
Hector Gervais - 1991. Curling.
Cheryl Gibson - 1986. Swimming.
Charles Graham - 1970. Boxing.
Wilf Greaves - 1958. Boxing.
Gail Greenough - 1994. Equestrian.
Susan Halak - 1978. Swimming.
Leroy Haliburton - 1960. Track and field.
William Hardy - 1989. Hockey.
Ron Hayter - 1978. Boxing, baseball.
Fran Heath - 1995. Synchronized swimming.
Arnold Henderson - 1988. Basketball.
Cameron Henning - 1994. Swimming.
Clare Hollingsworth - 1976. Multisport.
Paul Hortie - 1991. Boxing.
Bill Hunter - 1988. Hockey.
Hazel Jamison - 1980. Golf, Curling.
Jesse Jones - 1980. Track and field.
Bill Kasting - 1976. Cycling, speedskating.

John Primrose has won many shooting championships over his long and distinguished career. (Photo courtesy City of Edmonton Archives)

Normie Kwong - 1980. Football.
Albert Lawrence - 1959. Track and field.
Juanita Lawrence - 1959. Track and field.
Moses Lieberman - 1980. Football.
Pierre Lueders - 1999. Bobsleigh.
Clifford Manahan - 1966. Curling.
Bill Manson - 1978. Wrestling.
Henry Martell - 1968. Golfing.
Bill McGrandle - 1990. Boxing.
Gary McPherson - 1993. Wheelchair sports.
Elmer "Rollie" Miles - 1980. Football.
Ron Minor - 1980. Wheelchair sports.
Frank Morris - 1994. Football.
Susan Nattrass - 1980. Shooting.
Les William Nelson - 1995. Swimming.
Helen Nicol - 1996. Multisport.

L.E. "Bud" Olson - 1982. Curling.
J. Percy Page - 1966. Basketball.
Miles Palmer - 1983. Football, boxing.
Jackie Parker - 1980. Football.
Jim Parsons - 1978. Boxing.
Bill Patrick - 1968. Diving.
Arthur Potter - 1968. Hockey.
Bill Price - 1986. Multisport.
John Primrose - 1974. Shooting.
Andrew Purcell - 1983. Tennis, hockey.
William Rankin - 1966. Boxing, football.
Lauritze Rasmussen - 1978. Softball.
Winnie Reid - 1989. Multisport.
John Reilly - 1968. Multisport.
Harold "Hal" Richard - 1987. Multisport.
Alex Romaniuk - 1974. Wrestling.
Gail Ross - 1982. Equestrian.
Jean Ross - 1968. Synchronized swimming.
Doreen Ryan - 1974. Speedskating.
Jim Ryan - 1983. Baseball.
Earl Samis - 1966. Multisport.
Glen Sather - 1996. Hockey.
Dianne Sharkey - 1976. Swimming (disabled).
Tom Sharkey - 1978. Swimming (disabled).
Eddy Shaske - 1990. Trapshooting.
Ross Sheppard - 1966. Track and field.
Arthur Skitch - 1961. Multisport.
Charlie Smallface - 1974. Boxing.
George Smith - 1976. Swimming.
Graham Smith - 1978. Swimming.
Gwen Smith - 1988. Swimming.
Johnny Smith - 1960. Boxing.
Rebecca "Becky" Smith - 1974. Swimming.
Sandra Smith - 1978. Swimming.
William "Don" Smith - 1974. Swimming.
Don Sprague - 1998. Multisport.

Robert Steadward - 1984. Wheelchair sports.
M.L. "Maury" Van Vliet - 1980. Multisport.
Francis Wetterberg - 1982. Fencing.
William "Deacon" White - 1990. Multisport.
Tom Wilkinson - 1996. Football.
Gerrald Williams - 1970. Boxing.
Ed Zemrau - 1976. University sports.
Ernest Zurch Jr. - 1960. Boxing.
Ernest Zurch Sr. - 1960. Boxing.
Frank Richard - 1961. Track and field.

Teams

1952 Edmonton Waterloo Mercurys Hockey Team - Inducted 1968:
George Abel, Jack Davies, Bill Dawe, Bruce Dickson, Monty Ford, Don Gauf, Bill Gibson, Ralph Harsch, Lou Holmes, Bob Myers, Dave Miller, Tom Pollock, Al Purvis, Gordon Robertson, Loz Secco, Frank Sullivan and Bob Watt.

1915-1940 Edmonton Grads Basketball Team - Inducted 1974:
Daisy Johnson, Nellie Perry, Eleanor Mountifield, Dorothy Johnson, Winnie Martin, Connie Smith, Abbie Scott, Elizabeth Elrick, Mary Dunn, Margaret Kinney, Elsie Bennie, Gladys Fry, Mildred McCormick, Doris Neale, Mae Brown, Margaret MacBurney, Babe Belanger, Helen Stone, Noel McDonald, Edith Stone, Mabel Munton, Evelyn Caulson, Jessie Innis, Helen McIntosh, Frances Gorden, Winnie Gallen, Betty Ross, Etta Dann, Helen Nothrup, Sophie Brown, Babe Daniel, Jean Williamson, Kay MacRitchie, Betty Bawden, Hattie Hopkins, Kate MacCrae, Marguerite

Bailey and Joan Johnstone.

Pat Ryan Curling Team - Inducted 1999: Pat Ryan (skip), Randy Ferby (third), Don Walchuk (second) and Don McKenzie (first).

1978-1982 Edmonton Eskimo Football Teams - Inducted 1997:
Robert Barber, Leo Blanchard, Nereo Bolzon, David Boone, Brian Broomell, Ian Bryant, Buck Buckanesky, Danny Briggs, Maurice Burton, Gregg Butler, Hugh Campbell, Rod Connop, Dave Cutler, Marco Cyncar, Dan Daniel, Mark deBrueys, Dennis Dickan, Ralph Dixon, Harry Doering, Ron Estay, Joe Faragalli, John Farlinger, Dave Fennell, Emilio Fraietta, Brian Fryer, Gene Gaines, Jim Germany, Danny Grant, Gary Hayes, York Hentschel, Larry Highbaugh, Joe Holliman, Bob Howes, Hank Ilesic, Ed Jones, Dan Kearns, Sean Kehoe, Brian Kelly, Danny Kepley, Stuart Kinio, John Konihowski, Stuart Lang, Pete Lavorato, Bruce Lemmerman, Mike Levenseller, Ken Lowe, Neil Lumsden, Craig Maflender, Bill Manchuk, Dwayne Mandrusiak, Greg Marshall, Willie Martin, Don Matthews, George McGowan, Mike McLeod, Jack McMahon, Ted Milian, Quincy Moffat, Warren Moon, Cal Murphy, Cliff Olander, James Parker, Mike Paush, John Pointer, Tom Towns, Hector Pothier, Dale Potter, Ernest Pough, Angelo Santucci, Tom Scott, Randy Simmrin, Waddell Smith, Bill Stevenson, Tom Towns, Charlie Turner, Tom Tuinei, Eric Upton, Mark Wald, Jim Walker, Ken Walser, Harry Walkers, Don Warrington, Larry Washington, Hank

Williams, Mike Williams, Wendell Williams, Dan Yochum, Dave Zacharko.

The Bell Memorial Award
Given annually to sports reporters, by the Alberta Sports Hall of Fame.
1975 - **Cecil "Tiger" Goldstick**. CFRN.
1976 - **Don Fleming**. The Edmonton Journal.
1977 - **Ernie Afaganis**. CBXT.
1985 - **Marty Knack**. The Edmonton Journal.
1987 - **Guy Coermier**. CBXFT.
1988 - **John Short**. The Edmonton Journal.
1991 - **Lisa Miller**. CFRN.
1993 - **Al McCann** - CFRN.

Ernie Afaganis has had a stellar career in sports broadcasting, including winning an ACTRA award.
(Photo courtesy Ernie Afaganis)

The Top 100

Edmonton is the City of Champions because of many people. Not only has the city produced many championship winners such as athletes and artists, it has been built into the strong and proud metropolis of today by many others with that same championship spirit. This list is not only of the award winners, but of the people who made all of Edmonton's accomplishments possible. These are the people who started award-winning traditions and events, who took Edmonton's winning attitude to accomplishments in other cities, and who inspired others to become winners.

The names and order were not chosen by the publishers, but were nominated and ranked by a panel of local business, history, civic and arts officials. This list is meant to recognize the importance of each of their respective contributions, and as a tribute to each of them. These 100 trailblazers represent the best of the many people who have made Edmonton the winning city it is today.

1 Wayne Gretzky

Generally regarded as the best hockey player of all time, Gretzky (right) is the holder of many records. Many of his records were achieved while he played for the Edmonton Oilers, while his career records were largely made up of his play in Edmonton. Gretzky is also remembered in Edmonton as the man who boosted the city's profile around the world. During his playing years in Edmonton, he was active in local affairs and acted as an unofficial ambassador for the city. His trade to Los Angeles sent the city into mourning. Edmontonians later had a statue of Gretzky erected in front of Skyreach Centre. More than a decade after he left, he is still what most non-residents think of when asked what they know about Edmonton. After his retirement, the city honoured Gretzky by giving the name Wayne Gretzky Drive to the freeway leading to the NHL arena Skyreach Centre.

Photo by Tom Braid, courtesy The Edmonton Sun.

2 The Ghermezians

This somewhat reclusive family of immigrants is best-known for building the world-renown West Edmonton Mall, which continues to be a world-record setter many years after it first caught the world's attention. Father Jacob, sons Eskandar, Raphael, Bahman and Nader (the most visible member of the family) brought Edmonton a profile and a sense of grandeur not seen before or since. Along with Gretzky, West Edmonton Mall's shopping and entertainment attraction is what most people think of when they hear the name 'Edmonton.'

3 Joe Shoctor

A lawyer and businessman, Shoctor is generally acknowledged as the father of Edmonton's Citadel Theatre - Canada's largest theatre complex. The main auditorium is named in his honor. Shoctor (right) is an active philanthropist, and has been involved in such winning enterprises as the Edmonton Eskimos, and the Edmonton Downtown Development Corporation. He was named to Order of Canada in 1978. He was also given the State of Israel Prime Minister's Medal.

Photo courtesy Citadel Theatre.

4 Frank Oliver

Oliver's power at the turn of the century was most felt through his political positions and connections. He was the first member from Alberta elected to the House of Commons. Oliver (left) spent 34 years as a parliamentarian, including time as Minister of the Interior, succeeding in having the Canadian Pacific Railway built through Edmonton, the naming of Edmonton as capital of Alberta, and Strathcona becoming home of the province's first university. He co-founded *The Edmonton Bulletin* with Alex Taylor.

Photo courtesy City of Edmonton Archives.

5 The Hole Family

Long a fixture on the Edmonton scene, the Hole family is most often recognized for its greenhouse business in St. Albert. Lois Hole (left) was named a Member of the Order of Canada in 1999, and is a best-selling author and chancellor of the University of Alberta. Her brother-in-law Jim Hole, best known for his work at the family's mechanical engineering firm Lockerbie and Hole, is one of the leading owners of the Edmonton Oilers. Henry Hole began the engineering business, and five of his nine children with wife Annie, became involved in the business. All nine children graduated from the university. Sons Ralph, Bob, Harry and Jim were all known for their philanthropic work as well as business, including helping to establish the Citadel Theatre, and setting up the Annie Hole Nutrition Fund for inner-city school food programs.

Photo courtesy Hole's.

6 Emily Murphy

One of the Famous Five, in 1916 Murphy (right) became the first woman police magistrate in the British Empire. She and four others successfully challenged the law (all the way to the British Privy Council) which didn't recognize women as persons. It was changed in 1929. Today, one of the city's leading river valley parks is named in her honour.

Photo courtesy City of Edmonton Archives.

7 Alex Taylor

Much of modern-day Edmonton was built on the foundation created by Alex Taylor (left), one of Alberta's pioneer farmers. He arrived in Edmonton in 1877, bringing the first telegraph to the city. He brought the first printing press to come to Edmonton, and with Frank Oliver founded the city's first newspaper, *The Edmonton Bulletin* (he later sold Oliver his share of the business). Taylor was also Edmonton's first weatherman, recording temperature and rainfall. Taylor is likely best known as the founder of the city's telephone system, which he set up in 1884 and operated for 18 years. He and his wife established the Edmonton Electric Light Company. His utilities businesses would eventually be bought by the city. He was the first school trustee to have a school named after him while serving on the board.

Photo courtesy City of Edmonton Archives.

8 Dr. G.R.A. Rice

Born in England in 1901, Dr. Rice became a broadcasting pioneer in Canada after he moved to Edmonton. Dr. Rice received many awards in his lifetime, including being named a Member of the Order of Canada in 1984. Rice also was inducted into the Canadian Broadcast Hall of Fame the same year. In 1922, he helped to found northern Alberta's first radio station, CJCA, and founded (with Hans Nielsen), CFRN radio. That station was the first in Western Canada to be granted an FM licence, in 1947. CFRN television followed in 1954, and in 1956 was the most powerful station of its kind in North America. Dr. Rice sold CFRN-TV in 1987 and retired.

9 John Rowand

John Rowand was the Hudson's Bay Company Chief Factor of Fort Edmonton and set the area's first business record. In the 1840s, the company's governor had all but decided to shut down the trading post and base the region's activity north or west (possibly Athabasca or Rocky Mountain House). Rowand challenged the company that Fort Edmonton was the more efficient location, and set a record for shipping goods, successfully persuading the company to leave Fort Edmonton where it was.

10 Peter Pocklington

Photo courtesy Ross Ongaro.

Edmonton's modern history would not be the same without Peter Pocklington's contributions. Alternately hailed and reviled by Edmontonians, Pocklington's (right) greatest achievements came as owner of the championship-winning Oilers, Trappers and Drillers sports teams.

11 J. Percy Page

Photo courtesy City of Edmonton Archives.

Page is best known for his many years as coach of the Edmonton Grads - the city's most successful sports team. The team won four Olympic titles, every national championship and all but one provincial title for which they competed in 25 years. After the team disbanded in 1940, Page (left) went on to a successful political career, winning seats in the provincial Legislature in 1940 and 1952. He was Alberta's Lt. Governor from 1959 to 1966.

12 Dr. Francis Winspear

Dr. Winspear came to Edmonton in 1928, and with his partners founded or operated more than 40 companies. Winspear was one of Edmonton's leading philanthropists, donating $6 million to the University of Alberta, and $6 million to build the world-class concert hall which bears his name (the largest private donation in Canada to an arts project). A vigilant champion of the arts, Winspear was the founder of the Edmonton Symphony Orchestra and the Edmonton Opera. Even after his death in 1997, his Winspear Foundation has continued his tradition of supporting benevolent, educational and artistic causes. Winspear is a Member of the Order of Canada.

13 Wilfrid 'Wop' May

Photo courtesy City of Edmonton Archives.

May is probably the best-known of the many bush pilots who flew out of Blatchford Field (now Edmonton City Centre Airport) in the first half of this century. May (right) had his most notable achievement in 1929, when he and fellow pilot Vic Horner risked their lives by flying an open-air aircraft 1,125 km (700 miles) in sub-zero cold to deliver desperately needed diptheria serum to Fort Vermillion. News of the mercy flight galvanized the city, with thousands greeting the men on their return. In 1935, he was made a Member of the Order of the British Empire.

14 Nellie McClung

McClung was part of the Famous Five group of women's-rights advocates who successfully fought for women to be recognized as persons under British Law. Among her decades of other achievements, McClung was also the first woman appointed to the Canadian Broadcasting Corporation's Board of Governors, in 1936. McClung is seen here (right) with her husband Wes.

Photo courtesy City of Edmonton Archives.

15 John Fry

Fry was Edmonton's longest-serving mayor, spending eight consecutive years as the city's top elected official. But it wasn't an easy term, since much of his time in office came during The Great Depression and World War Two. In keeping with the needs of the day, Fry was known as a constant fighter for Edmonton's interests, travelling often to Ottawa to push the city's needs. During the war, he helped to raise money and supplies for the war effort by helping to collect pots and pans to melt down and build military equipment. One of his daughters was a captain of the Edmonton Grads basketball team.

16 C.H. 'Punch' Dickens

Edmonton's leading pilot in the early days of flight, Dickens earned the Distinguished Flying Cross in World War One. He was the first pilot to fly into Edmonton's Blatchford Field, flew the first airmail plane on the prairies circuit (1929), was the first to fly over all of the Mackenzie River, and the first to fly across the barren lands. Dickens (right) was named to the Order of the British Empire, the Order of Canada, and was the first person inducted into Canada's Aviation Hall of Fame. He died in 1995.

Photo courtesy City of Edmonton Archives.

17 Tommy Banks

A musician and all-around entertainer, Banks has received numerous awards. In 1991 he was named Officer of the Order of Canada, and was made a member of the Alberta Order of Excellence in 1993. He nurtured the careers of many award-winning musicians, such as David Foster, and won a Juno award and received the Grand prix de Disque in 1979. He is also known for his landmark Tommy Banks Show. Banks was the winner of a Gemini Award in 1990 for best television variety show award, for a performance with k.d. lang during the Canadian Country Music Awards. Banks was honoured by the city in 1999 when a street outside the Yardbird Suite jazz club was renamed Tommy Banks Way.

18 John Walter

Walter was one of the town's leading businessmen in the late 1800s, creating innovative enterprises. Walter (right) established the first cable ferry service across the North Saskatchewan River at the foot of McDougall Hill in 1882. His home was the first telegraph office in the area. One of the city's first millionaires, he would build a succession of three larger homes (now designated as historical sites), reflecting his wealth and influence.

Photo courtesy City of Edmonton Archives.

19 John Ducey

Known for much of his life as Edmonton's 'Mr. Baseball,' Ducey (left) was a tireless supporter of the game. His time promoting and taking part led to his becoming one of the first six people inducted into the Canadian Baseball Hall of Fame. Aside from his performance as both a player and umpire, Ducey is remembered as the man most responsible for his long service in organizing and running the city's leading teams. After Edmonton became the home of a Triple-A team (a long-time dream of Ducey's), the Renfrew Park baseball field where he had spent so much of his life was renamed John Ducey Park in 1984. The facility has been greatly expanded and renovated, and re-christened Telus Field (over the objections of Ducey supporters), but a bronze bust of Ducey stands in the park, and the street outside was re-named John Ducey Way in his honour.

Photo courtesy City of Edmonton Archives.

20 Douglas Cardinal

An internationally famous architect, Cardinal has literally helped to change the look of modern Edmonton. As the designer of such award-winning landmarks as the Edmonton Space Science Centre and St. Albert Place, Cardinal built a reputation for cutting-edge, award-winning designs that blended with the natural world and his Metis cultural background. His best-known projects include the new Canadian Museum of Civilization in Hull, Quebec.

21 Hugh Campbell

After a playing career in Saskatchewan, the longtime Edmonton Eskimos coach and manager was the architect of the team during its most successful period. As head coach, Campbell (right) led the Eskimos to five consecutive Grey Cups, from 1977 to 1982.

Photo courtesy City of Edmonton Archives.

22 William Hawrelak

Edmonton's most colourful and longest-serving mayor since World War Two, Hawrelak presided over the city during its first major boom. He was first elected mayor in 1951, just after the Leduc oil discovery. During his first period in office (which lasted eight years), Hawrelak was a key player in Edmonton growth. An extremely popular mayor, he resigned after the 1959 Porter Inquiry found conflicts of interest between his business and civic affairs. Hawrelak was re-elected in 1963, but again had to resign under a cloud (he would eventually be exonerated in the 1965 SunAlta land scandal). Returning for a third term in 1974, Hawrelak died while in office in 1975. The city's major river valley park is named in his honour.

23 Angela Cheng

Edmonton's world-class Kiwanis Music Festival was the jumping-off point for classical pianist Cheng (right), who has won many international awards. She has won the Montreal International Piano Competition, the Medal of Excellence from the Mozarteum in Salzberg, Austria, and the Gold medal at the Arthur Rubenstein International Competition.

Photo by Michal Schmidt, Artists International, courtesy of The Dr. Anne Burrows Foundation.

24 Ernest Manning

Manning (right) was Canada's second-longest serving premier, running Alberta from 1943 to 1968. He served 46 years in office as MLA, premier, & senator. He helped William Aberhart found the Social Credit Party and was instrumental in rebuilding the province (and especially Edmonton) after The Great Depression.

25 Bill Comrie

Comrie is the founder of The Brick, the Edmonton-based chain that is the largest dollar-volume furniture retailer in Canada. Comrie has also been a leader in sporting events and organizations. The soccer team Brickmen took its name from the sponsor business, and the Brick Annual Super Novice Hockey Tournament is organized by the business. Comrie has also been an owner of the CFL's B.C. Lions.

26 Sandy Mactaggert

An entrepreneur and philanthropist, McTaggert has been named to both the Order of Canada and the Alberta Order of Excellence. In 1995, McTaggert won the prestigious Award for Distinguished Service to Education from the International Education Council in the United States - only the second Canadian recipient in 40 years. He was also inducted into the Junior Achievement of Northern Alberta's Hall of Fame in 1986.

27 Dr. Charles Allard

Allard had success in more than one field, as one of the city's top surgeons (he was Chief of Surgery for 25 years at Edmonton General Hospital), businessmen and entertainment entrepreneurs. He was instrumental in bringing the Edmonton Oilers to the city, including helping to finance the team in 1976. Likely his best-known accomplishment was the founding of CITV television station (the first independent television station in Western Canada), along with its siblings Superchannel, Allarcom studios, CKRB, and Studio Post & Transfer. The entertainment empire has produced many award-winning movies and television series, including SCTV.

28 Alex Mair

One of Edmonton's leading historical writers and a long-time journalist, Mair founded the groundbreaking Radio and Television Arts program at the Northern Alberta Institute of Technology - one of the first of its kind in Western Canada.

29 Jackie Parker

An Edmonton sports legend, this Eskimos player and coach is enshrined in both the CFL Hall of Fame and the Canadian Sports Halls of Fame. He is a three-time winner of the Schenley Award for being the most outstanding football player in Canada (1957, 1958 and 1960), and seven times was named the Western Divisions' most valuable player. As running back he helped the Eskimos to win three Grey Cups in a row (1954-56).

30 Matt McCauley

Elected as the first mayor of the Town of Edmonton in 1892, McCauley ran Edmonton's first cartage company and livery barn, and its first butcher shop. He was the first chairman of the board of trustees for the Edmonton Public School Board and helped introduce free education. From 1895 to 1902, he was a member of the North West Territory Assembly. One of his more dubious achievements came when he led a vigilante group that drove out squatters. The group accomplished the task by pushing the squatters' homes over the top of the river valley bank.

31 **Don Stanley**

The son of local hockey hero Russell 'Barney' Stanley, he played centre for the Waterloo Mercurys hockey team that won the world championship in 1950. In 1954, he formed Stanley Associates Engineering Ltd. Stanley Engineering has grown to become one of the top engineering companies in the world. He was named to the Alberta Order of Excellence as a leader in the field of engineering, and for his community, athletic, and professional endeavors.

32 **Gabby Haas**

This longtime radio broadcaster and musician is Canada's Polka King. Haas set the Guinness World record for longest running radio show. The Continental Musicale Show on CKUA began in 1946. He has also been making records for close to 40 years, and spent 35 years on TV. In 1987, the Alberta Recording Association gave him the Lifetime Achievement Award.

33 **The Muttart Family**

Gladys Muttart (right), who passed away in 1969, was president of the Canadian Diabetes Association. She helped establish 24 diabetes research branches across Canada and has donated money through the Muttart Foundation to diabetes research. Merrill Muttart (left) was one of the most successful businessmen in Edmonton, pioneering the use of prefabricated houses and drywall construction in Canada. The river valley's spectacular Muttart Botanical Conservatory is named in their honour.

Photos courtesy City of Edmonton Archives.

34 **Max Ward**

Ward carried Edmonton's tradition of aviation pioneering into the last half the century, and for decades was Canada's best-known aviator and executive. Ward founded his namesake Wardair airline in 1953. The airline won major awards for service, and operated for 36 years. He received many awards and in 1991 was inducted into Alberta Business Hall of Fame.

35 **Robinson Koipillai**

Koipillai isn't one of Edmonton's better-known community members, but his effect on modern-day life in the city has been felt by many. A longtime promoter of multiculturalism & racial harmony, he has won many awards: the Alberta Achievement Award, Man of the Year Award from the Federal Minister of Multiculturalism, and the Canada Council's National Award for Outstanding Educator. In 1996, he was named to the Order of Canada.

36 **Clarence 'Big' Miller**

This U.S.-born blues singer and trombonist was one of the world's foremost blues and big band musicians, playing with such artists as Duke Ellington and Count Basie. Coming to Canada in part to avoid racial conflict, Miller (right) came to Edmonton in 1970 and in 1979 won a Juno award. His most lasting contribution to Edmonton was helping to found the Jazz City Festival in 1981.

Photo courtesy Stony Plain Recording Company.

37 John and Barbara Poole

Named to the Edmonton Cultural Hall of Fame, the Pooles have worked to promote such award-winning organizations as the Provincial Museum of Alberta, Edmonton Art Gallery, Citadel Theatre, Edmonton Symphony Orchestra, Edmonton Opera, Alberta Ballet and the City Archives.

38 Holger Petersen

This musician and broadcaster is the owner of the award-winning Stony Plain Records, the largest and oldest independent record firm in Canada. The company has won eight Juno awards, many Canadian Country Music Association awards, and has produced several gold records. Petersen's (right) contributions to music were recognized in 1992 with five awards from the Alberta Recording Industry Association. He records and manages such award-winning musicians as blues guitarist Amos Garrett, Canadian music legend Ian Tyson, and Prairie Oyster.

Photo courtesy Stony Plain Recording Company.

39 Arthur Hiller

Edmonton's most successful arts export, Hiller is a movie director, and was president of the Academy of Motion Picture Arts and Sciences for many years, and president of the Director's Guild of America for four years. Born and raised in Edmonton, he went on to direct more than 30 feature films. After being invited to Hollywood, he directed such award-winning shows as *Matinee Theatre*, *Gunsmoke* and *Alfred Hitchcock Presents*. Many of his films have won awards, such as *The Out-of-Towners*, *Hospital*, *Love Story* (for which he won a Golden Globe as Best Director), *The Americanization of Emily*, and *Silver Streak*.

40 William F. 'Deacon' White

Generally acknowledged as the founder of modern sport in Edmonton, White (left) was an American baseball player who moved to Edmonton in 1906. It was White who came up with the team name Edmonton Eskimos for his 1909 baseball team, after Calgary sports writers mocked the colder northern weather and called the people of the capital 'Eskimeaux.' White is a member of the Edmonton Sports Hall of Fame. The name was later adopted by White's football team.

Photo courtesy City of Edmonton Archives.

41 Stanley Milner

Alderman and oil industry pioneer, Milner founded Chieftain International. He has also served as a director at leading Edmonton-based corporations. Milner was the main force behind the construction of the downtown library in 1967, which was named in his honour. In 1987 he was named the Canadian Business Leader of the Year by the University of Alberta Business Faculty.

42 Gerry Wright

Sometimes referred to as the father of the award-winning Old Strathcona, he was also instrumental in the creation of the world-class Fringe Theatre Festival and the farmer's market in the old Strathcona bus barn. He also played an important part in building the LRT mass-transit line, the first of its kind in Canada.

43 Heather Airth

Airth was one of many who organized relief efforts after the Black Friday tornado of 1987. That grew in to the establishment of the Edmonton Emergency Relief Agency, the first private emergency-relief agency in Canada. Now helping countless people affected by disasters such as fire and flooding, it is one of the largest such agencies in the country.

44 Glen Sather

An Edmonton hockey legend, Sather was coach and is now general manager of the Stanley Cup-winning Edmonton Oilers. Sometimes called the best deal-maker in hockey and acknowledged as the architect of the championship Oilers teams of the 1980s and 1990s, Sather was also a player on the Memorial Cup-winning Edmonton Oil Kings hockey club of the mid-1960s.

45 Jim Edwards

One of the city's first broadcasters - with CFRN radio - Edwards turned to politics, won multiple elections and was arguably the city's most influential M.P. during Conservative governments of the 1980s. He is now president and C.E.O. of Economic Development Edmonton.

46 Father Lacombe

Lacombe was a mediator between government and Indians. He founded the first church in Alberta, in 1861, and established several missions. He opened the first Indian Industrial School of Alberta (in 1884), helped build the first bridge in the West, and built an orphanage, school, and hospital. He is honoured with a statue in St. Albert.

47 John Michaels

Michaels (right) was a prominent businessman and a community booster. He is known for starting the Edmonton Newsboys' Band early in the century, as a way of combating juvenile delinquency. The band, made up entirely of newspaper delivery boys, would be hailed as the finest boys band in Canada. It was the only one in Canada selected to play in the 1924 British Imperial Exposition.

Photo courtesy City of Edmonton Archives.

48 Clare Drake

Often called the greatest coach in college hockey history, he was the University of Alberta Golden Bears coach for 28 years. As a coach he won six national championships and 16 Canada West Titles. In total, Drake (below-left) coached 1,030 games, and ended with a winning record of .695. He also coached university football in 1962, 1967, & 1968, with a record of 23 wins and four losses, including a CIAU championship in 1967, becoming the only coach in CIAU history to win national championships in two major sports. In international hockey, Drake was coach of the Canadian Olympic team at the 1980 Olympic Winter Games. Drake coached the Canadian student National team to the gold medal at the 1981 World Student Games, a gold medal at the Pacific Rim Tournament in Japan in both the 1977/78 and 1978/79 series, and in 1985 coached Team Canada to a gold medal in hockey's Spengler Cup. Internationally, he coached 160 games and finished with a

Photo courtesy University of Alberta.

winning percentange of .700. When he retired from the Bears, he had won more games as coach than anyone else in North American intercollegiate hockey. Drake's success led to his being named Coach of the Year by the CIAU (1974/75 and 1987/88), and by the CWUAA three times (1984/85, 1986/87 and 1987/88). He also coached the WHA Oilers during the 1975-76 season. Drake has been honored in many ways: The University Arena was renamed the Clare Drake Arena, he was inducted into the Alberta Sports Hall of Fame in 1980, to the University of Alberta's Wall of Fame in 1987, and to the Canadian Sports Hall of Fame in 1989. Mentor-coach for the Canadian National Women's Hockey Team since 1995, Drake has led them to the Pacific Rim Gold Medal in 1995, the 3 Nations Cup Gold Medal in 1996, and the world championship in 1997. Drake was also the player personnel scout and evaluator for the Canadian National Mens Team which won the world championship in 1997.

49 Alex Decoteau
Decoteau was Canada's first Native police officer, joining the Edmonton city force in 1911. An outstanding athlete, Decoteau was an Olympic-class middle-distance runner (the only Albertan to compete in the 1912 games), and set many records during his sporting career. He was killed in action during World War One.

50 Norm Kimball
Although football is a team sport, the modern success of the championship-winning Edmonton Eskimos could be greatly attributed to Kimball, who organized and ran the club to the point where it had the best win/loss record in the league during the 1970s. He led the team to six Grey Cup victories.

51 Ron Hayter
One of the longest-serving city council members (1971-1995), Hayter has been active in sports in Edmonton as a player, coach and promoter. Hayter was founding director of the 1978 Commonwealth Games. He has served on the Edmonton Boxing and Wrestling Commission, and played a key role in bringing world championship baseball events to the city. Hayter has won the Vanier Award for Outstanding Young Canadian (1975), the Certificate of Merit from the Canadian Federation of Amateur Baseball, and awards from the International Baseball Association and the Canadian Professional Boxing Federation (where he has served nine terms as president over the past 30 years). He is a member of the Alberta, Canada and Nicaragua sports halls of fame (for his work with the group which pushed for baseball being accepted as an Olympic sport).

52 Bessie Nichols

Photo courtesy City of Edmonton Archives.

Nichols (right) was the first woman to run for - and win - an election in Alberta. In 1912, she became a school trustee, winning the second-highest number of votes among the seven winning candidates.

53 Meyer Horowitz
Horowitz, who arrived at the University of Alberta from McGill (in Montreal) in 1969, has heavily influenced civic life in Edmonton. His efforts at promoting education were recognized with his winning the George Croskery Memorial Award for merit in education (the highest award from the Canadian College of Teachers). He was only the second Albertan to receive the honour. The Meyer Horowitz Theatre in The Citadel complex is named in his honour. He was named an Officer of the Order of Canada in 1991.

54 Henry 'Gizmo' Williams
This longtime Edmonton Eskimo football player is one of the most popular athletes in the city's history. His famous dedication and and drive have led to his holding the record for punt returns. He's even had more punt-return touchdowns called back because of teammates' penalties than anyone else has had in total. Williams is also known and respected for his longtime community activism, including speaking out regularly on children's issues.

55 Bill Smith

The current mayor of Edmonton, Smith played defensive halfback for the Eskimos from 1956 to 1963, and was named to the All Star Team in 1960. Best known for his tireless work championing and promoting the city in Canada and abroad, Smith is the first mayor in recent history to lead the city without first sitting as a council member.

56 Brian Paisley

Paisley (right) founded the Edmonton Fringe Theatre Festival in 1982. The Fringe is the biggest alternative theatre festival in North America. He also founded Chinook Theatre (now called Fringe Theatre Adventures), which is aimed at young audiences and is arguably the most successful touring company of its kind on the Prairies.

Photo courtesy Fringe Theatre Adventures.

57 Bill Hunter

The colourful former newspaperman was the first general manager of Edmonton Oilers, having been largely responsible for bringing the team into existence as a World Hockey Association francise. He was instrumental in building the Edmonton Coliseum (now Skyreach Centre).

58 Justice Tevie & Arliss Miller

This prominent couple steered many of the city's notable and award-winning organizations. Court of Queen's Bench Justice Tevie Miller was Chancellor of the University of Alberta, president of the Edmonton Symphony, chairman of the Alberta Award for Excellence, president of the Edmonton Bar Association, and president of the Edmonton Jewish Community Council. Arliss is active in the community, serving on civic and national boards. She was named to the Order of Canada in 1999. Tevie and Alriss Miller (left) were jointly honoured with the prestigious Torch of Learning Award from the Hebrew University of Jerusalem.

Photo courtesy Lisa and Arliss Miller.

59 Paul Kane

Kane is recognized as Canada's most famous early artist/explorer. His paintings of the life of Native peoples in the late 1800s, before the influx of Europeans made him Canada's first internationally recognized painter. Edmonton's Paul Kane Park is named after him. The park itself won several awards for excellence in landscaping.

60 Annie Jackson (Kelcher)

Jackson was a worker with the Children's Shelter when she became the city's first female police officer in 1912. Jackson was selected from an overall group of 47 applicants. Her work included what one news report called 'hustling hussies off the street.'

61 Kenneth W. MacKenzie

Photo courtesy City of Edmonton Archives.

The first mayor of the City of Edmonton, MacKenzie (right) served a one-year term, which was the standard term of the day. He served in 1904/1905.

62 Vernon Barford

Coming to Edmonton around the turn of the century, Barford founded and was musical director of the Edmonton Amateur Operatic Society, and co-founded the Edmonton Festival in 1908 - the first regional music festival in North America. The event is now known as the Kiwanis Music Festival, and has launched the careers of several international music stars. Vernon Barford Junior High School is named in his honour.

63 Louise McKinney

Photo courtesy City of Edmonton Archives.

McKinney was one of Edmonton's Famous Five, the group that successfully had the law changed to recognize women as persons. McKinney (left) was also the first woman elected to a legislature in the British Empire, serving as an Alberta MLA from 1917 to 1921.

64 Norm Kwong

Affectionately known as 'The China Clipper,' Kwong was a fixture of the Edmonton Eskimo Football Club during some of its most successful championship years of the mid-1950s. He was Canada's Athlete of the Year in 1955, and won several Schenley Awards. He was named a CFL All-Star five times, and was a key player in the Esks' 1954, 1955, 1956 Grey Cup victories.

65 John McDougall

McDougall (right) helped create one of Edmonton's first brick buildings, the Empire Block on Jasper Ave. His company McDougall-Secord is the city's oldest business partnership. He also started a financial house and mortgage corporation, was an alderman (1894 to 1895) and mayor (1897 to 1908). He was a promoter and the original director of the city's power company. John A. McDougall School was built in his honor.

Photo courtesy City of Edmonton Archives.

66 Dr. Don Smith

The father of Edmonton's most award-winning swimming family, Smith was an accomplished swimmer in his own right. Smith and his wife Gwen spurred greatness in their eight children, who won many swimming titles and set many records from the 1960s to the 1980s. The Kinsmen pool is named in his honour.

67 Kurt Browning

Originally from the southern Alberta town of Caroline, Browning (right) was an unofficial ambassador for Edmonton as he piled up an amazing record of national and world figure skating titles. He won Canadian and World Championship gold in 1989, 1990, 1991 and 1993, and was the first person in his sport to successfully land a quadruple jump in competition (in 1988). The Sports Federation of Canada named him the Top Male Athlete in Canada four times.

Photo courtesy Royal Glenora Club.

68 Dr. Anne Burrows

An accomplished musician and music teacher, Burrows (left) has led many efforts to support young Edmonton musicians. She published *Music Through Braille*, one of the first books to help integrate blind children into mainstream school classes. Burrows is a member of the Order of Canada.

Photo by Rod McCaskill, courtesy The Edmonton Journal.

69 Jack McCreath

McCreath won the Canadian Drama Award for contributions to drama in 1963. In 1959 he helped create Edmonton Theatre Associates, which evolved into the Walterdale Theatre. In 1978 he masterminded the opening ceremonies production for the Commonwealth Games, which was hailed as the best ceremonies the games had ever seen.

70 Joseph Clarke

Mayor of Edmonton for many years (right), Clarke's most lasting achievement was negotiating the lease of a parcel of federal land for recreation. The stadium built there now bears his name, and the land also houses Commonwealth Stadium and the world-class Commonwealth Sports and Fitness Centre. The stadium facilities were both the best of their kind when built, and were central to the successful bid for the 2001 World Track and Field Championships.

Photo courtesy City of Edmonton Archives.

71 Mo Leiberman

Leiberman was quarterback of the 1915 University of Alberta football team before playing for the Eskimos from 1919 to 1921. He helped organize the first western challenge for the Grey Cup. During his time as president of the Eskimos, the team won three consecutive Grey Cup titles and two league championships (1955 and 1956). He received an award from the Canadian Football League for outstanding contribution to football. Leiberman is pictured (below) in the middle of the centre row, between the two men in white, in this 1950s-era Esks photo.

Photo courtesy City of Edmonton Archives.

72 Pierre Lueders

Along with bobsleigh partner Dave MacEachern, Lueders has won the 1998 Olympic gold medal and two World Cup championships. In the various bobsleigh events, Lueders has won about 30 World Cup race medals.

73 Doug McNally

The former Edmonton police chief won the Police Exemplary Service Medal in 1986 for 20 years of service. During his 28-year career he received two awards for outstanding police work. Now retired, he has been involved in the community, such as being a driving force in Canada's first Success By 6 education program.

74 Alexander Rutherford

The first Premier of Alberta, Rutherford had many firsts to his name, and was instrumental in choosing Edmonton as provincial capital, and Strathcona as site of the University in Edmonton. The province's high school honours scholarships carry his name.

75 Izena Ross

Ross was the first woman elected to Edmonton City Council, winning a seat in 1921, and resigning at the end of her one-year term. She later went on to become a school trustee for 10 years.

76 Bruce Saville

Founder of Saville Systems, one of Canada's leading software companies, he made Edmonton a world player in the development of software for telephone companies. In 1996, Saville won the Prairie Region Entrepreneur of the Year Award. Saville Systems is in more than 17 countries.

77 John Bucyk

One of the all-time greats of hockey, Bucyk began his career with the Maple Leaf Athletic Club in Edmonton. After his successful time with the Edmonton Flyers, the player affectionately called 'The Chief' moved to the Boston Bruins of the NHL. He twice won both the NHL's Lady Byng Trophy as most gentlemanly player, and the Bruin's award as most valuable player.

78 Buster Brown

This native of Cranbrook, B.C. came to Edmonton in 1911. One of Edmonton's outstanding track and field athletes in the early part of the century, Brown (left) held provincial records and Alberta championships in the 100 yards, 220 yards junior and 220 yards senior races. He was a member of the 440 yards relay team that won the gold medal at the 1930 British Empire Games in Hamilton. Brown was also an outstanding hockey player, including being a member of the Edmonton Superiors.

79 John Norris

Working for the Hudson's Bay Company, Norris (right) and George Flett were put in charge of the first Red River Carts to travel from Winnipeg to Edmonton. Their pioneering trip took three and a half months, and set the route that would become the major trade passage between the cities.

80 William Tomison

An inland trader with the Hudson's Bay Company, Tomison is largely credited with having built the first Fort Edmonton/Edmonton House in 1795. The site changed locations several times before the final structure on the Legislature grounds was dismantled and eventually lost.

81 Brad Fraser

Playwright and director Brad Fraser has won many Alberta Culture Playwriting Competitions and had award winning plays run across Canada. His play *Human Remains and the True Nature of Love* is one of the biggest theatrical hits to come out of Edmonton. His plays have sold out performances in Canada and on Broadway in New York City.

82 Eric John Slatter

Slatter was involved in negotiations in the formation of the groundbreaking Old Strathcona Foundation on which he served as the representative of Heritage Canada. Through the 1970s and 1980s, Slatter helped to re-organize the city's philanthropic organizations, leading to the restructuring and refunding of the Edmonton Community Foundation, which administers a fund of more than $25 million for charities and the arts.

83 Eric Geddes

Founding chairman of Old Strathcona Foundation in 1975, Geddes (right) was instrumental in restoring the historic south-side district. Named to the Order of Canada in 1989, he was the first winner of the ASTech Award for Outstanding Contribution to the Alberta Science and Technology Community. Geddes was the first recipient of the University of Alberta's Faculty of Business Distinguished Alumni Award. Geddes was also awarded the University of Alberta Alumni Golden Jubilee Award in 1984.

84 Ruth Carse

An accomplished dancer, with 20 years of performing in Canada and abroad, she founded the Alberta Ballet Company in 1966, and the Alberta School of Ballet in 1971. She has won the Sir Frederick Haultain award (1983), the Queen's Silver Jubilee Medal (1977), and the Canada Dance Award (1990) which is the nation's most distinguished dance honour. Carse is a Member of the Order of Canada.

85 Violet Archer

Archer is one of Canada's best-known and highest ranked composers. She has close to 400 published works, and she is listed in 41 encyclopedias and dictionaries of music. Her work has earned her prestigious prizes such as the Order of Canada, the Queen's Silver Jubilee Medal, and Alberta's Sir Frederick Haultain award. The Violet Archer Festival in 1985 was the first of its kind to honour a Canadian composer.

86 Dr. Yashu Coe

The specialist in pediatric cardiology is the inventor of several devices now used in heart surgery around the world. His latest is a radio-frequency catheter used to open blocked pulmonary valves. It has a small tube inserted into an infant's heart through the arteries, where it uses radio waves to open a hole in the malformed valve.

87 Leslie, Erik & Gordon Nielsen

Each of these three brothers gained fame, but in different areas. Leslie has a 50-year show-business career, starring in more than 80 movies and 1,200 television shows. His television credits cover many years, including the popular but short-lived *Police Squad*. He has also appeared in movies such as *The Poseiden Adventure* and *Airplane!*. Leslie got his start when he won a scholarship for Neighbourhood Playhouse in New York. Erik was in the air force during the Second World War, winning the Distinguished Flying Cross as a member of the Royal Air Force 101 Squadron that had the highest casualty rate of any Allied squadron. After returning to Edmonton to teach, serving in the air force again, and then studying law, Erik was elected as a Member of Parliament. He would eventually serve for 30 years, the longest continuous term ever. Gordon achieved fame briefly as a seven-year-old, when he garnered local newspaper coverage for saving the life of a playmate trapped in a cave-in on a road construction site. He later moved to Vancouver, where he was a police officer and a businessman.

88 Malcolm Forsythe

University of Alberta music professor and world-famous Edmonton composer, he won the 1989 Canadian Composer of the Year award, and won Juno Awards in 1987 and 1995 for Best Classical Composition.

89 Walter Kaasa

Drama teacher, actor and politician, he served as deputy minister of Alberta Culture and helped fund the arts in his 26 years of government service. A theatre in the Jubilee Auditorium is named after him. He helped develop libraries, art curriculum in schools, historical resources, museums, and cultural heritage. In 1980, he won Speaker of the Year from the Canadian Speech Association. He was named to the Order of Canada in 1996.

90 Ralph Klein

While a Calgarian, Premier Ralph Klein has had an undeniable impact on Edmonton. As the province's top political leader (and therefore a resident of Edmonton) Klein's Conservative governments have led the nation in cost cutting, including being the first to make deficit budgets illegal. The moves have earned him respect for their success at balancing the provincial budget, although critics say they nearly crippled the city, which was more dependent on government employment than Calgary.

91 Pete Jamison

Jamison was a unique and instantly recognizable character, acting as Edmonton's unofficial town crier - the only one of his kind anywhere in North America. In 1978 he became the subject of the National Film Board documentary *Never a Dull Moment.* He was on radio every morning on CJCA. Known for his snappy suits and wearing one of his 219 hats to match, Jamison continued his passionate role well into his 70s, before dying in 1991 at age 82.

92 Georges Roy, Luke Kelly & Antonio Prince

Finding that the existing public school system didn't meet their needs as Catholics, these three became the city's first Edmonton Catholic Separate School trustees in 1888 after successfully campaigning to have voters approve the new system. (Roy is pictured top left, Kelly top right, Prince in the lower photograph.)

Photos courtesy City of Edmonton Archives.

93 Neil Reimer

Reimer (left) founded and was the first leader of the Alberta New Democratic Party, part of a lifelong dedication to workers' issues. He helped organize the Oil Workers International Union. He was named an officer of the Order of Canada, for work on occupational health & safety, and received an Alberta Achievement Award.

Photo courtesy City of Edmonton Archives.

94 Dr. Anne Anderson

Anderson (right) wrote the first Cree-English dictionary (completed by an associate after her death). She wrote more than 80 books and other publications in Cree. She became a member of the Order of Canada in 1991.

Photo courtesy City of Edmonton Archives.

95 Jane Ashe Poitras

A renowned native artist and activist, her work has won acclaim and been widely exhibited across Canada. Her paintings hang in museums across Canada and Europe.

96 Cecil 'Tiger' Goldstick

The longtime sporting figure is one of the most-recognized people in Edmonton's recent past. But it isn't just for his work with championship teams such as the Edmonton Flyers hockey team and local baseball teams. Goldstick (right) is also a proponent of children's sports programs, including a charity to get sports equipment into the hands of the city's poorer children. A city sports field is named in his honour.

Photo courtesy City of Edmonton Archives.

97 George Blondheim

One of Edmonton's top musical talents, Blondheim won a 1991 Genie Award for his song *Such Magic*, and has written the score for such big-budget movies as *Jewel of the Nile* and *9-1/2 Weeks*. He as also worked with such award-winning artists as k.d. lang and Tom Cochrane.

98 Ken Grierson

Grierson is one of Edmonton's most accomplished racquet-sports athletes. He won numerous city, provincial and national championships, playing both badminton and tennis. He won three gold medals in badminton at World Masters Games.

99 Irene Parlby & H. Muir Edwards

Two members of the Famous Five, they helped lead the charge for women's rights in the famous Persons Case.

100 Elizabeth Sterling

A pioneer of live theatre, in 1937 she became Canada's first female provincial drama director. Sterling (left) influenced drama in Alberta, helping to establish the Banff School of Fine Arts as well as many Edmonton theatre groups. Her work was recognized when the local drama awards were named in her honour.

Photo courtesy City of Edmonton Archives.

Acknowledgements

City of Champions would not have been possible without the help of many people and organizations who believe in Edmonton. Generous in their time and effort, they are among the people who make this city great. We would like to thank everyone who helped in the creation of this book, especially the following.

Bruce Ibsen, Johwanna Alleyne, Paddy Lamb and all the staff of the City of Edmonton Archives.
Chris McLeod, City of Edmonton.
Ernie Afaganis, Bob Bradburn, Al McCann, Buzz McClung, Doug McFarlane, Wes Montgomery, and Waldo Ranson.

By the Numbers
David Schneider, Val Stevens, Thelma Scannell, Wayne Wood, Patricia Dickson and Linda Hall, City of Edmonton. Kenn Bur, Cyndie Annette, and Rick Hersack, Economic Development Edmonton. Judy Berghofer, Old Strathcona Foundation. Marjorie Bencz, Edmonton's Food Bank. Jon Hall, Volunteer Centre of Edmonton. Jacques Laflamme, Environment Canada. David Phillips, *The day Niagara Falls ran dry!: Canadian weather facts and trivia.*

Professional Sports
Dave Jameson, Edmonton Eskimo Football Club. Joe Petrone and Ross Ongaro, Edmonton Drillers. Warren Suitor and Bill Tuele, Edmonton Oilers. Denyse Conroy, Edmonton Trappers.

Amateur Sports
Susan Bulmer, Canadian Amateur Diving Association. Dan Carle and Chantalle Beaudoin, University of Alberta. Kelly Anne Carter Erdman. Lisa Columbo, Alberta Bicycling Association. Audrey Greenough. Donna Hateley, Alberta Sports Hall of Fame and Museum. Ron Hayter. James Hood, Swim Alberta. Aart Looye. Eric Mahabir, Edmonton Cricket League. Bernie Masterson, Concordia University College of Alberta. Tamara McKernan, Ringette Alberta. Greg Meropolis, Northern Alberta Institute of Technology. Don Metz, Aquila Productions. Tina Moller, Synchro Alberta Association. Marylynn Morris, Northern Alberta Curling Association. Veli Niinimaa, Biathlon Alberta. Ian Paidon, Royal Glenora Club. Christine Purvis, City of Edmonton. Jacqueline Sealy, Grant MacEwan Community College. Clair Seyler, Ron Hodgson Pontiac Buick GMC. Gwen Smith. Diane Tessman, Canadian Figure Skating Association. Karen Waples, Tigers Baseball Association. Andy Wigston, Brick Minor Hockey Tournament.

Festivals
Larissa Banting, Northern Alberta International Children's Festival Paul Bourret, Kiwanis Music Festival. David Cheoros and Gerald Osborn, Fringe Festival. Dick Finkel and Darka Tarnawsky, Street Performers Festival. Robert Hardy, National Screen Institute - Canada. Jazz City. Tali Laurenson, Heritage Festival. Greg Lenuik, Cariwest. Cora Molstad. Cathy Schreiner, Canadian Birkebeiner Ski Festival. Linda Snider, First Night Festival. Jane and John Tames, Blueberry Bluegrass and Country Music Festival. Linda Wedman and Rae Cowley, The Works. Terry Wickham, Jocelyn Babcock, and Muffy Skywalker, Folk Festival. Bob Willans, Medieval Festival.

Arts and Leisure
Barry Anderson, Kevin Arnott, Mark Brostrom, Melissa Dodson, Terry Josey, Doug Kirchner, Val Mayes, Ruth Merriott, Laurie Pettigrew, Monique St. Louis, Crystal Steparyk, Jill Wright, City of Edmonton. Kerry Aldridge, Edmonton Opera. Miki Andrejevic and Lorraine Carson, Writers Guild of Alberta. Jean Archer, Whitemud Equine Centre. Tommy Banks. Margaret Barry. Ross Bradley, Alberta Foundation for the Arts. Barbara Bruce and Catherine Crowston, Edmonton Art Gallery. Kathy Classen, Theatre Alberta. Cora Doucette, University of Alberta. Doug Elves, Stroll of Poets. Susan Farnell, City of Edmonton. Helen Folkmann, Film and Video Arts Society of Alberta. Kyra Garlinski, Vinok. Jason Golinowski, Cheremosh. Corey Haberstock, Pro Coro Canada. Kyna Hamill, Free Will Players. Merle Harris, Canadian Children's Authors, Illustrators and Performers. Lana Hudon, West End Gallery. Gail Haughton, Brian Webb Dance Company. Kelly Isaac, National Film Board of Canada. Todd Janes and Heidi Taylor, Latitude 53. Anna Koziak, Polonez. Danielle LaBrie, Alberta Society of Artists. Kathy Lakan, Walterdale Theatre. Wayne Mackenzie, Electrum Design Studio. Larissa Makowsky, Karvonen Films. Dana McKort, Edmonton Symphony Orchestra and Francis Winspear Centre for Music. Bradley Moss, Theatre Network. Julie Naylor, Alberta Craft Council. Heather Redfern, Catalyst Theatre. Vincent Rees and Brad Walker, Shumka School of Dance. Philippe Renoir, Famous Players. Joe Shoctor, Troy Funk and Mararet Mooney, Citadel Theatre. Jetske Sybesma, Stella Chooi and Blair Brennan, University of Alberta. Yoko Sekiya, University of Alberta Press. Christina Tozer and Peni Christopher, Edmonton Arts Council. Varscona Theatre. Claire Verret and Laurie McInnes, Great North Productions. Bobbi Westman, Alberta Dance Alliance. Angus Wyatt, and David LaRiviere, Society of Northern Alberta Print Artists.

West Edmonton Mall
Travis Reynolds, West Edmonton Mall. Wendy Andrews.

Tourist Attractions
Jan Archbold, City of Edmonton. Elizabeth Buchanan, Muttart Conservatory. Robert Busse, Alberta Aviation Museum. Donalda DaSilva Pelton, Edmonton Space and Science Centre. Herb Dixon, Alberta Pioneer Railway Association. Arnold Grant, Ukranian Village. Ken Green, Elk Island National Park. Cheryl Herchen and Darcy Potratz, Northlands Park. Jane Ross, Provincial Museum of Alberta. Tim Willis, The Provincial Museum of Alberta.

Medicine
Dr. Beverly Bell, Cross Cancer Institute. Steve Buick and Candace Toews, Capital Health. Cathy Ducharme, Donna Angus, and Dr. Yashu Coe, University of Alberta Hospitals.

Education
Dale Armstrong, Jane Generoux, Lisa Toliver-Fuchs, and Dianne Greenough, Edmonton Public Schools. Melanie Busby, Grant MacEwan Community College. Scott Graham and Karen Lynch, Alberta College. Kathy Murie, Edmonton Catholic Schools. Brian Silzer and the staff of the Registrar's Office, University of Alberta.

Business
Kenn Bur, Cyndie Annett and Shelley Brown, Economic Development Edmonton. Liz Iggulden, Old Strathcona Foundation. Suzanne Lyrentzis, Peace Hills Trust.

Media
Dan Healing, Paul Stanway and Kathy Levesque, *Edmonton Sun*. Shannon Havard, Videon. Doug Ionson, CBC. Randy McDonald and Ursula Patlock, CFRN. Andrea Macnab, ACCESS. Karen Paulgaard, ITV. Sheila Pratt and Dave Makris, *Edmonton Journal*.

Top 100
The Hole family. Erik Neilson and Leslie Neilson. Mary Phillips, Gold Quill Productions. Jack and Michael Calkins, Victoria Comp. Archives.

About the publishers

Cal Nichols

Born in Paradise Hill, Saskatchewan, Cal started his business career as the Imperial Esso Agent in St. Walburg, Saskatchewan. In 1969, Cal and wife Edna moved to Edmonton. During the next 13 years Cal would pursue various business and career opportunities with Imperial Oil. He was the commission bulk agent for Esso in Edmonton from 1972 through 1981. In 1983, anticipating the de-regulation of the crude oil and natural gas markets, Cal and two associates founded Northridge Canada Inc. which was ultimately sold to TransCanada Pipelines. In 1985, Cal created Gasland Oil, with its head office in Edmonton. Gasland grew to have more than 50 branded petroleum outlets in Western Canada, many with convenience stores and other customer facilities. Cal sold substantially all of Gasland's petroleum marketing business in 1996, but retained the real estate. He has therefore shifted his focus to developing the company's real estate holdings. Being familiar with petroleum marketing and

environmental issues, Cal founded Nichols Environmental (Canada) Ltd. in late 1997, in Edmonton.

Cal is best known locally for his desire to retain NHL hockey in Edmonton. In 1996, Cal co-chaired the 'Friends of the Oilers' ticket drive campaign. Starting with a meagre 6,200 in season ticket sales, Nichols orchestrated the increase of that number to more than 13,000, thus averting the risk of the team moving. In 1997, when the franchise was put up for sale, Nichols spearheaded the bid from a local ownership group by co-ordinating the raising of the US$60 million in equity required to purchase the team. His motivation for this was solely to see Edmonton remain as a major league city.

Cal has always found a way to give back to the community in which he lives and works. Cal served as a town councillor and President of the Chamber of Commerce in St. Walburg. Numerous Edmonton charities have been the beneficiaries of his effort and money. Cal served for two years as Chairman of the Cross Cancer Institute/Glenn Anderson Golf Tournament and

continues to assist the organizing committee. For many years, Cal has been a member of the organizing committee for the annual Premier's Prayer Breakfast, hosted each year by the City of Edmonton, and in 1999 served as chairman.

Cal and Edna have two adult children, both graduates of the University of Alberta; Ken is involved in retail petroleum marketing and other entrepreneurial projects; Kris is an occupational therapist.

Cal has become one of the most recognized and trusted citizens of Edmonton.

Douglas G. Cumming

Douglas G. Cumming was born in Viking, Alberta and moved to Edmonton as a young man. Doug and his wife Marg have one son, Tom, an international lawyer currently on assignment with the Government of Canada in China.

Doug began with Acklands Limited in 1957, serving in increasingly responsible roles, including branch manager, General Manager Alberta, General Manager Western Canada, Vice-President Western Canada and Senior Vice-President Operations - Canada. In 1996, Acklands - Grainger Inc. became the Canadian subsidiary of W.W. Grainger Inc. and Doug was made its president. He was appointed chairman in 1999. He is responsible for Acklands - Grainger

Inc., Safety Supply, Bumper to Bumper, Westward Tools, Profast'ners and Cisco. In 1981, Doug graduated from Harvard University in the Advanced Management Program.

Doug has quietly and effectively served his home city of Edmonton as Chairman of Western Industrial Research and Training Centre. He is a past board member of the Alberta Cancer Foundation as well as leading an innovative substantial fundraising program for the Cross Cancer Institute. In 1985, he spearheaded a campaign to involve corporate funds and the Edmonton Oilers in thoughtful recognition of the needs of cancer patients. Later that year, Cal Nichols of Gasland Oil joined this initiative and the funds name was then changed to the Glenn Anderson/Acklands/Gasland Fund,

which has generated substantial donations for the care and treatment of those touched by cancer. Doug enjoys collecting antique hand tools, hunting, fishing and always saying "yes" to friends in need of a favour.

Index

About the editors

Jamie Wilson

Born in Toronto, Jamie graduated from Ryerson Polytechnic Institute with a B.A. in journalism in 1982.

After university, Jamie moved to Nova Scotia, where he quickly made a name for himself as a sports reporter and editor at two newspapers in one of the area's leading media companies. He was known not only for his design work, but for using his writing to promote local athletes. Other pieces included the uncovering of financial misdealings in local politics.

Moving back to Ontario, Jamie worked at news outlets in southwestern Ontario before taking his sister's advice and joining her in Edmonton in the late 1980s. Working at *The Edmonton Sun*, he was a writer on the police, environment and other beats, and a copy editor.

Leaving *The Sun* and spending time as a teacher's aide and graphic designer, Jamie has recently completed his first novel, and is the owner of a cartoon and news syndication company.

Allyson Quince

Allyson Quince is a freelance journalist, and an Edmonton enthusiast. She grew up in Windsor, Ontario, and graduated with an M.A. in English Literature from Queen's University in Kingston.

After graduating, Quince pursued her interest in newspaper journalism. She moved to the interior of British Columbia, and began working as a news reporter and photographer at the *Cranbrook Daily Townsman*.

Quince has since worked for newspapers in British Columbia, Saskatchewan and Alberta. She also has taught literature courses at the University of Regina.

Quince first moved to Edmonton with her husband and four children

in 1992. After spending a year in Toronto, they returned to live in Edmonton in 1998.

Welcome to

THE CITY OF

Edmonton

City of Cham